In cooperation with

NorthStar

Building Skills for the TOEFL® iBT

High Intermediate

D0160828

Helen S. Solórzano

Series Editors
Frances Boyd
Carol Numrich

PEARSON
Longman

NorthStar: Building Skills for the TOEFL iBT, High Intermediate

Pearson Education, 10 Bank Street, White Plains, NY 10606

Vice president, multimedia and skills: Sherry Preiss
Project manager: Debbie Sistino
Development manager: Paula H. Van Ells
Production coordinator: Melissa Leyva
Senior production editor: Robert Ruvo
Director of manufacturing: Patrice Fraccio
Senior manufacturing buyer: Dave Dickey
Photo research: Jessica Gorkin
Cover design: Rhea Banker
Cover art: Der Rhein bei Duisburg, 1937, 145(R 5) Rhine near Duisburg
    19 × 27.5 cm; water-based on cardboard; The Metropolitan Museum of
    Art, N.Y. The Berggruen Klee Collection, 1984. (1984.315.56)
    Photograph © 1985 The Metropolitan Museum of Art. © 2003 Artists
    Rights Society (ARS), New York / VG Bild-Kunst, Bonn
Text composition: Anthology, Inc.
Text font: 11/13 Sabon
Credits: see pages xii–xiii

Library of Congress Cataloging-in-Publication Data

Solórzano, Helen Sophia.
    Northstar. Building skills for the TOEFL iBT high intermediate/
Helen S. Solorzano.
        p. cm.
    ISBN 0-13-193708-1 (pbk.)—ISBN 0-13-198578-7 (pbk. : with
audio CD)
        1. English language—Textbooks for foreign speakers. 2. Test of
English as a foreign language—Study guides. 3. English language—
Examinations—Study guides. I. Title. II. Title: Building skills for the
TOEFL iBT high intermediate.
PE1128.S5957 2006
428'.0076—dc22

                                                                2005023860

ISBN: 0-13-193708-1 (Student Book)
        0-13-198578-7 (Student Book with Audio CDs)

ETS, the ETS logo, and TOEFL are registered
trademarks of Educational Testing Service (ETS),
used under license by Pearson Longman.

LONGMAN ON THE WEB

Longman.com offers online resources for teachers and students. Access our Companion Websites, our online catalog, and our local offices around the world.

Visit us at **longman.com**.

Printed in the United States of America
2 3 4 5 6 7 8 9 10—VHG—09 08 07 06

Contents

Welcome to NorthStar

Building Skills for the TOEFL® iBT

In Cooperation with ETS®

Pearson Longman and *ETS* combine their expertise in language learning and test development to create an innovative approach to developing the skills assessed in the new TOEFL Internet-based test (iBT). *NorthStar Building Skills for the TOEFL iBT*, a new three-level series, links learning and assessment with a skill-building curriculum that incorporates authentic test material from the makers of the TOEFL iBT.

Each book in the series has 10 thematic units that are organized like the TOEFL iBT into listening, reading, speaking and writing sections. Each unit includes focused integrated skill practice to develop critical thinking and communicative competence. Authentic TOEFL iBT practice sets developed by ETS offer practice and further assessment.

Purpose

The TOEFL test has changed, so preparation for it must change, too. *NorthStar: Building Skills for the TOEFL iBT* takes a new approach—an instructional approach—to test preparation. In this approach, students develop academic skills in English, while building test-taking confidence.

The TOEFL iBT requires students to show their ability to use English in a variety of campus and academic situations such as listening to lectures on unfamiliar topics, orally paraphrasing and integrating information that they have just read and listened to, and writing a well-organized essay with detailed examples, correct grammar, and varied vocabulary. The speaking and writing tasks require clear and confident expression. With these books, students move progressively, sharpening language skills *and* test-taking abilities.

The three *Building Skills* texts are intended as stepping stones from classroom instruction in English to TOEFL and academic readiness. In language instruction, students will benefit most from an integrated-skills, content-based curriculum, with a focus on critical thinking. In instructional test preparation with these books, students will encounter the same content-rich material, tasks, and question types that appear on the test. Using these books in the classroom will improve students' communicative skills, keep their interest, sharpen awareness of their skills, and build their confidence.

Extensive Support to Build the Skills Assessed on the TOEFL iBT

The *Building Skills* books strengthen English language skills while they familiarize students with the type of content, questions and tasks on the *TOEFL iBT*. Practice and mastery of these skills can help learners build confidence to communicate successfully in an academic environment.

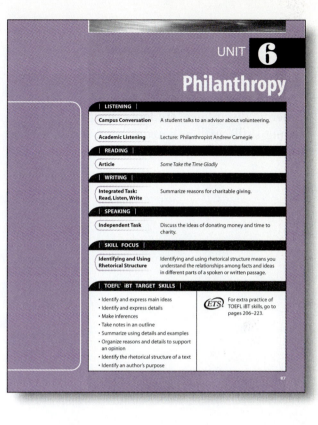

High-Interest Listening Selections

Campus conversations introduce students to practical vocabulary, conversations, and situations encountered in everyday life in a college or university.

Academic listenings present lectures, reports, and interviews, helping students understand a wide variety of styles and topics.

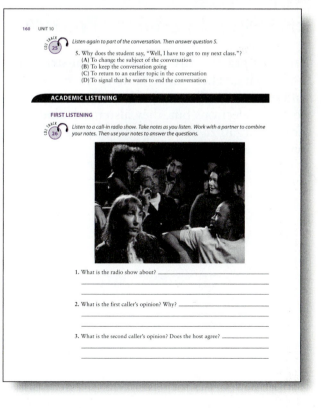

High-Interest Academic Reading Selections

Through engaging readings from many different academic disciplines, students sharpen critical reading skills such as categorizing, summarizing, and analyzing.

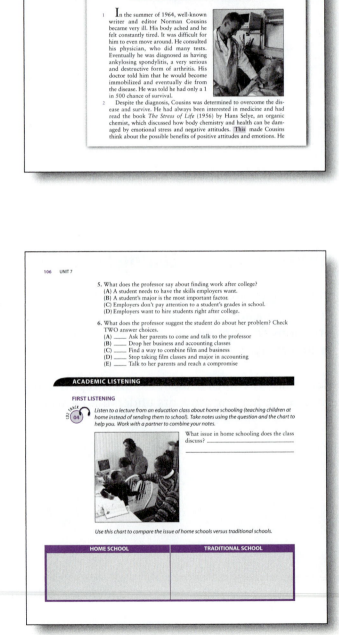

Extensive Note-taking Practice

Students practice structured and semi-structured note-taking. These kinds of activities not only enhance comprehension of both listening and reading selections but, they also teach students how to organize information for speaking and writing responses.

New TOEFL-Type Items and Item Analysis

Extensive TOEFL-type practice items familiarize students with the kinds of questions and tasks they will encounter in the TOEFL iBT. Analysis activities help them understand the purpose of each item.

Education   111

8. In paragraph 6, the word *persist* is closest in meaning to
   (A) quit
   (B) explain
   (C) finish
   (D) learn

9. According the paragraph 7, why might children be more successful in school if they can resist impulses?
   (A) They are more popular with their teachers.
   (B) They can focus on their work and not get distracted.
   (C) They easily understand new information.
   (D) They have more friends at school.

10. Look at the four squares ☐ that indicate where the following sentence could be added to the passage. Where would the sentence best fit? Circle the letter that shows the point where you can insert this sentence.

    Research like this shows how important Emotional Intelligence can be in a person's life.

    ☐A☐ Of all the attributes of Emotional Intelligence, the ability to postpone immediate gratification and to persist in working toward some greater future gain is most closely related to success—whether one is trying to build a business, get a college degree, or even stay on a diet. ☐B☐ One researcher examined whether this trait can predict a child's success in school. ☐C☐ The study showed that 4-year-old children who can delay instant gratification in order to advance toward some future goal will be "far superior as students" when they graduate from high school than will 4-year-olds who are not able to resist the impulse to satisfy their immediate wishes (Shoda et al., 1990). ☐D☐

11. Select the appropriate phrases from the answer choices and match them to the personal components of Emotional Intelligence to which they relate. TWO of the answer choices will NOT be used.
    (A) communicate with others about our feelings
    (B) control our impulses
    (C) express our emotions appropriately
    (D) recognize our feelings
    (E) understand the feelings of others
    (F) understand why we feel the way we do
    (G) work toward a future goal

    Awareness and Management of Emotions   **Self-Motivation**
    • _____   • _____
    • _____   • _____
    • _____

---

112   UNIT 7

ANALYSIS

It is helpful to know the purpose of a test item. There are four types of questions in the reading section.

1. Basic Comprehension
   • main ideas
   • details
   • the meaning of specific sentences

2. Organization
   • the way information is structured in the text
   • the way ideas are linked between sentences or between paragraphs

3. Inference
   • ideas are not directly stated in the text
   • author's intention, purpose, or attitude not explicitly stated in the text

4. Vocabulary and Reference
   • the meaning of words
   • the meaning of reference words such as *his, them, this,* or *none*

Go back to the reading questions and label each question with 1, 2, 3, or 4. Then work with a partner to see if you agree. Check the Answer Key for the correct answers. Which questions did you get right? Which did you get wrong? What skills do you need to practice?

❸ Speaking

INTEGRATED TASK: READ, LISTEN, SPEAK

In this section, you will read a short passage and listen to an excerpt on the same topic. Then you will speak about the relationship between the two.

READING

Read the excerpt on the next page from a psychology textbook. With a partner, complete the task.

Guided Practice in Integrated and Independent Tasks

Integrated tasks require students to synthesize information from two sources and then speak or write a response. Students practice critical thinking, as well as note-taking and other practical steps for producing a quality response.

Definition of Culture Shock: _____

Stage 1: _____

    Feelings: _____

Stage 2: _____

    Feelings: _____

Stage 3: _____

    Feelings: _____

Stage 4: _____

    Feelings: _____

LISTENING

CD2 TRACK 22

Listen to the excerpt from Lucy *by Jamaica Kincaid. Use the questions to take notes as you listen.*

1. How does Lucy feel? _____
_____

2. What does she miss from home? _____
_____

SPEAKING

Work with a partner to create a role play. Follow the steps below to prepare.

One partner plays Lucy and the other partner plays Lucy's friend. Lucy explains her feelings of culture shock, using examples from the listening. Lucy's friend explains how her feelings are an example of culture shock.

Step 1

With your partner, skim the reading and your notes from the reading and listening tasks (pages 148–149). Fill in an outline for your speaking task:

1. How does Lucy feel? Explain using examples.

EMOTION	EXAMPLES

---

3 Speaking

INTEGRATED TASK: READ, LISTEN, SPEAK

In this section, you will read a short passage and listen to an excerpt on the same topic. Then you will speak about the relationship between the two.

READING

Read the passage and then complete the outline on the next page.

What Is Culture Shock?

Culture shock refers to the feelings of discomfort experienced as a person adjusts to a new culture. It is caused by having to cope with many new and unfamiliar situations and traditions. Newcomers feel helpless because they cannot understand all the new things they experience. However, understanding the stages of culture shock—and knowing that it is only temporary—can help newcomers make the transition.

There are four stages of culture shock, although the length of time each stage lasts will differ for each person. The first stage is the honeymoon stage. During this time, when you first enter a new culture, everything is interesting and exciting. You are curious about the new culture and eager to learn. Everything seems interesting, the people are friendly, the food is delicious, and you are eager to explore your new surroundings. However, after some time, the distress stage begins. The newcomer starts to feel uncomfortable and unhappy in the new culture. Everything seems very difficult: shopping, getting around, and making friends all seem confusing. You may begin to feel homesick and want to return home. Feelings of anger and sadness are common, and you may be overwhelmed by small problems. However, these feelings are only temporary. Gradually, the newcomer becomes more comfortable in the culture and enters the recovery stage. The new customs seem clearer, and everyday interactions are easier. You begin to enjoy the new culture once more. Finally, the stability stage begins. Life becomes more normal, and your sense of humor returns. You may not like everything about the new culture, but it doesn't make you so unhappy. You begin to feel at home in the new culture.

Independent tasks help students build the skills they need to express and support opinions.

2. What stage of culture shock is she experiencing? _____

Define the stage.
_____
_____
_____

3. Give examples from Lucy's experience.
_____
_____
_____

Step 2

Take turns practicing a two-minute role play between Lucy and her friend. Use the information in your outline to help you.

Step 3

Work with another pair. Take turns performing your two-minute role play.

> To evaluate your partner's response, use the Speaking Evaluation Form on page 174.

4 Writing

INDEPENDENT TASK

Write on the following topic. Follow the steps below to prepare.

Do you agree or disagree with the following statement?
"Immigrants should try to become part of the culture in their new home, and not hold onto the traditions of their home culture."

Step 1

Outline your response. First write down your opinion in response to the prompt. Then brainstorm reasons for your opinion. Think of specific details or examples to support your reasons.

Opinion: _____

    Reason: _____

    Details/Examples: _____

    Reason: _____

    Details/Examples: _____

Essential Academic Skills for TOEFL iBT Success

The Skill Focus section in each book raises students' awareness of a key academic language skill. At each level of the series, students deepen and broaden mastery of these ten essential skills:

- Skimming and Scanning

- Identifying and Using Main Ideas and Details

- Making Inferences

- Identifying and Using Rhetorical Structure

- Using Context Clues

- Paraphrasing

- Summarizing

- Using Detailed Examples

- Comparing and Contrasting

- Identifying and Using Cohesive Devices

---

28   UNIT 2

5 Skill Focus

PARAPHRASING

EXAMINATION

1 *Read the excerpt from the Academic Listening. Look at the answer choices to the question. Do the choices use the same words as the report, or are the ideas expressed in other words?*

> The group kept a diary of their travels online, and even when the going got tough, they buckled down, turning to each other for inspiration as they continued on the trail to the peak.

What did the climbers do during their climb?
(A) They wrote about their experience on the Internet.
(B) They took a lot of photographs.
(C) They videotaped each other.
(D) They talked to the media about their experience.

2 *Read the question from the reading. Do the answer choices use the same wording as the reading text, or are the ideas expressed in other words?*

Which of the sentences below best expresses the essential information in the passage excerpt? Incorrect choices change the meaning in important ways or leave out essential information.

> She was impatient and hungry for words, and her teacher's scribbling on her hand would never be as fast, she thought, as the people who could read the words with their eyes.

(A) Helen Keller wanted to communicate more quickly.
(B) Helen Keller didn't understand her teacher.
(C) Helen Keller's teacher wrote in her hand.
(D) Helen Keller didn't get enough to eat.

3 *Review what you wrote for the Integrated Task on page 26. Did you use the same words to describe the ideas in the reading and listening, or did you express the ideas in your own words?*

Overcoming Obstacles   **29**

Tips

To do well on the TOEFL, it is essential to learn how to read, write, and speak paraphrased information. When you are reading, you have to recognize when phrases and sentences have the same meaning as another phrase or sentence. When you are writing or speaking, you need to restate ideas from another source in your own words, without changing the meaning.

An effective paraphrase:

- contains the same information as the original statement.

- is expressed in different words.

- may leave out less important details.

Recognizing paraphrased information

When you are answering multiple-choice questions about the main idea or details of a text, you can often get the correct answer by choosing the best paraphrase of the information in the text.

Using paraphrasing in speaking or writing

When you write or speak about ideas in a text, you need to paraphrase the ideas you heard or read.

In writing, if you don't paraphrase, you must use quotation marks to show that you are quoting the same language as the original text. Otherwise, you may be committing plagiarism—taking words from someone else's work and pretending they are your own—an act that is prohibited in colleges and universities.

Example: The law protects people with disabilities from employment discrimination.

Quote: "The law protects people with disabilities from employment discrimination."

Paraphrase: The ADA stops employers from discriminating against disabled people.

In the Examination exercise, you noticed that the answer for the first item is (A) because it conveys the same meaning as the sentences in the listening excerpt. In the second item, the answer is (A) because it is the best restatement of the essential information in the reading passage excerpt.

ETS Practice Section

Developed by ETS especially for this new series,
TOEFL iBT tasks offer authentic practice and
further assessment.

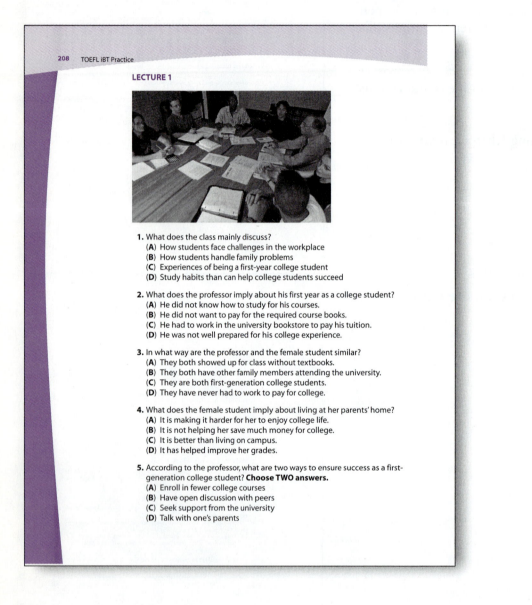

208   TOEFL iBT Practice

LECTURE 1

1. What does the class mainly discuss?
   (A) How students face challenges in the workplace
   (B) How students handle family problems
   (C) Experiences of being a first-year college student
   (D) Study habits than can help college students succeed

2. What does the professor imply about his first year as a college student?
   (A) He did not know how to study for his courses.
   (B) He did not want to pay for the required course books.
   (C) He had to work in the university bookstore to pay his tuition.
   (D) He was not well prepared for his college experience.

3. In what way are the professor and the female student similar?
   (A) They both showed up for class without textbooks.
   (B) They both have other family members attending the university.
   (C) They are both first-generation college students.
   (D) They have never had to work to pay for college.

4. What does the female student imply about living at her parents' home?
   (A) It is making it harder for her to enjoy college life.
   (B) It is not helping her save much money for college.
   (C) It is better than living on campus.
   (D) It has helped improve her grades.

5. According to the professor, what are two ways to ensure success as a first-generation college student? **Choose TWO answers.**
   (A) Enroll in fewer college courses
   (B) Have open discussion with peers
   (C) Seek support from the university
   (D) Talk with one's parents

Measuring Skills

To develop fluency and accuracy in English, students need practice and feedback. Students can complete Writing and Speaking Evaluation Forms to assess each other's written and spoken responses.

Evaluation Forms for Integrated and Independent Tasks

WRITING

Exchange papers with a partner. Evaluate each other's writing using the grid below. Discuss strengths and weaknesses. Use the evaluation to revise and edit your writing. Write a second draft and give it to your teacher.

4 = always   **3 = most of the time**   **2 = some of the time**   **1 = rarely or never**

UNIT	1	2	3	4	5	6	7	8	9	10
CONTENT										
The response …										
addresses the topic.										
is organized.										
shows connections between ideas.										
LANGUAGE										
The writing incorporates …										
effective vocabulary.										
correct grammar.										
correct spelling and punctuation.										
TOTAL:										

173

234   TOEFL IBT

TOEFL® iBT Test—Independent Speaking Rubrics

Score	General Description	Delivery	Language Use	Topic Development
4	The response fulfills the demands of the task, with at most minor lapses in completeness. It is highly intelligible and exhibits sustained, coherent discourse. A response at this level is characterized by all of the following:	Speech is generally clear, fluid and sustained. It may include minor lapses or minor difficulties with pronunciation or intonation. Pace may vary at times as speaker attempts to recall information. Overall intelligibility remains high.	The response demonstrates good control of basic and complex grammatical structures that allow for coherent, efficient (automatic) expression of relevant ideas. Contains generally effective word choice. Though some minor (or systematic) errors or imprecise use may be noticeable, they do not require listener effort (or obscure meaning).	The response presents a clear progression of ideas and conveys the relevant information required by the task. It includes appropriate detail, though it may have minor errors or minor omissions.
3	The response addresses the task appropriately, but may fall short of being fully developed. It is generally intelligible and coherent, with some fluidity of expression, though it exhibits some noticeable lapses in the expression of ideas. A response at this level is characterized by at least two of the following:	Speech is generally clear, with some fluidity of expression, but it exhibits minor difficulties with pronunciation, intonation or pacing and may require some listener effort at times. Overall intelligibility remains good, however.	The response demonstrates fairly automatic and effective use of grammar and vocabulary, and fairly coherent expression of relevant ideas. Response may exhibit some imprecise or inaccurate use of vocabulary or grammatical structures or be somewhat limited in the range of structures used. Such limitations do not seriously interfere with the communication of the message.	The response is sustained and conveys relevant information required by the task. However, it exhibits some incompleteness, inaccuracy, lack of specificity with respect to content, or choppiness in the progression of ideas.
2	The response is connected to the task, though it may be missing some relevant information or contain inaccuracies. It contains some intelligible speech, but at times problems with intelligibility and/or overall coherence may obscure meaning. A response at this level is characterized by at least two of the following:	Speech is clear at times, though it exhibits problems with pronunciation, intonation or pacing and so may require significant listener effort. Speech may not be sustained at a consistent level throughout. Problems with intelligibility may obscure meaning in places (but not throughout).	The response is limited in the range and control of vocabulary and grammar demonstrated (some complex structures may be used, but typically contain errors). This results in limited or vague expression of relevant ideas and imprecise or inaccurate connections. Automaticity of expression may only be evident at the phrasal level.	The response conveys some relevant information but is clearly incomplete or inaccurate. It is incomplete if it omits key ideas, makes vague reference to key ideas, or demonstrates limited development of important information. An inaccurate response demonstrates misunderstanding of key ideas from the stimulus. Typically, ideas expressed may not be well connected or cohesive so that familiarity with the stimulus is necessary in order to follow what is being discussed.
1	The response is very limited in content or coherence or is only minimally connected to the task. Speech may be largely unintelligible. A response at this level is characterized by at least two of the following:	Consistent pronunciation and intonation problems cause considerable listener effort and frequently obscure meaning. Delivery is choppy, fragmented, or telegraphic. Speech contains frequent pauses and hesitations.	Range and control of grammar and vocabulary severely limits (or prevents) expression of ideas and connections among ideas. Some very low-level responses may rely on isolated words or short utterances to communicate ideas.	The response fails to provide much relevant content. Ideas that are expressed are often inaccurate, limited to vague utterances, or repetitions (including repetition of prompt).
0	Speaker makes no attempt to respond OR response is unrelated to the topic.			

Teachers can use the authentic TOEFL iBT Scoring Rubrics developed by ETS to assess student responses to Integrated and Independent Tasks.

Teachers' Manuals

Teachers' Manuals for each level provide unit-by-unit suggestions as well as evaluation tools to track students' progress. The Teachers' Manuals also include actual student responses to speaking and writing tasks at all score levels. Provided by ETS, these authentic samples enable teachers to assess proficiency.

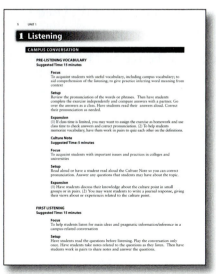

1   UNIT 1

1 Listening

CAMPUS CONVERSATION

PRE-LISTENING VOCABULARY
Suggested Time: 15 minutes

Focus
To acquaint students with useful vocabulary, including campus vocabulary; to aid comprehension of the listening; to give practice inferring word meaning from context

Setup
Review the pronunciation of the words or phrases. Then have students complete the exercise independently and compare answers with a partner. Go over the answers as a class. Have students read their answers aloud. Correct their pronunciation as needed.

Expansion
(1) If class time is limited, you may want to assign the exercise as homework and use class time to check answers and correct pronunciation. (2) To help students memorize vocabulary, have them work in pairs to quiz each other on the definitions.

Culture Note
Suggested Time: 5 minutes

Focus
To acquaint students with important issues and practices in colleges and universities

Setup
Read aloud or have a student read aloud the Culture Note so you can correct pronunciation. Answer any questions that students may have about the topic.

Expansion
(1) Have students discuss their knowledge about the culture point in small groups or in pairs. (2) You may want students to write a journal response, giving their views about or experiences related to the culture point.

FIRST LISTENING
Suggested Time: 15 minutes

Focus
To help students listen for main ideas and pragmatic information/inference in a campus-related conversation

Setup
Have students read the questions before listening. Play the conversation only once. Have students take notes related to the questions as they listen. Then have students work in pairs to share notes and answer the questions.

Acknowledgments

Many people at ETS contributed to this project, but Longman would especially like to thank Phil Everson, Matt Chametzky, Kate Kazin, Will Jared, and Frank Heron.

Credits

page 4 "CornCam" Copyright NPR© 2001. The text and audio of the news report by NPR's Cheryl Corley was originally broadcast on National Public Radio's *Morning Edition*© on August 2, 2001, and is used with the permission of National Public Radio, Inc. Any unauthorized duplication is strictly prohibited.; **page 6** "Focus on Bomb Suspect Brings Tears and a Plea" Copyright 1996 by The New York Times Co. Reprinted with permission.; **page 18** "The Achilles Heel Track Club" Footage Courtesy of WWOR News, WWOR-TV, Inc. All rights reserved.; **page 21** "The Miracle" © 1999 TIME Inc. reprinted by permission.; **page 37** "Get Back in Bed" Satellite Sisters LLC. Used by permission.; **page 57** "Monologue of Isabel Watching It Rain in Macondo" from LEAF STORM AND OTHER STORIES by Gabriel Garcia Marquez.; **page 75** "Interview with Medicine Priest" Used with permission of David Winston, Herbalist AHG ; **page 93** "Some Take the Time Gladly" by Mensah Dean from *The Washington Times*. Copyright © 1997 News World Communication, Inc. Reprinted with permission from *The Washington Times*.; **page 109** "Emotional Intelligence" From Ellen R. Green Wood, Samuel E. Wood *The World of Psychology*, 2/e. Published by Allyn and Bacon, Boston, MA. Copyright © 2002 by Pearson Education. Reprinted by permission of the publisher.; **page 124** "Food in a Bowl" Satellite Sister, LLC. Used by permission.; **page 127** "'Slow Food' Movement Aims at Restoring the Joy of Eating" From USA TODAY, a division of Gannett Co., Inc. Reprinted with Permission.; **page 140** "Poor Visitor" (1) Excerpt from "Poor Visitor" from LUCY by Jamaica Kincaid. Copyright © 1990 by Jamaica Kincaid. Reprinted by permission of Farrar, Straus and Giroux, LLC. (2) © Jamaica Kinkaid 1990. Reprinted with the permission of the author c/o The Wylie Agency Inc.; **page 143** "Coming to America" From SCHOLASTIC UPDATE November 15, 1996. Copyright © 1996 by Scholastic Inc. Reprinted by permission of Scholastic, Inc.; **page 163** "Thoreau's Home" by Henry D. Thoreau, from *Walden*. Text is reprinted from a first edition of *Walden, or Life in the Woods* 1854, published by Ticknor and Fields, Boston.; **page 166** "Inside the House" (Newsweek 11/27/95), from THE ROAD AHEAD by Bill Gates, copyright © 1995, 1996 by William H. Gates III. Used by permission of Viking Penguin, a division of Penguin Group (USA), Inc.

We acknowledge Tess Ferree and Kim Sanabria for use of their material from *Northstar: Listening and Speaking High Intermediate,* Second Edition and Andrew K. English and Laura Monahaon English for use of their material from *Northstar: Reading and Writing High Intermediate,* Second Edition.

Photo Credits

page 4, © Jim Foster/Corbis; **page 6,** © S. Martin-Atlanta Journal/Corbis Sygma; **page 17,** © Mary Kate Denny/ PhotoEdit; **page 21,** © Hulton Archive/Getty Images; **page 35,** © Cathrine Wessel/Corbis; **page 39,** © Royalty-Free/Corbis; **page 53,** © Royalty-Free/Corbis; **page 57,** © Bettmann/Corbis; **page 71,** © Jason/zefa/Corbis; **page 72,** © A. Stegmeyer Photography/Photo courtesy of Solar Survival Architecture; **page 90,** © Charlie Borand/IndexStock; **page 93,** © Mug Shots/Corbis; **page 106,** © Pat Clear Photography/PhotoEdit; **page 113,** © Royalty-Free/Corbis; **page 124,** © David Young—Wolff/PhotoEdit; **page 127,** © David Young—Wolff/PhotoEdit; **page 140,** © Alan Schein Photography/Corbis; **page 144,** © Underwood & Underwood/Corbis; **page 160,** © Emmanuel Faure/Getty Images; **page 206,** © Bill Aron/ PhotoEdit; **page 208,** © Bonnie Kamin/PhotoEdit; **page 209,** © Gary Conner/PhotoEdit; **page 211,** © Larry Williams & Associates/zefa/Corbis.

NorthStar Practice Units for the TOEFL® iBT

Media

TOEFL® iBT TARGET SKILLS	

- Identify and express main ideas
- Identify and express details
- Make inferences
- Organize information
- Complete outlines
- Express and support an opinion
- Skim and scan for key information

(ETS) For extra practice of TOEFL iBT skills, go to pages 206–223.

1 Listening

CAMPUS CONVERSATION

PRE-LISTENING VOCABULARY

Read the sentences. Guess the meaning of the boldfaced words and phrases. Choose the best definition or synonym. Work with a partner and compare your answers.

1. I don't know what to write my paper about. I can't **come up with** any ideas.
   a. talk about
   b. think of
   c. write about

2. I like taking advanced classes because we **go into more depth** and I learn more about the subject.
   a. examine more completely
   b. spend less time
   c. study at a later date

3. Advertisers try to **influence** us. They want us to buy things that we don't really need.
   a. agree with
   b. have an effect on
   c. understand

4. With my high-speed wireless web connection, I don't have to dial in and wait to get on the Internet. I get **instant** access to it.
   a. expensive
   b. immediate
   c. slow

5. I have a list of ten classes I'd like to take next semester, but I have to **narrow down** the list and choose only four.
   a. expand
   b. reduce
   c. select

6. If you need to look at a dictionary, go to the **reference desk** in the library, and the librarians will show you where it is.
   a. a place to buy a book
   b. a place to study quietly
   c. a place to get information

> **Culture Note:** College and university professors are required to have office hours when they are available to talk to students. Some professors may ask students to make appointments in advance, but many allow students to stop by during office hours without an appointment. When students ask questions about class materials or assignments, professors see it as a positive sign that they are engaged and interested in the class.

FIRST LISTENING

Read the questions. Listen to the conversation between a student and a professor. Take notes after each question. Share your notes with a partner. Then use your notes to answer the questions.

1. What problems does the student have? _____

_____

2. How does the professor help her? _____

_____

SECOND LISTENING

Read the questions. Listen to the conversation again. Add details to your notes. Then use your notes to answer the questions. Work with a partner and compare your answers.

1. Why does the student go to see her professor?
   (A) To explain why she missed a class
   (B) To ask a question about a topic discussed in class
   (C) To get a homework assignment
   (D) To get help choosing a topic for her class project

2. What topic does the professor suggest for the student's term paper?
   (A) Traditional journalism
   (B) Newspapers and magazines
   (C) Internet news sources
   (D) Reference resources

3. What did the student do at the library?
   (A) She tried to find an article for the class.
   (B) She got help from the librarian on her term paper.
   (C) She looked at Internet news.
   (D) She used the media center.

Listen again to part of the conversation. Then answer question 4.

4. Why does the professor say, "Really?"?
   (A) He is doubtful.
   (B) He is annoyed.
   (C) He is happy.
   (D) He is surprised.

Listen again to part of the conversation. Then answer question 5.

5. What can you infer about the professor?
   (A) He expects the student to agree with the article.
   (B) He is concerned that the student won't understand the article.
   (C) He disagrees with the author of the article.
   (D) He thinks the student should read the article.

ACADEMIC LISTENING

FIRST LISTENING

Listen to the radio report. Take notes as you listen using the questions. Work with a partner to combine your notes. Then use your notes to answer the questions.

1. What is CornCam? _____

   _____

   _____

2. Where is CornCam located? _____

   _____

   _____

3. Who watches CornCam? _____

   _____

   _____

SECOND LISTENING

Read the questions. Listen to the report again. Add details to your notes. Then use your notes to answer the questions. Work with a partner and compare your answers.

1. What is the report mainly about?
   (A) Farmers who live in the Midwest
   (B) Internet sites around the world
   (C) Methods for growing corn
   (D) A website that shows corn growing

2. In the report, the man mentions types of people who watch CornCam. Indicate whether each type of person is mentioned in the report. Check the correct box for each phrase.

	YES	NO
(A) People in England		
(B) Children in school		
(C) People in big cities		
(D) Commercial farmers		
(E) Scientists who study corn		

Listen again to part of the report. Then answer question 3.

3. What can you infer about the woman when she says, "Can it be that riveting, really? What's the appeal?"?
   (A) She has never seen CornCam.
   (B) She agrees with the man about CornCam.
   (C) She is surprised that CornCam is popular.
   (D) She disagrees with the man about CornCam.

4. According to the man, what is one reason people watch CornCam?
   (A) They think it is relaxing.
   (B) They want to learn about corn.
   (C) They have trouble sleeping.
   (D) They can see new farming methods.

Listen again to part of the report. Then answer question 5.

5. What does the man mean when he says this?
   (A) Good weather is very important for growing corn.
   (B) Corn only grows during the summer months.
   (C) Corn usually grows six inches a day.
   (D) The corn can grow very quickly in good conditions.

2 Reading

FOCUS ON BOMB SUSPECT BRINGS TEARS AND A PLEA

PRE-READING

Read the title of the article and look at the picture. Skim (read quickly) the first sentence of each paragraph. Then scan (look for without reading) to find the names of the people in the questions below. With a partner, discuss the questions.

1. Who is Richard Jewell?
2. Who is Barbara Jewell?

READING

Read the article and answer the questions. Then work with a partner and compare your answers. When you disagree, go back to the text to find helpful information.

Focus on Bomb Suspect Brings Tears and a Plea

(By Rick Bragg, from the *New York Times*)

1   Barbara Jewell stared into the unblinking eyes of the television cameras she has come to despise and spoke in tears today of how life had changed for her son, Richard, since he was named a month ago as a suspect in the bombing in Centennial Olympic Park. "Now my son has no real life," said Mrs. Jewell, a little gray-haired woman, speaking out for the first time since her 33-year-old son was suspected—but never arrested or charged—in the bombing that killed one person and injured 111 others.

2   "He is a prisoner in my home," Mrs. Jewell said at a news conference this afternoon. "He cannot work. He cannot know any type of normal life. He can only sit and wait for this nightmare to end."

3   She begged President Clinton to clear her son's name and asked reporters to spread the word that her son was innocent of any wrongdoing in the July 27 bombing. After her tearful request, her son's lawyers said they would file civil lawsuits over reporting on the case.

4   Richard A. Jewell, a security guard in Centennial Olympic Park and a former sheriff's deputy, was at first hailed as a hero for discovering the bomb and helping to clear

people from the area. Then news accounts, including a special edition of the *Atlanta Journal*, named him as a suspect. Since then, television and news executives have repeatedly debated the intense attention focused on Mr. Jewell, with most deciding that too many people knew he was a suspect for his name to be avoided or suppressed.

5   "I do not think any of you can even begin to imagine what our lives are like. Richard is not a murderer," said Mrs. Jewell, an insurance claims coordinator. But, she said, "He has been convicted in the court of public opinion."

6   Meanwhile, the Jewells continue to be besieged by reporters. "They have taken all privacy from us," Mrs. Jewell said. "They have taken all peace. They have rented an apartment which faces our home in order to keep their cameras trained on us around the clock. They watch and photograph everything we do. We wake up to photographers, we go to sleep with photographers. We cannot look out the windows. We cannot walk our dogs without being followed down the sidewalk."

7   Mrs. Jewell said she was not just saddened and hurt by the ordeal, but was also angry.

Richard Jewell was later cleared of any suspicion in the Olympic Park bombing. The federal government publicly apologized to him in 1997, and in 2005 another man pleaded guilty to the crime. However, Jewell's life has never been the same since.

1. What is the main idea of this text?
   (A) Richard Jewell was named as a suspect in the Olympic Park Bombing.
   (B) Richard Jewell's mother thinks news reports are hurting her son.
   (C) Richard Jewell does not like being followed by the media.
   (D) Richard Jewell's mother talked to President Clinton.

2. What does the author suggest about Barbara Jewell in this sentence?

   Barbara Jewell stared into the unblinking eyes of the television cameras she has come to despise and spoke in tears today of how life had changed for her son, Richard, since he was named a month ago as a suspect in the bombing in Centennial Olympic Park.

   (A) She is nervous.
   (B) She is tired.
   (C) She is excited.
   (D) She is sad.

3. What is Richard Jewell's occupation?
   (A) Lawyer
   (B) Insurance claims coordinator
   (C) Security guard
   (D) Television reporter

4. In paragraph 3, the word **begged** is closest in meaning to
   (A) asked
   (B) looked at
   (C) forced
   (D) helped

5. In paragraph 4, the word **most** refers to
   (A) reporters and journalists
   (B) television and news executives
   (C) police officers
   (D) people in Atlanta

6. In paragraph 6, the word **besieged** is closest in meaning to
   (A) interviewed
   (B) ignored
   (C) hated
   (D) surrounded

7. In paragraph 6, all of the following are mentioned by Barbara Jewell EXCEPT
   (A) The Jewells have no privacy or peace.
   (B) Photographers watch everything the Jewells do.
   (C) The Jewells are followed when they walk their dog.
   (D) Someone threatened to hurt Richard Jewell.

8. Look at the four squares ☐ that indicate where the following sentence could be added to the passage. Where would the sentence best fit? Circle the letter that shows the point where you would insert this sentence.

   As a result, most media outlets are now naming Mr. Jewell as a suspect.

   ⒜ Richard A. Jewell, a security guard in Centennial Olympic Park and a former sheriff's deputy, was at first hailed as a hero for discovering the bomb and helping to clear people from the area. ⒝ Then news accounts, including a special edition of the *Atlanta Journal*, named him as a suspect. ⒞ Since then, television and news executives have repeatedly debated the intense attention focused on Mr. Jewell, with most deciding that too many people knew he was a suspect for his name to be avoided or suppressed. ⒟

9. Write 1 to 4 to put the events in the order in which they occurred.
   (A) _____ Richard Jewell discovered a bomb in the Olympic park.
   (B) _____ The press started following Richard Jewell everywhere.
   (C) _____ Barbara Jewell criticized the press for their treatment of her son.
   (D) _____ Richard Jewell was named a suspect in the bombing.

ANALYSIS

It is helpful to know the purpose of a test item. There are four types of questions in the reading section:

1. Basic Comprehension

- main ideas
- details
- the meaning of specific sentences

2. Organization

- the way information is structured in the text
- the way ideas are linked between sentences or between paragraphs

3. Inference

- ideas are not directly stated in the text
- author's intention, purpose, or attitude not explicitly stated in the text

4. Vocabulary and Reference

- the meaning of words
- the meaning of reference words such as *his*, *them*, *this*, or *none*

Go back to the reading questions and label each question with 1, 2, 3, or 4. Then work with a partner to see if you agree. Check the Answer Key for the correct answers. Which questions did you get right? Which did you get wrong? What skills do you need to practice?

3 Speaking

INTEGRATED TASK: READ, LISTEN, SPEAK

In this section, you will read a short text and listen to an excerpt on the same topic. Then you will speak about the relationship between the two.

READING

Read the excerpt on the next page. Then complete the outline.

Technology and the News

Due to the development of new technology such as satellite communication and the Internet, people in the 21st century are better informed about world events than ever before. We no longer have to wait until the evening news hour or publication of the daily newspaper to find out about current events. Instead, we can get updates on the latest breaking news stories as soon as they happen via 24-hour cable TV broadcasts and Internet news sources. You can even subscribe to services that send news directly to your e-mail address or cell phone. As a result, we can always be informed about important events. In addition, news coverage is no longer limited by geography and distance. Modern Internet and satellite technology allows broadcasters to send video and audio reports around the world, so events that were once local now have a global audience, and we can learn about breaking news in every corner of the world.

Main Idea: _____

    Detail: _____

         _____

         _____

    Detail: _____

         _____

LISTENING

CD1 TRACK 08

Listen to the excerpt from a lecture. Use the outline to take notes as you listen.

Main Idea: _Modern news reporting makes us dumber._

    Detail: _____

         _____

         _____

    Detail: _____

         _____

SPEAKING

Speak on the following topic. Follow the steps below to prepare.

> Does modern news reporting make us better informed? Debate the two points of view in the reading and the lecture.

Step 1

Work with a partner. Review your notes on the reading and the listening and organize them in the chart.

	READING	LISTENING
Frequent news updates		
International news		

Step 2

Choose your roles in the debate. You must take opposing points of view. Take turns making a one-minute oral argument for your position. Use the outlines on page 10 to help you.

Step 3

Change partners. Take turns giving a one-minute response to the topic again.

> To evaluate your partner's response, use the Speaking Evaluation Form on page 174.

4 Writing

INDEPENDENT TASK

Write on the following topic. Follow the steps on the next page to prepare.

> What is the best source of news (newspaper, cable TV, the Internet, magazines)? Why do you prefer it to other news sources?

Step 1

- Think of reasons why you prefer the news source.

- Work in groups. Take turns describing your opinion. Use details and examples to support your opinion.

- React to what you have heard. What news sources do your classmates prefer? Why do they feel that way?

Step 2

Write for 20 minutes. Leave the last 5 minutes to edit your work.

To evaluate a partner's writing, use the Writing Evaluation Form on page 173.

Step 3

Use your partner's evaluation to help you revise and edit your writing. Write a second draft and give it to your teacher.

5 Skill Focus

SKIMMING AND SCANNING

EXAMINATION

Look at the following items from the unit. Work with a partner and answer these questions about the items.

- How much of the text did you reread to answer the questions? Did you reread it quickly or slowly?

- What strategy would be best for answering each question: reading the whole text quickly or looking for a specific piece of information in the text?

Item 1 (Reading, p. 7)

What is Richard Jewell's occupation?
(**A**) Lawyer
(**B**) Insurance claims coordinator
(**C**) Security guard
(**D**) Television reporter

Item 2 (Reading, p. 8)

Write 1 to 4 to put the events in the order in which they occurred.
(A) _____ Richard Jewell discovered a bomb in the Olympic park.
(B) _____ The press started following Richard Jewell everywhere.
(C) _____ Barbara Jewell criticized the press for their treatment of her son.
(D) _____ The media named Richard Jewell as a suspect in the bombing.

Tips

To do well on the TOEFL, it is essential to learn how to skim and scan. When you *skim* a text, you are reading quickly to understand the general meaning, the gist. When you *scan* a text, you are reading quickly to find specific information, such as facts, names, and dates.

Skimming Tips

- Go back to the text and reread it quickly.

- Read the first and last sentences of paragraphs.

Scanning Tips

- It is not necessary to read each word.

- Look at the text quickly to find key word(s).

In **Item 1**, you probably scanned the whole text to find the specific words or phrases related to jobs. Then you probably skimmed the nearby sentences to help you find the best answer, which is (C) *security guard*.

In contrast, in **Item 2**, you probably skimmed and scanned the whole text to answer the question. When you skimmed, you wanted to get the main ideas, which are paraphrased in the item choices. You probably also scanned for time markers, such as *today, a month ago, July 27*, etc. From using both skills, you learned that the order of items is (A), (D), (B), (C).

PRACTICE

1 *Work with a partner. Read the questions. Decide which strategy is best for finding the answer: skimming or scanning. Circle the best strategy.*

1. What is the main topic of the reading?   skim   scan

_____

2. What percent of Americans spend more than
   two hours per day paying attention to the news?   skim   scan

_____

3. What does the author say about the tabloid media?   skim   scan

_____

4. What are "news resistors"?   skim   scan

_____

5. What does paragraph 3 discuss?   skim   scan

_____

2 *Look at the reading. Go back and write the answers to the questions in Exercise 1 using the strategy you circled. Do not read every word.*

News in Society

1   People in the United States have many sources of news, some of which are available 24 hours a day. Some say that Americans have become addicted to the news. In a recent survey, more than 65 percent of American respondents said that they spend from one-half to two hours per day watching, listening to, or reading the news. Twenty percent said they pay attention to the news for more than two hours each day. News comes from every angle, not only from printed sources, but from TV, radio, and the Internet as well.

2   With the increased availability of news, serious questions have emerged about the role of the news media in society. Should the media report every detail about every story, even when the information does not seem timely or relevant? Critics are concerned that by focusing on everything at once, the media increasingly ignore the more important social, political, and economic issues that we face. We become distracted from what's important by reading about what is not. One extreme example of this is the type of information covered by the tabloid media, which focus on negative stories of violence, crime, and scandal.

3   How can people deal with all the news that is available to them? Some become "news resistors" and choose to turn their backs on news, resisting the urge to turn on the TV and read the paper every day. They argue that although daily news reports may provide us with many facts, they do not include the background or context that we need to understand news events. They suggest that instead of daily reports, we look for information from news sources that have more in-depth analysis of the news, such as monthly magazines.

3 *Read the article and check your answers. Did you answer the questions correctly by skimming and scanning?*

Overcoming Obstacles

LISTENING	
Campus Conversation	A student and professor discuss classes the student missed.
Academic Listening	A television news report: *Disabled Athletes Climb Mount Kilimanjaro*

READING	
Essay	*The Miracle*

WRITING	
Integrated Task: Read, Listen, Write	Discuss how the Americans with Disabilities Act helps disabled people in the workplace.

SPEAKING	
Independent Task	Describe a difficult experience and how you overcame it.

SKILL FOCUS	
Paraphrasing	Paraphrasing is the ability to restate ideas from other sources in your own words without changing the meaning.

TOEFL® iBT TARGET SKILLS	

- Identify and express main ideas
- Identify and express details
- Make inferences
- Recognize a speaker's or writer's attitude
- Paraphrase and summarize
- Summarize a text and relate it to a listening

ETS® For extra practice of TOEFL iBT skills, go to pages 206–223.

1 Listening

PRE-LISTENING VOCABULARY

Read the sentences. Guess the meaning of the boldfaced words and phrases. Then match each word or phrase with a definition or synonym from the list below. Work with a partner and compare your answers.

_____ 1. Poverty is a big problem, and there are many *aspects* to it. One is poor-quality housing, and another is lack of food.

_____ 2. I don't like her *attitude* toward me. She seems to dislike me for some reason.

_____ 3. You finished your report already? Wow! You*'re on top of* the work for this class!

_____ 4. I didn't work on my project last night, so I have to *catch up on* it today!

_____ 5. If you can't *deal with* a problem you're having at school, it's a good idea to talk to an advisor and get some help with it.

_____ 6. The professor offered to give the student *an extension* because he couldn't finish his work by the end of the semester.

_____ 7. I have a test today, so I'm going to *go over* my notes once more before class.

_____ 8. My friend is *paralyzed* from the waist down, so he uses a wheelchair to get around.

_____ 9. The Americans with Disabilities Act makes sure that disabled people have the same *rights* as everyone else, such as the right to get a job or to live where they want.

a. extra time

b. feelings about someone

c. freedoms and abilities

d. get to the same level as everyone else

e. in control of

f. manage

g. parts

h. review

i. unable to move part of one's body

Culture Note: In many university classes, students are expected to participate actively in class discussions and group projects. Grades are often based on participation as well as exams. Attendance is not optional. Therefore, when a student misses class for any reason, the student is expected to speak to the professor about the absence and make up any work.

FIRST LISTENING

Read the questions. Listen to the conversation between a student and a professor. Take notes after each question. Share your notes with a partner. Then use your notes to answer the questions.

1. Why does the student go to see the professor? _____

   _____

2. How does the professor help the student? _____

   _____

SECOND LISTENING

Read the questions. Listen to the conversation again. Add details to your notes. Then use your notes to answer the questions. Work with a partner and compare your answers.

1. Why does the student go to see his professor?
   (A) To say he needs to take some time off from school
   (B) To find out why he didn't do well on a test
   (C) To explain that he is late finishing an assignment
   (D) To explain that he was sick and missed several classes

2. What are the students required to do at the end of the term?
   (A) Make a group presentation about their research
   (B) Take a final exam
   (C) Write a term paper about their research
   (D) Do an independent study project

Listen again to part of the conversation. Then answer question 3.

3. Select the sentence that best expresses how the professor probably feels.
   (A) She's embarrassed because she can't find the handouts.
   (B) She's unhappy that Tom picked up the handouts.
   (C) She's impressed that the student already has the handouts.
   (D) She's pleased that the student is doing so well in class.

4. With which research group does the student want to work?
   (A) Housing and Transportation
   (B) Health care
   (C) Education
   (D) Employment

Listen again to part of the conversation. Then answer question 5.

5. What does the professor imply?
   (A) Getting an extension is a bad idea.
   (B) The student has a problem.
   (C) The student will need an extension.
   (D) She can help the student during the winter break.

ACADEMIC LISTENING

FIRST LISTENING

Listen to a news report about a group of disabled athletes from the Achilles Track Club who climbed Mount Kilimanjaro. Take notes using the questions below. Work with a partner and combine your notes.

1. What words describe the disabilities the climbers have? Circle all that apply.

   paralyzed   blind   deaf   amputee[1]

2. What did they do during the climb?

   _____

   _____

[1] *amputee:* someone who has had a leg or arm surgically removed

3. How did they feel during the climb?

_____

_____

SECOND LISTENING

Read the questions. Listen to the report again. Add details to your notes. Then use your notes to answer the questions. Work with a partner and compare your answers.

1. What disabilities did the climbers have?
(A) Most of them were deaf.
(B) Most of them were blind.
(C) Most of them were paralyzed.
(D) Most of them were amputees.

Listen again to part of the report. Then answer question 2.

2. What does the woman mean when she says, "Because behind accomplishing this physical challenge for myself, I knew there was a greater message we were all carrying."?
(A) She's tired because they had to carry a lot of heavy equipment.
(B) She wants people to know what disabled people can do.
(C) Finishing the climb was a relief.
(D) The climb was a spiritual journey.

3. What did the climbers do during their climb?
(A) They wrote about their experience on the Internet.
(B) They took a lot of photographs.
(C) They videotaped each other.
(D) They talked to the media about their experience.

Listen again to part of the report. Then answer question 4.

4. What does the woman mean when she says, "Getting to the top was definitely the high point."?
(A) Getting to the top of Mount Kilimanjaro was really difficult.
(B) It was very high at the top of Mount Kilimanjaro.
(C) The best part of the trip was reaching the top of Mount Kilimanjaro.
(D) The best part of the trip was climbing up Mount Kilimanjaro.

5. What can you infer about all the climbers?
(A) The climb was easier than they expected.
(B) They wish they had stayed home.
(C) They are glad they went on the climb.
(D) They are planning another climb soon.

ANALYSIS

It is helpful to know the purpose of a test item. There are three types of questions in the listening section.

1. Basic Comprehension

- main ideas
- details
- the meaning of specific sentences

2. Organization

- the way information is structured
- the way ideas are linked

3. Inference

- ideas are not directly stated
- speaker's intention, purpose, or attitude not explicitly stated

Go back to the listening questions and label each question with 1, 2, or 3. Then work with a partner to see if you agree. Check the Answer Key for the correct answers. Which questions did you get right? Which did you get wrong? What skills do you need to practice?

2 Reading

THE MIRACLE

PRE-READING

You will read an article by Diane Shuur, an accomplished jazz musician who is blind. In the reading, she compares her struggles and triumphs to those of Helen Keller, a famous writer and activist who was not only blind, but deaf as well.

Work with a partner. Read the sentences from the article and make predictions about what they mean.

Sentence 1

[Helen Keller] proved how language could liberate[1] the blind and the deaf.

How do you think Helen Keller proved this? _____

_____

[1]*liberate:* allow someone to go free

Sentence 2

I am a beneficiary of [Helen Keller's] work.

How do you think the author has benefited? _____

_____

READING

Read the text and answer the questions. Then work with a partner and compare your answers. When you disagree, go back to the text to find helpful information.

The Miracle

She altered our perception of the disabled and remapped the boundaries of sight and sense.

by Diane Schuur (from *Time*)

1   Helen Keller was less than two years old when she came down with a fever. It struck dramatically and left her unconscious. The fever went just as suddenly. But she was blinded and, very soon after, deaf. As she grew up, she managed to learn to do tiny errands, but she also realized that she was missing something. "Sometimes," she later wrote, "I stood between two persons who were conversing and touched their lips. I could not understand, and was vexed. I moved my lips and gesticulated frantically without result. This made me so angry at times that I kicked and screamed until I was exhausted." She was a wild child.

2   I can understand her rage. I was born two months prematurely and was placed in an incubator. The practice at the time was to pump a large amount of oxygen into the incubator, something doctors have since learned to be extremely cautious about. But as a result, I lost my sight. I was sent to a state school for the blind, but I flunked[1] first grade because Braille[2] just didn't make any sense to me. Words were a weird concept. I remember being hit and slapped. And you act all that in.[3] All rage is anger that is acted in, bottled in for so long that it just pops out. Helen had it harder. She was both blind and deaf. But, oh, the

---

[1] *flunked:* failed
[2] *Braille:* a form of printing with raised round marks that blind people can read by touching
[3] *act all that in:* keep your emotions inside you

transformation that came over her when she discovered that words were related to things! It's like the lyrics of that song: "On a clear day, rise and look around you, and you'll see who you are."

3   I can say the word *see*. I can speak the language of the sighted. That's part of the first great achievement of Helen Keller. She proved how language could liberate the blind and the deaf. She wrote, "Literature is my utopia. Here I am not disenfranchised."[4] But how she struggled to master language. In her book *Midstream*, she wrote about how she was frustrated by the alphabet, by the language of the deaf, even with the speed with which her teacher spelled things out for her on her palm. She was impatient and hungry for words, and her teacher's scribbling on her hand would never be as fast, she thought, as the people who could read the words with their eyes. I remember how books got me going after I finally grasped Braille. Being in that school was like being in an orphanage. But words—and in my case, music—changed that isolation. With language, Keller, who could not hear and could not see, proved she could communicate in the world of sight and sound—and was able to speak to it and live in it. I am a beneficiary of her work. Because of her example, the world has given way a little. In my case, I was able to go from the state school for the blind to regular public school from the age of 11 until my senior year in high school. And then I decided on my own to go back into the school for the blind. Now I sing jazz.

---

[4] *disenfranchised:* not having rights, not feeling a part of society

1. How did Helen Keller become blind and deaf?
   (A) She had a fever.
   (B) She was in an accident.
   (C) She was born blind and deaf.
   (D) She received too much oxygen.

2. In paragraph 1, what does the word *this* mean in the sentence beginning "This made me so angry . . ."?
   (A) Getting a fever
   (B) Standing between two people
   (C) Kicking and screaming
   (D) Not understanding people who were talking

3. Based on the information in paragraph 2, what can be inferred about premature babies born today?
   (A) They will probably be less healthy.
   (B) They will probably not be given too much oxygen.
   (C) They will probably not be put in an incubator.
   (D) They will probably be treated by fewer doctors.

4. The word *transformation* in paragraph 2 is closest in meaning to
   (A) emotion
   (B) image
   (C) change
   (D) problem

5. According to paragraph 2, what does the author imply about her childhood?
   (A) She learned to read easily.
   (B) She was angry because she was blind.
   (C) She was not a good student.
   (D) She went to school with seeing children.

6. Which of the sentences below best expresses the essential information in the passage excerpt? Incorrect choices change the meaning in important ways or leave out essential information.

   > She was impatient and hungry for words, and her teacher's scribbling on her hand would never be as fast, she thought, as the people who could read the words with their eyes.

   (A) Helen Keller wanted to communicate more quickly.
   (B) Helen Keller didn't understand her teacher.
   (C) Helen Keller's teacher wrote in her hand.
   (D) Helen Keller didn't get enough to eat.

7. The word *isolation* in paragraph 3 is closest in meaning to
   (A) feeling of being alone
   (B) feeling of belonging
   (C) ability to communicate
   (D) ability to make friends

8. Which of the following statements about the author can be inferred from paragraph 3?
   (A) The author feels sorry for Helen Keller.
   (B) The author was good friends with Helen Keller.
   (C) The author was inspired by Helen Keller's achievements.
   (D) The author wishes she were more like Helen Keller.

9. The organization of the text can best be described as
   (A) a comparison of the author's life and Helen Keller's life
   (B) a chronological description of events in the author's life
   (C) an argument in favor of educating blind people
   (D) a cause-and-effect analysis of losing one's sight

10. Look at the four squares ☐ that indicate where the following sentence could be added to the text. Where would the sentence best fit? Circle the letter that shows the point where you would insert this sentence.

> Because of this mistreatment, I became very angry.

I can understand her rage. I was born two months prematurely and was placed in an incubator. **A** The practice at the time was to pump a large amount of oxygen into the incubator, something doctors have since learned to be extremely cautious about. But as a result, I lost my sight. I was sent to a state school for the blind, but I flunked first grade because Braille just didn't make any sense to me. Words were a weird concept. I remember being hit and slapped. **B** And you act all that in. All rage is anger that is acted in, bottled in for so long that it just pops out. Helen had it harder. **C** She was both blind and deaf. But, oh, the transformation that came over her when she discovered that words were related to things! It's like the lyrics of that song: "On a clear day, rise and look around you, and you'll see who you are." **D**

11. Select the appropriate phrases from the answer choices and match them to the person to whom they relate. TWO of the answer choices will NOT be used.

Helen Keller   **Diane Schuur**

_____   _____

_____   _____

_____   _____

Answer Choices

(**A**) Became handicapped at age two   (**E**) Had parents who were blind

(**B**) Became handicapped at birth   (**F**) Went to a regular high school

(**C**) Failed first grade   (**G**) Wrote a book about her life

(**D**) Got her sight back later in life   (**H**) Was blind and deaf

3 Writing

INTEGRATED TASK: READ, LISTEN, WRITE

In this section, you will read a short text and listen to an excerpt on the same topic. Then you will write about the relationship between the two.

READING

Read the passage. Complete the outline below. Work with a partner and compare your answers.

The Americans with Disabilities Act of 1990

The Americans with Disabilities Act (ADA) became law in the United States in 1990. The law protects people with disabilities from employment discrimination. An employer must give disabled people an equal chance to be hired and promoted, and a person cannot be fired from a job because they have a disability.

In addition, employers are required to provide "reasonable accommodations" to help employees with disabilities perform their jobs. These reasonable accommodations include:

- getting special equipment (e.g., buying a TTY machine so a deaf person can use the telephone)
- allowing flexible work schedules (e.g., letting en employee come in late or leave early from work)
- making the workplace accessible to people with disabilities (e.g., installing a ramp so that people in wheelchairs can enter a building)

Most accommodations are low-cost and easy for an employer to make. For example, allowing an employee to work flexible hours may cost the employer nothing at all. However, if the accommodations are too expensive or too difficult to make, the employer is not required to provide them.

Main Idea: _____

_____

Detail: _____

_____

Detail: _____

_____

LISTENING

Listen to the radio report. Use the questions on the next page to take notes as you listen.

1. Who is Brian Wong?

_____

_____

2. What accommodations has Brian's employer made for him?

• accessibility: _____

• equipment: _____

• work schedule: _____

3. How does the company benefit?

_____

WRITING

Write on the following topic. Follow the steps below to prepare.

Describe the Americans with Disabilities Act and use examples from the radio report to explain how it helps disabled people in the workplace.

Step 1

Work with a partner. Skim the reading and your notes from the listening. Use the questions below to organize the information. Try to express the information in your own words, instead of copying directly from the reading.

1. What is the Americans with Disabilities Act (ADA)?

_____

2. What is the purpose of the ADA?

_____

3. What do employers have to do under the ADA?

_____

4. How does the ADA benefit Brian Wong?

• equipment: _____

• work schedule: _____

• accessibility: _____

Step 2

Write for 20 minutes. Leave the last 5 minutes to edit your work.

> To evaluate a partner's writing, use the Writing Evaluation Form on page 173.

Use your partner's evaluation to help you revise and edit your writing. Write a second draft and give it to your teacher.

4 Speaking

INDEPENDENT TASK

Speak on the following topic. Follow the steps below to prepare.

Describe a difficult experience and how you overcame it. Include details and examples in your explanation.

Step 1

Quickly brainstorm a list of difficult experiences you have faced, such as moving to a new country, taking a difficult class, entering a new school, or dealing with an illness or death in the family. Choose one experience that you want to speak about. Write some notes about your experience by answering the questions.

1. What happened? _____

   _____

2. What problems did this cause? _____

   _____

3. How did you overcome the problems? _____

   _____

Step 2

Work with a partner. Take turns practicing a one-minute oral response to the speaking topic. Use the information in your chart to help you.

Step 3

Change partners. Take turns giving a one-minute response to the topic again.

> To evaluate your partner's response, use the Speaking Evaluation Form on page 174.

5 Skill Focus

PARAPHRASING

EXAMINATION

1 *Read the excerpt from the Academic Listening. Look at the answer choices to the question. Do the choices use the same words as the report, or are the ideas expressed in other words?*

> The group kept a diary of their travels online, and even when the going got tough, they buckled down, turning to each other for inspiration as they continued on the trail to the peak.

What did the climbers do during their climb?
(A) They wrote about their experience on the Internet.
(B) They took a lot of photographs.
(C) They videotaped each other.
(D) They talked to the media about their experience.

2 *Read the question from the reading. Do the answer choices use the same wording as the reading text, or are the ideas expressed in other words?*

Which of the sentences below best expresses the essential information in the passage excerpt? Incorrect choices change the meaning in important ways or leave out essential information.

> She was impatient and hungry for words, and her teacher's scribbling on her hand would never be as fast, she thought, as the people who could read the words with their eyes.

(A) Helen Keller wanted to communicate more quickly.
(B) Helen Keller didn't understand her teacher.
(C) Helen Keller's teacher wrote in her hand.
(D) Helen Keller didn't get enough to eat.

3 *Review what you wrote for the Integrated Task on page 26. Did you use the same words to describe the ideas in the reading and listening, or did you express the ideas in your own words?*

Tips

To do well on the TOEFL, it is essential to learn how to read, write, and speak paraphrased information. When you are reading, you have to recognize when phrases and sentences have the same meaning as another phrase or sentence. When you are writing or speaking, you need to restate ideas from another source in your own words, without changing the meaning.

An effective paraphrase:

- contains the same information as the original statement.

- is expressed in different words.

- may leave out less important details.

Recognizing paraphrased information

When you are answering multiple-choice questions about the main idea or details of a text, you can often get the correct answer by choosing the best paraphrase of the information in the text.

Using paraphrasing in speaking or writing

When you write or speak about ideas in a text, you need to paraphrase the ideas you heard or read.

In writing, if you don't paraphrase, you must use quotation marks to show that you are quoting the same language as the original text. Otherwise, you may be committing plagiarism—taking words from someone else's work and pretending they are your own—an act that is prohibited in colleges and universities.

Example: The law protects people with disabilities from employment discrimination.

Quote: "The law protects people with disabilities from employment discrimination."

Paraphrase: The ADA stops employers from discriminating against disabled people.

In the Examination exercise, you noticed that the answer for the first item is (A) because it conveys the same meaning as the sentences in the listening excerpt. In the second item, the answer is (A) because it is the best restatement of the essential information in the reading passage excerpt.

PRACTICE

1 *Read about Frank McCourt, who overcame a difficult childhood to become a successful teacher and write the Pulitzer Prize-winning memoir* Angela's Ashes. *Read McCourt's biography. Then choose the best paraphrase for the numbered sentences.*

Frank McCourt was born in New York in 1930. ¹**Although his parents, Angela and Malachy, had moved to New York from Ireland in search of a better life, the family had a difficult time in New York because his father could not earn enough money to support them.** The McCourts returned to Ireland hoping that their life would improve. Again, it didn't. Life in Ireland was equally hard if not harder than in New York. Three of Frank's siblings died as babies. ²**Eventually, his father abandoned the family, forcing his four sons and Angela to live a very meager existence.**

Frank's childhood was filled with misery. ³**There was never enough food, and their house was small, dirty, and very cold in the wintertime. ⁴When it rained, the floor would flood with water.** Frank and his brothers yearned for a better life.

Frank did, however, have ways to escape from his tormented childhood. ⁵**He loved to read, and even though his dilapidated house had no electricity, he would read under the street lamp outside his home.** He also had a strong sense of humor. ⁶**Humor was the McCourt's defense against their life of relentless poverty and hopelessness, so even in the worst of times, the McCourts could find something to laugh about.**

Sentence 1
- (A) The McCourt family still had economic troubles after moving from Ireland to New York to improve their lives.
- (B) The McCourt family moved from Ireland to New York because they wanted to improve their lives.

Sentence 2
- (A) Frank's father left the family because they were so poor.
- (B) Frank's family was very poor after his father left.

Sentences 3 and 4
- (A) The McCourt's house got flooded whenever it rained.
- (B) The McCourts lived in very bad conditions and often went hungry.

Sentence 5
- (A) Frank enjoyed reading, even when it was difficult to find enough light.
- (B) Frank's house didn't have any electricity, so he couldn't read inside.

Sentence 6
- (A) The McCourts looked for humor, even when life was difficult.
- (B) The McCourts didn't take life seriously.

2 *Work with a partner. Compare your answers to the questions in Exercise 1.*

1. Underline the phrases in the numbered sentences and in the paraphrase that have the same meaning.

2. Discuss why the alternative paraphrase is not an effective paraphrase. Does it change the meaning of the numbered sentence, leave out important information, or use too many of the same words as the original sentence?

3 *Work with a partner. Read the following statements about Frank McCourt and write a paraphrase of each one. The first one is done for you. Then share your paraphrases with the class. Discuss the differences between them. (There may be more than one correct paraphrase.)*

1. Steward Park High School sat in the middle of dilapidated tenement buildings on Manhattan's Lower East Side.

Paraphrase: *Steward Park High School was is a poor neighborhood in Manhattan.*

2. When McCourt began teaching at Stuyvesant High School in 1972, he joked that he'd finally made it to paradise.

Paraphrase: _____

_____

3. On Fridays the students read their compositions aloud.

Paraphrase: _____

_____

4. McCourt was past 50 and painfully aware of the passage of time.

Paraphrase: _____

_____

5. In September 1996, *Angela's Ashes* hit bookstores.

Paraphrase: _____

_____

6. But despite his growing frustration at this unfinished book, he never tired of his students' work.

Paraphrase: _____

_____

4 *Review your work for the Integrated Task on pages 25–26. Read the notes you took for the radio report and reread your written responses to the questions. Discuss these questions:*

1. What information from the radio report did you include in your notes or written response?

2. How effectively did you paraphrase the information?

Rewrite one paraphrase so that it is more effective.

Medicine

TOEFL iBT TARGET SKILLS®

- Identify and express main ideas
- Identify and express details
- Make inferences
- Listen and take notes in an outline
- Summarize and discuss two points of view using main ideas and details

(ETS) For extra practice of TOEFL iBT skills, go to pages 206–223.

1 Listening

CAMPUS CONVERSATION

PRE-LISTENING VOCABULARY

Read the conversations. Guess the meaning of the boldfaced words and phrases. Then match each word or phrase with a definition or synonym from the list on the next page. Work with a partner and compare your answers.

_____ 1. A: Did you see the news about the house that **collapsed**?
                 B: Yes, they said the heavy rain had washed away the land under it.

_____ 2. A: I don't understand this math problem. I've been looking at it for 15 minutes!
                 B: Why don't you just **skip** it and finish the other problems first.

_____ 3. A: It's only 11:00 P.M.! It's too early to go to bed!
                 B: I'd better go to sleep now, or else I'll **end up** falling asleep in class tomorrow!

_____ 4. A: Hey, want to come over to my place and **hang out** for a while?
                 B: Sure! Maybe we can watch a movie or something.

_____ 5. A: You joined the **intramural** volleyball team? Does that mean you have to play against teams from other colleges?
                 B: No, we just play other teams from this school.

_____ 6. A: Wait, let me look in my bag. I want to **make sure** I have my textbook.
                 B: Good idea. The professor said we'd need the book today in class!

_____ 7. A: Why are we stopping at the security office?
                 B: We need to get a **clearance**, or security won't let us into the building.

_____ 8. A: When's the last time you had a **physical**?
                 B: Let's see . . . I saw the doctor about a year ago, and she gave me a complete exam.

_____ 9   A: I'm thinking about dropping a class. What's the **policy** on that?
                 B: If you drop it in the first two weeks of school, you can get most of your money back.

_____ 10. A: I heard you are taking six classes this semester. You must be really busy!
                 B: Oh, it's really **no big deal**. A couple of them are just fun classes.

_____ 11. A: Did you hear about Janelle's family? They were in a car accident. Her younger brother was killed, and her mom and dad are in the hospital.
                 B: I know. It's a real **tragedy**.

a. very sad event

b. approval for something

c. an examination of someone's body and general health by a doctor

d. official way of doing something

e. check on something or verify it

f. happening within one school

g. finish by having an unplanned result

h. not complicated or important

i. not do something

j. spend time with someone

k. suddenly fell down

> **Culture Note:** Many colleges and universities have student health clinics that provide medical care for students. Students can get physical exams, see mental health counselors, and receive emergency care when they are sick. When students enroll at a school, they are required to purchase health insurance that pays for health services on campus or at a hospital.

FIRST LISTENING

Read the questions on the next page. Listen to the conversation between a basketball coach and a student. Take notes after each question. Share your notes with a partner. Then use your notes to answer the questions.

1. What does the student want to do? _____

_____

2. What does the coach tell him? _____

_____

SECOND LISTENING

Read the questions. Listen to the conversation again. Add details to your notes. Then use your notes to answer the questions. Work with a partner and compare your answers.

1. What does the student want to do?
(**A**) Play intramural basketball
(**B**) See the doctor about an injury
(**C**) Ask the coach a question about a class
(**D**) Meet the other players on his basketball team

Listen again to part of the conversation. Then answer question 2.

2. Select the sentence that best expresses how the student probably feels.
(**A**) He is bored because he can't play basketball.
(**B**) He is nervous about seeing the doctor.
(**C**) He is upset that he needs a health clearance.
(**D**) He is happy that he can join the basketball team.

Listen again to part of the conversation. Then answer question 3.

3. Why does the coach say, "Yeah, I know. I can see you're anxious to get started."?
(**A**) To explain the university's policy
(**B**) To express his agreement with the policy
(**C**) To show he is sympathetic to the student
(**D**) To indicate that he is angry at the student

Listen again to part of the conversation. Then answer question 4.

4. What does the coach imply about getting a health clearance?
(**A**) It takes a long time to get an appointment with the doctor.
(**B**) The student must pay a fee to get a health clearance.
(**C**) Several other students also need health clearances.
(**D**) It is not difficult to get a health clearance.

5. What does the student decide to do at the end of the conversation?
   (**A**) Watch the basketball team practice
   (**B**) Talk to a different coach
   (**C**) Go to Health Services right away
   (**D**) Look for information about another sport

ACADEMIC LISTENING

FIRST LISTENING

Listen to an interview from the Satellite Sisters, *a radio show featuring conversation among five sisters who live in five different cities. Lian, one of the sisters, is talking to Dr. Joyce Walsleben, director of New York University's Sleep Disorders Center. Take notes using the outline below. Work with a partner and combine your notes.*

What is Lian's personal experience with sleep?

_____

_____

How serious a problem is sleep deprivation?

_____

_____

Example: _____

Example: _____

How does Lian feel without sleep?

_____

_____

What happens by Friday?

_____

_____

SECOND LISTENING

Read the questions. Listen to the interview again. Add details to your notes. Then use your notes to answer the questions. Work with a partner and compare your answers.

1. What is the report mainly about?
   (A) The type of people who suffer from sleep loss
   (B) The causes and effects of sleep loss
   (C) Ways to avoid sleep loss
   (D) Accidents caused by sleep loss

2. Why does Lian mention her experience as a parent?
   (A) To explain her children's sleep habits
   (B) To give advice about how to get more sleep
   (C) To compare sleep loss problems in adults and children
   (D) To give an example of the causes and effects of sleep loss

3. Which effects of sleep deprivation were mentioned in the report? Check the items that were mentioned.
   (A) _____ Poor job performance
   (B) _____ Weight gain
   (C) _____ Car accidents
   (D) _____ Not making good decisions
   (E) _____ Falling asleep at work

Listen again to part of the conversation. Then answer question 4.

4. What does Dr. Walsleben imply when she says, "I think it's great of you to have recognized that."?
   (A) She feels that there are more tired drivers now than in the past.
   (B) She understands why people drive when they are tired.
   (C) She thinks that most drivers do not recognize when they are too tired to drive.
   (D) She wants Lian to explain more about her driving habits.

5. What does Dr. Walsleben imply about tired drivers?
   (A) They should not drive.
   (B) They should take time off from work.
   (C) They should follow traffic regulations.
   (D) They should drink coffee to wake up.

2 Reading

NORMAN COUSINS'S LAUGH THERAPY

PRE-READING

Read the title of the article. Then read the first and last sentences of each paragraph.

What is the main idea of the article? _____

_____

READING

Read the article and answer the questions. Then, work with a partner and compare your answers. When you disagree, go back to the text to find helpful information.

Norman Cousins's Laugh Therapy

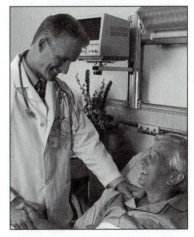

1   In the summer of 1964, well-known writer and editor Norman Cousins became very ill. His body ached and he felt constantly tired. It was difficult for him to even move around. He consulted his physician, who did many tests. Eventually he was diagnosed as having ankylosing spondylitis, a very serious and destructive form of arthritis. His doctor told him that he would become immobilized and eventually die from the disease. He was told he had only a 1 in 500 chance of survival.

2   Despite the diagnosis, Cousins was determined to overcome the disease and survive. He had always been interested in medicine and had read the book *The Stress of Life* (1956) by Hans Selye, an organic chemist, which discussed how body chemistry and health can be damaged by emotional stress and negative attitudes. This made Cousins think about the possible benefits of positive attitudes and emotions. He

thought, "If negative emotions produce (negative) changes in the body, wouldn't positive emotions produce positive chemical changes? Is it possible that love, hope, faith, laughter, confidence, and the will to live have positive therapeutic value?"

3   He decided to concentrate on positive emotions as a remedy to heal some of the symptoms of his ailment. In addition to his conventional medical treatment, he tried to put himself in situations that would elicit positive emotions. "Laugh therapy" became part of his treatment. He scheduled time each day for watching comedy films, reading humorous books, and doing other activities that would bring about laughter and positive emotions. Within eight days of starting his "laugh therapy" pro-gram, his pain began to decrease and he was able to sleep more easily. His body chemistry even began to change, and doctors were able to see an improvement in his condition! He was able to return to work in a few months' time and actually reached complete recovery after a few years.

4   Skeptical readers may question the doctor's preliminary diagnosis, and argue that Cousins was not really healed because he didn't have the disease in the first place. However, Cousins believes his recovery is the result of a mysterious mind-body interaction. His "laugh therapy" is a good example of one of the many alternative, or nonconventional, medical treatments people look to today.

1. Which of the sentences below best expresses the essential information in the passage excerpt? Incorrect choices change the meaning in important ways or leave out essential information.

> He had always been interested in medicine and had read the book *The Stress of Life* (1956) by Hans Selye, an organic chemist, which discussed how body chemistry and health can be damaged by emotional stress and negative attitudes.

(A) Hans Selye was an organic chemist who wrote a book called *The Stress of Life*.
(B) Cousins read a book about the effects of negative emotions on body chemistry.
(C) Stress and negative attitudes can cause changes in body chemistry.
(D) Cousins was interested in medicine, so he read the book *The Stress of Life*.

2. In paragraph 2, the word *This* refers to
(A) the practice of medicine
(B) the thesis of Hans Selye's book
(C) the idea of body chemistry
(D) the problem of emotional stress

3. Based on paragraph 2, how did reading the book *The Stress of Life* affect Norman Cousins?
   (A) It made Cousins decide to write a book about his illness.
   (B) It influenced Cousins to refuse conventional medical treatment.
   (C) It caused Cousins to become interested in medicine.
   (D) It gave Cousins the idea of using positive emotions to heal illness.

4. The word *elicit* in paragraph 3 is closest in meaning to
   (A) produce
   (B) end
   (C) question
   (D) ignore

5. All of the following are mentioned in paragraph 3 as benefits of Cousins's laugh therapy EXCEPT
   (A) He had less pain.
   (B) He became stronger.
   (C) His body chemistry started to change.
   (D) He could return to work.

6. Look at the four squares ☐ that indicate where the following sentence could be added to the text. Where would the sentence fit best? Circle the letter that shows the point where you would insert this sentence.

   Soon his therapy began to have a positive effect.

   A He decided to concentrate on positive emotions as a remedy to heal some of the symptoms of his ailment. B In addition to his conventional medical treatment, he tried to put himself in situations that would elicit positive emotions. "Laugh therapy" became part of his treatment. He scheduled time each day for watching comedy films, reading humorous books, and doing other activities that would bring about laughter and positive emotions. C Within eight days of starting his "laugh therapy" program, his pain began to decrease and he was able to sleep more easily. His body chemistry even began to change, and doctors were able to see an improvement in his condition! He was able to return to work in a few months' time and actually reached complete recovery after a few years. D

7. The word *skeptical* in paragraph 4 is closest in meaning to
   (A) angry
   (B) doubting
   (C) confused
   (D) intelligent

8. According to paragraph 4, what does the author say about laugh therapy?
   (A) Doctors understand why laugh therapy works.
   (B) Laugh therapy works on all types of illnesses.
   (C) Not everyone believes that laugh therapy works.
   (D) Laugh therapy works better than conventional medicine.

9. Which of the following best describes the author's presentation of information about Norman Cousins's laugh therapy?
(A) The author describes events in Cousins's life in the order they occurred.
(B) The author compares conventional medical treatment and laugh therapy.
(C) The author discusses two opinions about laugh therapy.
(D) The author argues in favor of using laugh therapy.

10. Read the first sentence of a summary of the article. Then complete the summary by circling THREE answer choices that express the most important ideas in the article. Some sentences do not belong in the summary because they express ideas that are not presented in the passage or are minor ideas in the passage.

Norman Cousins used laugh therapy to cure himself of a deadly disease.

Answer Choices

(A) Doctors are studying laugh therapy to understand how it works.

(B) Cousins invented laugh therapy to use positive emotions for healing.

(C) Cousins made a complete recovery and went back to work.

(D) The book *The Stress of Life* was written by chemist Hans Selye.

(E) Cousins was diagnosed with a deadly form of arthritis.

(F) Cousins watched comedy films and read humorous books.

ANALYSIS

It is helpful to know the purpose of a test item. There are four types of questions in the reading section.

1. Basic Comprehension

- main ideas
- details
- the meaning of specific sentences

2. Organization

- the way information is structured in the text
- the way ideas are linked between sentences or between paragraphs

3. Inference

- ideas are not directly stated in the text
- author's intention, purpose, or attitude not explicitly stated in the text

4. Vocabulary and Reference

- the meaning of words

- the meaning of reference words such as *his*, *them*, *this*, or *none*.

Go back to the reading questions and label each question as 1, 2, 3, or 4. Then work with a partner to see if you agree. Check the Answer Key for the correct answers. Which questions did you get right? Which did you get wrong? What skills do you need to practice?

3 Speaking

INTEGRATED TASK: READ, LISTEN, SPEAK

In this section, you will read a short passage and listen to an excerpt on the same topic. Then you will speak about the relationship between the two.

READING

Read a university newspaper's announcement about a new late-night study center. Then take notes on the important information.

Late-Night Study Center

The new Late-Night Study Center will open next semester on the first floor of the library. The goal is to provide a safe and quiet study space for students who wish to study after normal library hours end. The center will be open Sunday through Thursday, 11:00 P.M. to 8:00 A.M., with expanded hours during study periods and finals week. During late-night study, the reserves desk and group study rooms will be open, and photocopiers and the public computers will be available. Other library services will be closed. The eat-in lounge will be open, but food and drink must stay in that area.

Late-Night Study Center

Purpose: _____

Location: _____

Hours: _____

Services available: _____

LISTENING

Listen to the conversation. Use the outline to take notes as you listen.

CD1 TRACK 22

Opinion: The woman (supports / does not support) creation of the Late-Night Study Center.

Reasons: 1. _____

_____

_____

2. _____

_____

_____

SPEAKING

Speak on the following topic. Follow the steps below to prepare.

The woman expresses her opinion of the announcement in the university newspaper. State her opinion and explain the reasons she gives for holding that opinion.

Step 1

Work with a partner. Skim your notes on the reading and the listening. Prepare for the speaking task by answering the questions.

1. What is the Late-Night Study Center? _____

_____

2. What is the woman's opinion about it? _____

_____

3. What are the reasons for her opinion? _____

_____

Step 2

With your partner, take turns practicing a one-minute oral response. Use the answers to the questions from Step 1 to help you.

Step 3

Change partners. Take turns giving a one-minute response to the topic again.

To evaluate your partner's response, use the Speaking Evaluation Form on page 174.

4 Writing

INDEPENDENT TASK

Write on the following topic. Follow the steps below to prepare.

Discuss how emotions can affect a person's health. Be sure to state a main idea. Use details and examples to explain your opinion.

Step 1

- Think of reasons for your opinion.

- Work in groups. Take turns describing your opinion.

- React to what you have heard. What was your classmate's opinion? Why does your classmate have that opinion?

Step 2

Write for 20 minutes. Leave the last 5 minutes to edit your work.

> To evaluate a partner's writing, use the Writing Evaluation Form on page 173.

5 Skill Focus

IDENTIFYING AND USING MAIN IDEAS AND DETAILS

EXAMINATION

*Look at the following questions from the unit. Mark the items that ask you to identify main ideas (**MI**) and items that ask you to identify detail (**D**).*

Item 1 (Campus Conversation, p. 36)

_____ What does the student want to do?
  (A) Play intramural basketball
  (B) See the doctor about an injury
  (C) Ask the coach a question about a class
  (D) Meet the other players on his basketball team

Item 2 (Academic Listening, p. 38)

_____ What is the report mainly about?
(A) The type of people who suffer from sleep loss
(B) The causes and effects of sleep loss
(C) Ways to avoid sleep loss
(D) Accidents caused by sleep loss

Item 3 (Academic Listening, p. 38)

_____ Which effects of sleep deprivation were mentioned in the report? Check the items that were mentioned.
(A) _____ Poor job performance
(B) _____ Weight gain
(C) _____ Car accidents
(D) _____ Not making good decisions
(E) _____ Falling asleep at work

Item 4 (Reading, p. 41)

_____ All of the following are mentioned in paragraph 3 as benefits of Cousins's laugh therapy EXCEPT
(A) He had less pain.
(B) He became stronger.
(C) His body chemistry started to change.
(D) He could return to work.

Item 5 (Reading, p. 42)

_____ Read the first sentence of a summary of the article. Then complete the summary by selecting THREE answer choices that express the most important ideas in the article. Some sentences do not belong in the summary because they express ideas that are not present in the passage or are minor ideas in the passage.

Norman Cousins used laugh therapy to cure himself of a deadly disease.

Answer Choices

(A) Doctors are studying laugh therapy to understand how it works.

(B) Cousins invented laugh therapy to use positive emotions for healing.

(C) Cousins made a complete recovery and went back to work.

(D) The book *The Stress of Life* was written by chemist Hans Selye.

(E) Cousins was diagnosed with a deadly form of arthritis.

(F) Cousins watched comedy films and read humorous books.

Tips

To do well on the TOEFL, it is essential to identify and use main ideas and details.

Main Ideas

When you read or listen to a text, first identify the topic. Ask yourself: Who or what is this text about? Then try to determine what the author's or speaker's most important point about the topic is. This will help you identify the main idea.

Details

Detail questions can focus on specific examples, facts, explanations, or reasons. They often ask *wh-* questions *(who, what, when, where, why, how?).*

When you read or listen to a text, you must distinguish between relevant and irrelevant information. Ask yourself, "Is this detail important? Does it support the main idea?" Not all details in a text or segment of speech are equally important.

Some TOEFL questions about details also ask you to eliminate something that is not mentioned in the text:

- All of the following are mentioned in paragraph 2 EXCEPT . . .

- Which of the following is NOT mentioned in paragraph 2?

Item 1 from the Campus Conversation is a main idea question about the entire conversation: playing intramural basketball.

From the Academic Listening, **Item 2** is a main idea question that asks about the main topic of the listening. Answer choices (A) and (B) are incorrect because they are details in the report, not main ideas. **Item 3** is a detail question about examples used to support the main idea. The question contains a list of possible effects, and you must listen for the ones mentioned in the report.

From the Reading, **Item 4** is a detail question about possible benefits of laugh therapy. You have to eliminate the incorrect answer choice. **Item 5** is a main idea question. You must choose the three statements that express the most important ideas in the passage. Answer choice (A) is incorrect because the topic was not discussed in the article. Answer choices (D) and (F) are incorrect because they are minor details in the passage, not main ideas.

PRACTICE

1 *You will read an article about sleep deprivation. Before reading the article, read the questions below. Identify whether they ask about the main idea (**MI**) or a detail (**D**).*

_____ 1. What is this article mainly about? _____

_____

_____ 2. Why did Jonas Robards go into the hospital? _____

_____

_____ 3. Which of the following people is NOT mentioned in the article?

(A) Jonas Robards

(B) Robards's doctor

(C) A medical intern

(D) A nurse

_____ 4. According to paragraph 2, how many 10-hour days had the intern worked before the accident? _____

_____ 5. Based on paragraph 3, what are hospitals doing to reduce staff errors?

_____

_____ 6. What problem is discussed in the article? _____

_____

2 *Read the article on the next page. Underline the sections of the text where you can find the answers to the questions above. Then answer the questions. Discuss your answers with a partner.*

Sleep Deprivation Causes Medical Error

1   Two weeks ago, 10-year-old Jonas Robards was admitted to a private hospital in Colorado for routine surgery. In preparation for the operation, he was accidentally given an overdose of his medication. He became very ill for several days, but fortunately he recovered. However, this case illustrates the serious problem of medical errors caused by staff who are suffering from sleep deprivation.

2   Investigations revealed that the intern who ordered the medication that night, as well as the nurse who administered it, were both seriously sleep deprived. They had both been on duty for 15 hours when Robards received his medicine. The intern had worked 10 hours per day for the past eight days, while the nurse had worked the same shifts for six days in a row. Just before checking on the boy and ordering his medicine, both the intern and the nurse had spent five hours in the operating room working on victims of a car accident emergency.

3   Because of stories like these, many hospitals are considering limiting the number of hours a doctor or nurse can work per week. They are also instituting new rules, such as prohibiting staff from giving medication if they have been on duty for more than 12 hours. With these new restrictions, hospitals hope to reduce the number of errors made by staff members who have not gotten enough sleep.

3 *Look back at the sets of listening questions in this unit. Identify the main idea and detail questions. (Each set of listening questions has one main idea question and one or more detail questions.)*

Natural Disasters

LISTENING	
Campus Conversation	A student and a computer technician discuss a computer problem.
Academic Listening	A radio report: *Hurricane Hunters*

READING	
Fiction Excerpt	*Monologue of Isabel Watching It Rain in Macondo*

WRITING	
Integrated Task: Read, Listen, Write	Compare hurricanes and tornadoes.

SPEAKING	
Independent Task	Describe a time when you experienced a natural disaster or unusual weather event.

SKILL FOCUS	
Making Inferences	Inferences are guesses, predictions, or conclusions about information that is not stated directly.

TOEFL® iBT TARGET SKILLS

- Identify and express main ideas
- Identify and express details
- Infer a speaker's or writer's intention or purpose
- Skim for important facts
- Compare and contrast related text and listening
- Organize main ideas and details

(ETS) For extra practice of TOEFL iBT skills, go to pages 206–223.

1 Listening

CAMPUS CONVERSATION

PRE-LISTENING VOCABULARY

Read the short passages. Guess the meaning of the boldfaced words and phrases. Then match each word or phrase with a definition or synonym from the list below. Work with a partner and compare your answers.

If you use a computer, (1) **chances are** that you will have a problem at some point. Some solutions are simple, like remembering to (2) **plug in** your computer before you turn it on. Other problems can be very complicated. That's why it's important to (3) **back up** your work frequently, so if something happens, you will have a saved copy of it.

My car is really old and (4) **in bad shape**. First it got a (5) **leak** around the windshield, so I get wet every time I drive in the rain. The hood is getting rusty. Now the (6) **battery** is dead, so I can't even start the car!

Once I lived at the bottom of a hill. One day, a road construction crew accidentally broke a major water pipe. Then (7) **all of a sudden**, the water poured down the hill right to my house. The rushing water was (8) **intense**. All my (9) **stuff** got wet: my furniture, my clothing, my computer, everything! I was afraid that my house might wash away in the water!

_____ **a.** opening where water enters

_____ **b.** an object that supplies electricity

_____ **c.** things that belong to someone

_____ **d.** having a strong effect

_____ **e.** connect to an electrical supply

_____ **f.** it's likely

_____ **g.** not in good condition

_____ **h.** save on a computer hard drive or other storage media

_____ **i.** unexpectedly

Culture Note: Most colleges and universities provide computer services including wireless or high-speed Internet access, e-mail services, computer labs where students can use computers and printers, and classes on using different computer software. Many campuses also have a computer support center, staffed by student consultants who can help with simple computer problems.

FIRST LISTENING

Read the questions. Listen to the conversation between a student and a student consultant. Take notes as you listen. Share your notes with a partner. Then use your notes to answer the questions.

1. What is the student's problem? _____

_____

2. How does the student consultant help the student? _____

_____

SECOND LISTENING

Read the questions. Listen to the conversation again. Add details to your notes. Then use your notes to answer the questions. Work with a partner and compare your answers.

1. What is the student's problem?
   (A) His computer got wet in a flood.
   (B) His computer won't turn on.
   (C) He lost some work on his computer.
   (D) He needs a new computer program.

Listen again to part of the conversation. Then answer question 2.

2. When the student says, "This is great . . . " he probably feels
   (A) unhappy about his computer problem
   (B) hopeful that his computer will be fixed
   (C) angry at the student consultant
   (D) relieved by what the student consultant told him

3. What happened to the student's roommate?
   (A) The rain woke him up.
   (B) His laptop also stopped working.
   (C) He stepped in a big puddle.
   (D) His desk got wet from the rain.

Listen again to part of the conversation. Then answer question 4.

4. Why does the student consultant say, "But about your computer . . . "?
   (A) To disagree with the student
   (B) To answer a question
   (C) To end the conversation
   (D) To change the subject

Listen again to part of the conversation. Then answer question 5.

5. What does the student consultant mean when she says, "Well, the bookstore has some computer stuff . . . you can try looking there . . . "?
   (A) She doubts that the bookstore has computer batteries.
   (B) She believes the bookstore has a lot of computer equipment.
   (C) She is unsure whether the bookstore is open.
   (D) She is certain the student can buy a computer battery at the bookstore.

6. What does the student consultant suggest the student do in the future?
   (A) Buy a new computer
   (B) Always back up his work
   (C) Leave his computer to be repaired
   (D) Save his notes in case this happens again

ACADEMIC LISTENING

FIRST LISTENING

Listen to the radio report about Hurricane Hunters. Take notes as you listen. Work with a partner to combine your notes. Then use your notes to answer the questions.

1. What are the Hurricane Hunters doing?

   _____

   _____

2. What are conditions inside the hurricane?

   eye wall: _____

   inside the eye: _____

3. What does the crew do inside the eye?

_____

_____

4. Why do people need to be on the airplane?

_____

SECOND LISTENING

Read the questions. Listen to the report again. Add details to your notes. Then use your notes to answer the questions. Work with a partner and compare your answers.

1. Where does the Hurricane Hunters' airplane travel?
   (A) Around the outside of the hurricane
   (B) Through the eye of the hurricane
   (C) On the ocean's surface
   (D) Directly behind the hurricane

Listen again to part of the conversation. Then answer question 2.

2. Why does the reporter Alex Zhao say, "But wait . . . "?
   (A) To correct a mistake
   (B) To show that he is paying attention
   (C) To indicate that something has suddenly changed
   (D) To interrupt the other speaker

3. According to crew member Miguel Rios, why is it necessary for people to be on the airplane?
   (A) They have to steer the airplane.
   (B) They can make observations that can't be made with technology.
   (C) They need to run the machines on the airplane.
   (D) They can make decisions about where to travel inside the hurricane.

Listen again to part of the conversation. Then answer question 4.

4. Select the sentence that best expresses Andrea Davis's reply to the reporter.
   (A) "My job can be frightening, but the work is very important."
   (B) "My job is dangerous, so I have to be brave."
   (C) "I don't think about danger when I'm doing my job."
   (D) "When I'm flying, I can't wait to get back on land."

5. What do the Hurricane Hunters do with the information they collect?
   (A) They make predictions about the hurricane.
   (B) They give it to weather forecasters.
   (C) They tell authorities where to evacuate the coastline.
   (D) They use it to study the behavior of hurricanes.

ANALYSIS

It is helpful to know the purpose of a test item. There are three types of questions in the listening section.

1. Basic Comprehension

- main ideas
- details
- the meaning of specific sentences

2. Organization

- the way information is structured
- the way ideas are linked

3. Inference

- ideas are not directly stated
- speaker's intention, purpose, or attitude not explicitly stated

Go back to the listening questions and label each question with 1, 2, or 3. Then work with a partner to see if you agree. Check the Answer Key for the correct answers. Which questions did you get right? Which did you get wrong? What skills do you need to practice?

2 Reading

MONOLOGUE OF ISABEL WATCHING IT RAIN IN MACONDO

PRE-READING

In this piece of fiction by Nobel Prize winner Gabriel García Márquez, the narrator, Isabel, describes the rainfall at the beginning of what will eventually be an enormous flood.

Read the sentences from the passage and try to guess the answers to the questions on the next page.

- It rained all afternoon in a single tone.
- My stepmother and I went back to look at the garden.
- A trickle of water began to run off the flowerpots.
- My father occupied the same spot where he had been on Sunday afternoon, but he didn't talk about the rain.
- And he stayed there, sitting by the railing with his feet on a chair and his head turned toward the empty garden.

- I saw the small garden, empty for the first time, and the jasmine bush against the wall, faithful to the memory of my mother.

- Suddenly I felt overcome by an overwhelming sadness.

    1. Where does the story take place? _____

    2. Who are the characters in the story? _____

    3. How do the characters feel? _____

READING

Read the passage and answer the questions. Then work with a partner and compare your answers. When you disagree, go back to the text to find helpful information.

MONOLOGUE OF ISABEL WATCHING IT RAIN IN MACONDO

BY GABRIEL GARCÍA MÁRQUEZ
(from *Leaf Storm and Other Stories*)

1   It rained all afternoon in a single tone. In the uniform and peaceful intensity you could hear the water fall, the way it is when you travel all afternoon on a train.

5   But without our noticing it, the rain was penetrating too deeply into our senses. Early Monday morning, when we closed the door to avoid the cutting, icy draft that blew in from the courtyard, our

10   senses had been filled with rain. And on Monday morning they had overflowed. My stepmother and I went back to look at the garden. The harsh gray earth of May had been changed overnight into a

15   dark, sticky substance like cheap soap. A trickle of water began to run off the flowerpots. "I think they had more than enough water during the night," my stepmother said. And I noticed that she had stopped smiling and that her joy of the previous day had changed during the night into a lax and

20 tedious seriousness. "I think you're right," I said. "It would be better to
have the Indians put them on the veranda[1] until it stops raining." And
that was what they did, while the rain grew like an immense tree over
the other trees. My father occupied the same spot where he had been on
Sunday afternoon, but he didn't talk about the rain. He said: "I must
25 have slept poorly last night because I woke up with a stiff back." And he
stayed there, sitting by the railing with his feet on a chair and his head
turned toward the empty garden. Only at dusk, after he had turned down
lunch, did he say: "It looks like it will never clear." And I remembered the
months of heat. I remembered August, those long and awesome siestas[2]
30 in which we dropped down to die under the weight of the hour, our
clothes sticking to our bodies, hearing outside the insistent and dull
buzzing of the hour that never passed. I saw the washed-down walls, the
joints of the beams all puffed up by the water. I saw the small garden,
empty for the first time, and the jasmine bush against the wall, faithful to
35 the memory of my mother. I saw my father sitting in a rocker, his painful
vertebrae resting on a pillow and his sad eyes lost in the labyrinth[3] of the
rain. I remembered the August nights in whose wondrous silence nothing
could be heard except the millenary sound that the earth makes as it spins
on its rusty, unoiled axis. Suddenly I felt overcome by an overwhelming
40 sadness.

---

[1] *veranda:* area on the side or front of a house with a floor and roof but no walls; porch
[2] *siesta:* a short sleep in the afternoon
[3] *labyrinth:* maze

1. Where does the story take place?
(A) At a friend's house
(B) In a hotel
(C) In a hospital
(D) In the narrator's house

2. The word *substance* in line 15 is closest in meaning to
(A) idea
(B) material
(C) connection
(D) perfume

3. Why does the narrator's stepmother want to move the flowerpots?
(A) She doesn't like how the plants look.
(B) She thinks the plants are in the way.
(C) She thinks the plants have gotten too much water.
(D) She likes having plants in the house.

4. The word *immense* in line 22 is closest in meaning to
(A) dark
(B) cold
(C) huge
(D) wide

5. The word *them* in line 21 refers to
   (A) senses
   (B) rain drops
   (C) flowerpots
   (D) Indians

6. Which of the sentences below best expresses the essential information in the passage excerpt? Incorrect choices change the meaning in important ways or leave out essential information.

   > I remembered August, those long and awesome siestas in which we dropped down to die under the weight of the hour, our clothes sticking to our bodies, hearing outside the insistent and dull buzzing of the hour that never passed.

   (A) The month of August seemed very long and hot.
   (B) There was a buzzing sound outside the house.
   (C) The narrator liked to take naps when it was hot.
   (D) The narrator wanted to wash her clothes.

7. Which of the following characters is NOT mentioned in the passage?
   (A) The narrator's mother
   (B) The narrator's brother
   (C) The narrator's father
   (D) The narrator's stepmother

8. How does the narrator's father feel about the rainy weather?
   (A) He is depressed by the rain.
   (B) He is relaxed watching the rain fall.
   (C) He is worried that the roof will leak.
   (D) He is bored by sitting in the house.

9. What can you infer about the narrator's family?
   (A) Her father and mother are divorced.
   (B) Her mother lives far away.
   (C) Her stepmother is sick.
   (D) Her mother is dead.

10. Look at the four squares ☐ that indicate where the following sentence could be added to the passage. Where would the sentence best fit? Circle the letter that shows the point where you would insert this sentence.

    > It looked completely different after the rain.

    A My stepmother and I went back to look at the garden. **B** The harsh gray earth of May had been changed overnight into a dark, sticky substance like cheap soap. A trickle of water began to run off the flowerpots. "I think they had more than enough water during the night," my stepmother said. **C** And I noticed that she had stopped smiling and that her joy of the previous day had changed during the night into a lax and tedious seriousness. **D**

11. Select the appropriate phrases from the answer choices and match them to the person described in the passage. TWO of the answer choices will NOT be used.

The narrator's father

- _____

- _____

- _____

The narrator's stepmother

- _____

- _____

- _____

Answer Choices

(A) asked the Indians to move the flowerpots

(B) didn't eat any lunch

(C) had a stiff back

(D) put the flowerpots on the veranda

(E) remembered what happened last August

(F) sat and watched the rain

(G) wasn't smiling anymore

(H) went to look at the garden

3 Writing

INTEGRATED TASK: READ, LISTEN, WRITE

In this section, you will read a short passage and listen to an excerpt on the same topic. Then you will write about the relationship between the two.

READING

Read the passage on the next page. Take notes to answer the questions that follow. Work with a partner and compare your notes.

Tornadoes

Tornadoes are nature's most violent storms. Tornadoes (also called *twisters*) are formed over land during thunderstorms, when a column of rapidly circling air forms under a thunderstorm and extends down to the ground. Tornadoes can be extremely destructive, with winds reaching 480 kilometers (or 300 miles) per hour and lasting up to an hour. In a destructive tornado, the damage path can be up to one and a half kilometers (or one mile) wide and over 97 kilometers (or 60 miles) long. The strong winds can uproot trees, lift cars, and damage buildings. They are often deadly and can destroy entire neighborhoods.

Predicting a tornado is difficult because they form very quickly, with little or no warning. Authorities may post a **tornado watch** or **tornado warning**. A tornado watch means that tornadoes are possible, usually because there are strong thunderstorms in the area, and people should watch for tornadoes to form. A **tornado warning** means that tornadoes have been seen in the area and people should take cover immediately. Unfortunately, there is usually little time for people to evacuate once a tornado has formed.

The United States has the highest number of tornadoes in the world each year, mostly in the Midwest and southern states. They occur most often in the spring and early summer, especially during the afternoon and early evening when thunderstorms are more common. Tornadoes are also common in Australia and Bangladesh.

1. What is a tornado? _____

_____

2. How destructive are tornadoes? _____

_____

3. How well can tornadoes be predicted? _____

_____

4. Where and when do tornadoes form? _____

_____

LISTENING

CD1 TRACK 30

Listen to the excerpt from a lecture. Take notes as you listen, using these questions to help you. The notes have been started for you.

1. What is a hurricane? _large storm —forms over ocean_ _____

_____

2. Where and when do hurricanes form? _____

_____

3. How well can hurricanes be predicted? _____

_____

4. How destructive are hurricanes? _____

_____

WRITING

Write on the following topic. Follow the steps below to prepare.

❙ Compare and contrast the features of hurricanes and tornadoes.

Step 1

Work with a partner. Skim the reading and your notes from the reading and listening tasks (pages 60–62). Fill in the chart below.

	HURRICANES	TORNADOES
What are they?		
Where and when do they form?		
How well can they be predicted?		
How destructive are they?		

Work on your own to complete the outline. First, choose the details you want to use in your written response. Then list the similarities and differences between hurricanes and tornadoes on the next page.

Similarities   1. _____

2. _____

Differences   1. _____

2. _____

3. _____

4. _____

Step 2

Write for 20 minutes on the topic. Leave the last 5 minutes to edit your work.

> To evaluate a partner's writing, use the Writing Evaluation Form on page 173.

4 Speaking

INDEPENDENT TASK

Speak on the following topic. Follow the steps below to prepare.

Describe a time when you experienced a natural disaster or unusual weather event. Explain what happened and how it affected you.

Step 1

• Think of a natural disaster or unusual weather event such as an earthquake, hurricane, snowstorm, drought, or rainstorm. Use the cluster diagram to brainstorm about the details of your experience.

• Write the type of event, and when and where it happened, in the center circle.

• Then, in the outer circles, write ideas about what you saw, heard, felt, and did during the experience.

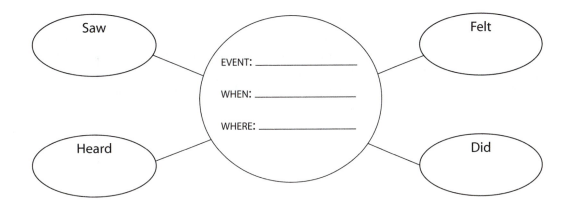

Step 2

Work with a partner. Take turns practicing a one-minute oral response to the topic. Use the information in your cluster diagram to help you.

Step 3

Change partners. Take turns giving a one-minute response to the topic again.

To evaluate your partner's response, use the Speaking Evaluation Form on page 174.

5 Skill Focus

MAKING INFERENCES

EXAMINATION

1 *Listen again to the excerpts and read the questions. How did you know the answer to the questions? Was it the words the speaker used or the way the speaker said the words? Mark the items WDS (words) or WAY (way).*

Item 1 (Campus Conversation, p. 53)

Listen again to part of the conversation. Then answer the question.

_____ When the student says, "This is great . . . " he probably feels
(A) unhappy about his computer problem
(B) hopeful that his computer will be fixed
(C) angry at the student consultant
(D) relieved by what the student consultant told him

Item 2 (Campus Conversation, p. 54)

Listen again to part of the conversation. Then answer the question.

_____ What does the student consultant mean when she says, "Well, the bookstore has some computer stuff . . . you can try looking there . . . "?
(A) She doubts that the bookstore has computer batteries.
(B) She believes the bookstore has a lot of computer equipment.
(C) She is unsure whether the bookstore is open.
(D) She is certain the student can buy a computer battery at the bookstore.

Item 3 (Academic Listening, p. 55)

Listen again to part of the conversation. Then answer the question.

_____ Why does the reporter Alex Zhao say, "But wait . . ."?
(A) To correct a mistake
(B) To show that he is paying attention
(C) To indicate that something has suddenly changed
(D) To interrupt the other speaker

2 *Read the questions and look back at the reading on page 57. How did you know the answers to these questions? Were they stated directly in the text or explained in other ways? Mark the items* **SD** *(stated directly) or* **OT** *(other ways).*

Item 1 (Reading, p. 59)

_____ How does the narrator's father feel about the rainy weather?
(A) He is depressed by the rain.
(B) He is relaxed watching the rain fall.
(C) He is worried that the roof will leak.
(D) He is bored by sitting in the house.

Item 2 (Reading, p. 59)

_____ What can you infer about the narrator's family?
(A) Her father and mother are divorced.
(B) Her mother lives far away.
(C) Her stepmother is sick.
(D) Her mother is dead.

Tips

To do well on the TOEFL, you have to think about more than the word-for-word meaning of a text. There are several comprehension questions in the listening and reading sections that are not literal; these are called inference questions. Inference questions ask you to make guesses or predictions, or draw conclusions about information that is not stated directly in a listening or reading passage. There are several different types of information you can infer from a text. Here are three main types:

1. Factual information not stated directly

• What information can you guess based on what you have heard or read?

• What conclusions can you draw?

(continued on next page)

2. The speaker/author's purpose

- Why is the speaker/author making this statement?

- What does the speaker/author want the listener/reader to do?

3. The speaker/author's attitudes or beliefs

- How does the speaker/author feel about the situation?

- Does the speaker/author believe something is true or false?

- How certain is the speaker/author?

To make inferences, pay attention to:

- context (who the people are, where they are, and what is happening)

- word choice (which words the speaker/author chooses to use)

- (listening only) intonation and tone of voice (how a speaker says something)

In the Examination Exercise 1, Items 1 and 2 are both questions about the speaker's attitudes or beliefs. **Item 1** asks about the speaker's feelings—whether he is unhappy, hopeful, angry, or relieved. You can tell by his tone that he is unhappy about his computer problem.

Item 2 asks about the speaker's certainty about her statement—whether she is doubtful or certain about her statement. You can tell by the tone of voice she uses when she says "the bookstore has some computer stuff" that she doubts that the store has the computer batteries.

Item 3 is a question about the speaker's purpose for making the statement. You can tell from the context that he is saying "But wait . . . " because something has suddenly changed as they enter the eye of the hurricane.

In Exercise 2, Items 1 and 2 are both questions about factual information not directly stated in the text. Item 1 asks about how the narrator's father feels. You can infer from several parts of the passage (he stays in the same place all day, he doesn't talk to anyone, he doesn't want to eat, he feels the rain will never clear, he is in pain) that he is depressed. (It is not a question about attitude and beliefs because it doesn't ask about the author's feelings.)

For **Item 2**, you can infer from clues in the passage that the narrator's mother is dead. (The narrator has a stepmother, and the jasmine bush was planted in memory of her mother.)

PRACTICE

Listening

1 *Look at the charts below. Listen to the excerpts and answer the questions **T** (true) or **F** (false).*

2 *Listen again. Pay attention to context, word choice, and intonation and tone of voice. Which clues helped you answer the questions? Write down the words or phrases that helped you identify the answer.*

CD1 TRACK 34

Listening 1

Situation: Two friends, Mark and Linda, are getting ready for a hurricane.

			INFERENCING CLUES
1. Linda feels ready for the hurricane.	T	F	
2. Linda wants Mark to give her a flashlight.	T	F	
3. Mark wants to give his flashlight to Linda.	T	F	

CD1 TRACK 35

Listening 2

Situation: A professor is giving a lecture about earthquakes.

			INFERENCING CLUES
1. The professor doubts that anyone can predict earthquakes.	T	F	
2. The professor is certain that Rosalyn Brown wrote the article in *Science Review*.	T	F	
3. The professor thinks the students should read the article in *Science Review*.	T	F	

3 *Discuss your answers with the class. Explain how the clues helped you answer the questions.*

Reading

1 *Look at the charts below. Read the excerpts from* Drought *by Jill Kerr Conway. The story describes how Conway's family survived a long period without rain in New South Wales, Australia. Complete each statement in the charts by circling the appropriate phase.*

2 *Read the excerpts again. Pay attention to the context and word choice. Which clues helped you answer the questions? Write down the words or phrases that helped you identify the answer.*

Excerpt 1

A dust storm usually lasts days, blotting out the sun…. It is dangerous to stray far from shelter, because the sand and grit lodge in one's eyes, and a visibility often reduced to a few feet can make one completely disoriented. … There is nothing anyone can do but stay inside, waiting for the calm after the storm…. Meals are gritty and sleep elusive. Rising in the morning, one sees a perfect outline of one's body, an afterimage of white where the dust had not collected on the sheets.

	INFERENCING CLUES
1. The author lived through (one sand storm / several sand storms).	
2. The author thought that dust storms were (exciting / horrible).	

Excerpt 2

My mother was hard to awaken. She had, in her stoic way, endured over the years two bad cases of ear infection, treated only with our available remedies, hot packs and aspirin. One ear was totally deaf as a result of a ruptured eardrum, and her hearing in the other ear was much reduced.

	INFERENCING CLUES
1. The Conway family lived (close to / far away from) doctors and hospitals.	

3 *Discuss your answers with the class. Explain how the clues helped you answer the questions.*

Conservation

| LISTENING |

Campus Conversation — A resident assistant and a student discuss recycling on campus.

Academic Listening — A lecture about ecological home building

| READING |

Reading — *Interview with a Medicine Priest*

| SPEAKING |

Integrated Task: Read, Listen, Speak — Role play a conversation about living in an ecologically built city. Use detailed examples.

| WRITING |

Independent Task — Discuss things that people should do in their daily lives to conserve natural resources and preserve the environment.

| SKILL FOCUS |

Using Detailed Examples — Using detailed examples shows your ability to illustrate an idea and to support general statements with concrete information.

| TOEFL® iBT TARGET SKILLS |

- Identify and express main ideas
- Identify and express details
- Make inferences
- Listen and take notes
- Scan for information and paraphrase it
- Categorize information
- Express an opinion using detailed examples

(ETS) For extra practice of TOEFL iBT skills, go to pages 206–223.

1 Listening

CAMPUS CONVERSATION

PRE-LISTENING VOCABULARY

Read the sentences. Guess the meaning of the boldfaced words and phrases. Then match each word or phrase with a definition or synonym from the list below. Work with a partner and compare your answers.

_____ 1. Many modern buildings are energy **efficient**, so they don't use much electricity or fuel for heating.

_____ 2. Most college students live on campus in **dormitories** during their freshman and sophomore years, but they often move to off-campus apartments later in college.

_____ 3. If you go to the bookstore today, **keep in mind** that it's really busy at the beginning of the semester, so the lines will be long.

_____ 4. When reading a new assignment, it's important to **look at the big picture**. Don't just think about the information in each article; think about how the article fits in with everything else you've learned in the class.

_____ 5. The paper isn't due until next month, but the professor is **pushing** us to hand it in early if we can.

_____ 6. When mail comes into the post office, it is **sorted** by address so it can be delivered.

_____ 7. I'm so **stressed out**! This week I have two papers due and exams in three of my classes! I need a vacation!

_____ 8. The students had to do a group project, so they **worked out** who would work on each part of the project.

a. consider the whole situation, not just the details

b. decided

c. divided into groups

d. encouraging

e. large buildings where students live

f. remember

g. works effectively without waste

h. worried and tired

> **Culture Note:** Campus dormitories, or "dorms," often employ Resident Assistants (RAs), which are third- or fourth-year students who live in the dormitory and are part of the Residence Staff that manages on-campus housing. RAs help supervise the students in the dorms as well as provide assistance and support if students have personal or academic troubles.

FIRST LISTENING

Read the questions. Listen to the conversation between a student and a resident assistant. Take notes as you listen. Share your notes with a partner. Then use your notes to answer the questions.

1. What topic is the Resident Assistant discussing with the student?

   _____

2. Do they agree or disagree about the topic? Why?

   _____

SECOND LISTENING

Read the questions. Listen to the conversation again. Add details to your notes. Then use your notes to answer the questions. Work with a partner and compare your answers.

1. What is the Resident Assistant doing during the conversation?
   (A) Giving the student directions around campus
   (B) Helping the student solve a problem
   (C) Showing the student around her new dorm
   (D) Asking the student about her experience in the dorm

Listen again to part of the conversation. Then answer question 2.

2. Why does the Resident Assistant say, "Recently, they built some new 'green' buildings that are really energy efficient. And this year, they're really pushing us to do recycling campus-wide."?
   (A) To change the topic of the conversation to architecture
   (B) To encourage the student to learn more about conservation
   (C) To explain about different types of conservation programs
   (D) To give examples of how the university supports conservation

Listen again to part of the conversation. Then answer question 3.

3. What can be inferred about the resident assistant when he says, "Well, no one's forcing you to do it. But really, it's not that much work . . . "?
   (A) He agrees with the student.
   (B) He is annoyed with the student.
   (C) He is pleased by the student's comment.
   (D) He isn't sure what the student means.

4. What does the student think about her dorm room?
   (A) It's comfortable.
   (B) It's not good for studying.
   (C) It's good for watching TV.
   (D) It's too small.

5. What is the student's objection to recycling?
   (A) She thinks that it will take too much time.
   (B) She doesn't like handling garbage.
   (C) She doesn't understand how to do it.
   (D) She thinks someone else should do it.

ACADEMIC LISTENING

FIRST LISTENING

Listen to a lecture from an ecology class. Take notes using the questions below. Work with a partner and combine your notes.

Earthship Homes

1. Where are they built? _____

   _____

   _____

2. How are they made? _____

   _____

   _____

3. What are three advantages of Earthship homes?

   a. _____

   b. _____

   c. _____

SECOND LISTENING

 Read the questions. Listen to the lecture again. Add details to your notes. Then use your notes to answer the questions. Work with a partner and compare your answers.

1. What are the primary materials used to build Earthship homes?
   (A) Red brick and concrete
   (B) Regular concrete and dirt
   (C) Recycled tires and dirt
   (D) Wood and recycled tires

 Listen again to part of the lecture. Then answer question 2.

2. Why does the professor ask, "So what makes these Earthship homes so unusual?"?
   (A) To emphasize her point
   (B) To introduce a new topic
   (C) To see if the students know the answer
   (D) To start a class discussion

 Listen again to part of the lecture. Then answer question 3.

3. What does the professor mean when she says, "Well, I don't know about that!"?
   (A) "I don't agree with you."
   (B) "I'm not sure I understand."
   (C) "Let's discuss that later."
   (D) "Please, don't interrupt me."

4. What point does the professor illustrate by mentioning the tire recycling program in Alberta, Canada?
   (A) Earthship homes are energy efficient because they are built with tires.
   (B) There are many uses for old tires besides building Earthship homes.
   (C) Many communities don't recycle tires to use in Earthship homes.
   (D) Some communities are encouraging construction of Earthship homes.

5. How does the government of Alberta, Canada, encourage people to recycle old tires?
   (A) It pays people to use them in recycling projects.
   (B) It sells them to people who build Earthship homes.
   (C) It sends them to another part of the country.
   (D) It teaches people how to build Earthship homes.

6. What advantages did the professor mention for building Earthship homes? Check all that apply.
   (A) _____ They are inexpensive to build.
   (B) _____ They are large and comfortable.
   (C) _____ They don't need to be heated in winter.
   (D) _____ They are easy to maintain and repair.
   (E) _____ They help get rid of old tires.

2 Reading

INTERVIEW WITH A MEDICINE PRIEST

PRE-READING

You will read an interview with David Winston, a Cherokee medicine priest, or spiritual leader. The Cherokee are a Native American tribe from the southeastern United States.

Scan the article to find answers to these questions. Write the answers by paraphrasing (using your own words).

1. What does David Winston talk about in the interview?

   _____

   _____

2. What are the three great Laws of Nature?

   _____

   _____

   _____

3. What is the Great Life?

   _____

READING

Read the passage on the next page and answer the questions. Then work with a partner and compare your answers. When you disagree, go back to the text to find helpful information.

INTERVIEW WITH A MEDICINE PRIEST

1 **Barbara Cassin:** Hi. I'm Barbara Cassin, and I'm with David Winston, a Cherokee medicine priest. David, thank you for agreeing to talk to us today.

2 **David Winston:** Oh, you're very welcome.

3 **BC:** Could you tell us a little bit about the Cherokee beliefs regarding the environment and conservation?

4 **DW:** Yes, I'd be happy to. Basically, Cherokee tradition tells us that we are part of nature and we depend on nature for our life, so we don't compete with it and we're not trying to tame it. We're trying to live with it. We are as important as everything else, but certainly no more important than anything else.

5 **BC:** Could you tell us a little more about that?

6 **DW:** We believe that there are three great Laws of Nature, and those are the laws that tell us how we have to live in relationship to everything else. The First Law of Nature is that you don't take any life without a real reason. And a real reason would be for food, for medicine, for protection—those would be the reasons for taking life. But basically, life is sacred.

7 **BC:** So you shouldn't kill needlessly. Would that include plants?

8 **DW:** Absolutely. We believe everything is alive. In fact, we believe stones are alive, trees are alive, plants are alive, animals are obviously alive, connected. And so to us, taking the life of a plant is just as grave a responsibility as taking the life of an animal. So all of those things should be done in a sacred way, in a good way. So for instance, when you go to gather a plant, you don't want to go and say, "Hey, here's a whole patch of plants," and go and gather them all. You gather a few, and then you gather a few from another spot, leaving the majority of the plants so that they can continue to grow and provide not only for themselves, but for us, and our children, and for their children.

9 **BC:** Interesting. And what about the Second Law?

10 **DW:** The Second Law is that everything we do should serve the Great Life.

11 **BC:** The Great Life. What do you mean by that?

12 **DW:** Well, we believe that there's one spirit that fills all things: humans, plants, rocks, whatever. And the sum of all of that, and more, is what we call the Great Life. We all are part of this same Great Life: Everything we do affects the Great Life, and everything that happens within the Great Life affects us. So it's very, very important that within the Second Law of Nature, that what we do will not harm other parts of the Great Life.

13 **BC:** I wonder if you could give an example.

14 **DW:** Well, I could give a lot of examples. On a simple, personal level, lots of people go out and get an electric toothbrush. Maybe it works a little bit better, and it's certainly easier to use: the toothbrush does all the work for you! But I have a manual toothbrush, and I've used one my whole life, and it works just fine. To use the electricity necessary to power that electric toothbrush requires coal or nuclear power that harms the air, it harms the water, it harms the Great Life.

(continued on next page)

15 **BC:** I see, so we don't really need it. What about the Third Law?

16 **DW:** The Third Law is that we don't pollute where we live. And where we live is not just our home, it's not just our intimate, small community, it's not just our country. It's this planet, this sacred altar we call the Earth.

We don't pour chemical waste down the drain because it all winds up in the water. So basically, we don't pollute the Earth.

17 **BC:** Well, you've certainly given us a lot to think about today. Thanks, David Winston, for talking to us.

18 **DW:** You're welcome. Un dun Koh ha hee.

1. What are the three great Laws of Nature?
   (A) Government regulations for using natural resources
   (B) Proposals for how people should live in the future
   (C) Scientific theories about conserving natural resources
   (D) Spiritual beliefs about how people should live

2. The word *tame* in paragraph 4 is closest in meaning to
   (A) control
   (B) pollute
   (C) support
   (D) expand

3. The word *we* in paragraph 6 refers to
   (A) all people
   (B) the Cherokee people
   (C) David Winston and the reader
   (D) David Winston and Barbara Cassin

4. The word *protection* in paragraph 6 is closest in meaning to
   (A) anger
   (B) fun
   (C) profit
   (D) safety

5. Based on paragraphs 6 to 8, what can be inferred about David Winston?
   (A) He doesn't hunt animals for sport.
   (B) He doesn't eat meat.
   (C) He doesn't keep animals as pets.
   (D) He doesn't wear animal skins.

6. All of the following are mentioned in paragraph 8 as being alive EXCEPT
   (A) air
   (B) rocks
   (C) plants
   (D) animals

7. Which of the sentences below best expresses the essential information in this passage from the article?

> So for instance, when you go to gather a plant, you don't want to go and say, "Hey, here's a whole patch of plants," and go and gather them all. You gather a few, and then you gather a few from another spot, leaving the majority of the plants so that they can continue to grow and provide not only for themselves, but for us, and our children, and for their children.

   (A) People should gather plants from many different places.
   (B) People should use all the resources they need for their families.
   (C) People should use resources carefully so there is enough for future generations.
   (D) People should pick plants from one area and leave the rest alone.

8. The word *manual* in paragraph 14 is closest in meaning to
   (A) not effective
   (B) not expensive
   (C) not mechanical
   (D) not useful

9. In paragraph 14, why does David Winston mention his toothbrush?
   (A) To analyze the reasons people use electric toothbrushes
   (B) To explain how we make choices when shopping
   (C) To describe what he does every morning
   (D) To give an example of the Second Law of Nature

10. Based on the passage, which statement most accurately reflects David Winston's opinion about the environment and conservation?
   (A) Conservation is difficult for many people because it requires lifestyle changes.
   (B) Conservation is an important part of the Cherokee belief system.
   (C) People today know more about conservation than in the past.
   (D) The Cherokee people have the best approach to conservation.

11. Select the appropriate phrases from the answer choices and match them to the law to which they relate. TWO of the answer choices will NOT be used.

First Law of Nature   **Second Law of Nature**   **Third Law of Nature**

- _____   - _____   - _____

- _____   - _____   - _____

Answer Choices

(A) Be kind to other people.   (E) Everything on Earth is alive.

(B) Our home is the entire planet.   (F) Don't kill anything without a reason.

(C) Don't pollute the place we live. (G) Take good care of your children.

(D) Everything we do should   (H) There is one spirit that fills all things.
    help the Great Life.

ANALYSIS

It is helpful to know the purpose of a test item. There are four types of questions in the reading section.

1. Basic Comprehension

- main ideas
- details
- the meaning of specific sentences

2. Organization

- the way information is structured in the text
- the way ideas are linked between sentences or between paragraphs

3. Inference

- ideas are not directly stated in the text
- author's intention, purpose, or attitude not explicitly stated in the text

4. Vocabulary and Reference

- the meaning of words
- the meaning of reference words such as *his*, *them*, *this*, or *none*

Go back to the reading questions and label each question with 1, 2, 3, or 4. Then work with a partner to see if you agree. Check the Answer Key for the correct answers. Which questions did you get right? Which did you get wrong? What skills do you need to practice?

3 Speaking

INTEGRATED TASK: READ, LISTEN, SPEAK

In this section, you will read a short passage and listen to an excerpt on the same topic. Then you will speak about the relationship between the two.

READING

Read the passage and then answer the questions.

Ecocities

Some urban planners are designing ecocities, cities that are built to be environmentally friendly. For example, there is easy access to public transportation, so residents don't need to own cars, and the community is connected by many bicycle and pedestrian walking paths. In addition, ecocities use sustainable energy by incorporating solar and wind power rather than relying solely on fossil fuels. Ecocities also have green space, including parks and forests that provide a natural habitat for wildlife, and community gardens where residents can grow fruits and vegetables. Furthermore, the buildings in an ecocity are constructed using ecological building materials, such as recycled materials and wood from certified sustainable forestry operations. By incorporating all of these features into ecocities, urban planners believe we will be able to start restoring our environment so there will be something left for our grandchildren.

1. What are ecocities?

_____

2. How do they help conserve natural resources?

- _____
- _____
- _____
- _____

LISTENING

Listen to the conversation between two students. Use the chart on the next page to take notes as you listen.

WOULD THE STUDENTS LIKE TO LIVE IN AN ECOCITY?	STUDENT 1	STUDENT 2
Opinion:		
Point:	• *cheaper*	
Examples:	• *lower utility bills*	
Point:		
Examples:		

SPEAKING

Speak on the following topic. Follow the steps below to prepare.

The two students express their opinions about ecocities. Create a role play of a similar conversation, with one partner speaking in favor of living in an ecocity and the other partner speaking against it. Use examples from the reading and conversation.

Step 1

Work with a partner. Choose which role you will take in the role play. Skim the reading and your notes from the listening. Make a list of the arguments for and against living in an ecocity. Then note the examples given for each argument.

ARGUMENTS FOR LIVING IN AN ECOCITY	EXAMPLES

ARGUMENTS AGAINST LIVING IN AN ECOCITY	EXAMPLES

Step 2

With your partner, take turns practicing your conversation. Use the information in your chart to help you.

Step 3

Change partners. Take turns giving a one-minute response to the topic again.

To evaluate your partner's response, use the Speaking Evaluation Form on page 174.

4 Writing

INDEPENDENT TASK

Write on the following topic. Follow the steps below to prepare.

Discuss things that people should do in their daily lives to conserve natural resources and preserve the environment.

Focus your answer on one general topic. Be sure to use detailed examples to support your opinion.

Step 1

Work with a partner. Brainstorm a list of ideas for how people can conserve natural resources and preserve the environment. Then think of a few specific examples to illustrate each idea. The first one is done for you.

CONSERVATION IDEAS	EXAMPLES
Recycling	newspapers bottles and cans from drinks old batteries

Work with another pair. Take turns describing your ideas. React to what you have heard. What are the best ideas? Why?

Step 2

Write for 20 minutes. Leave the last 5 minutes to edit your work.

To evaluate a partner's writing, use the Writing Evaluation Form on page 173.

5 Skill Focus

USING DETAILED EXAMPLES

EXAMINATION

Look at the questions from the unit. What point is being illustrated by the examples? What examples are used? Write the point and examples below. The first one is started for you.

Item 1 (Campus Conversation, p. 71)

Listen again to part of the conversation. Then answer the question.

RESIDENT ASSISTANT: Well, keep in mind that the university has a strong commitment to conservation. Recently, they built some new "green" buildings that are really energy efficient. And this year, they're really pushing us to do recycling campus-wide.

Why does the Resident Assistant say, "Recently, they built some new 'green' buildings that are really energy efficient. And this year, they're really pushing us to do recycling campus-wide."?
(A) To change the topic of the conversation to architecture
(B) To encourage the student to learn more about conservation
(C) To explain about different types of conservation programs
(D) To give examples of how the university supports conservation

Point: ___*The university supports conservation.*_____

Examples: ___*They built new "green" buildings.*_____

_____

Item 2 (Academic Listening, p. 73)

PROFESSOR: In fact, some communities are actively encouraging this kind of development [the construction of Earthship homes], not only because it generates new low-cost housing, but also because it is a way to dispose of old tires, which is a big problem in many places. In Alberta, Canada, for example, the government started a recycling program that encourages people to recycle tires in innovative ways. They do this by paying people to use the tires—two dollars per tire!

What point does the professor illustrate by mentioning the tire recycling program in Alberta, Canada?
(A) Earthship homes are energy efficient because they are built with tires.
(B) There are many uses for old tires besides building Earthship homes.
(C) Many communities don't recycle tires to use in Earthship homes.
(D) Some communities are encouraging construction of Earthship homes.

Point: _____

Examples: _____

Item 3 (Reading, p. 77)

In paragraph 14, why does David Winston mention his toothbrush?
(A) To analyze the reasons people use electric toothbrushes
(B) To describe choices we make when shopping
(C) To explain part of his daily life
(D) To give an example of the Second Law of Nature

Point: _____

Examples: _____

Tips

To do well on the TOEFL, you will have to use detailed examples to support your ideas and opinions in writing and speaking. Without detailed examples, an idea may not be clear:

DW: …But basically, life is sacred.

BC: So you shouldn't kill needlessly. Would that include plants?

DW: Absolutely. We believe everything is alive. And so to us, taking the life of a plant is just as grave a responsibility as taking the life of an animal. So all of those things should be done in a sacred way, in a good way.

The conversation above lacks details. When detailed examples are added, the point is easier to understand, and the explanation more interesting.

DW: …But basically, life is sacred.

BC: So you shouldn't kill needlessly. Would that include plants?

DW: Absolutely. We believe everything is alive. *In fact, we believe stones are alive, trees are alive, plants are alive, animals are obviously alive, connected.* And so to us, taking the life of a plant is just as grave a responsibility as taking the life of an animal. So all of those things should be done in a sacred way, in a good way. *So for instance, when you go to gather a plant, you don't want to go and say, "Hey, here's a whole patch of plants," and go and gather them all. You gather a few, and then you gather a few from another spot, leaving the majority of the plants so that they can continue to grow and provide not only for themselves, but for us, and our children, and for their children.*

(continued on next page)

Listening and Reading

Pay attention to the examples used in the texts and write the examples in your notes. Then think about how the examples are being used in the text:

- What points are the examples being used to illustrate?
- How do the examples help explain each point?

Writing and Speaking

Including detailed examples in your responses to the writing and speaking tasks has two purposes: to help explain your ideas clearly, and to hold the reader's or listener's interest.

1. Use examples to support your main points.

    General Statement: Ecocities are environmentally friendly.

    Examples: • public transportation

    • sustainable energy

    • green space

    • ecological building materials

2. Include specific details such as places, people, dates, times, and numbers to explain your examples.

    Ecocities also have green space, including *parks and forests* that provide a *natural habitat for wildlife,* and *community gardens* where *residents* can *grow fruits and vegetables.*

    In *Alberta, Canada,* for example, the government started a recycling program that encourages people to recycle *tires* in innovative ways. They do this by paying people to use the tires—*two dollars per tire!*

3. Use signal words to show that you are introducing an example:

    for example   for instance   such as   including

4. Follow the directions for the specific TOEFL Task. In the TOEFL Integrated Speaking/Writing Task, use examples from the readings and listenings. In the Independent Speaking/Writing Task, use examples from your own experience.

PRACTICE

1 *Work with a partner. Look at the reading from the unit.*

1. Number the four examples used to support the main point.

2. Underline the specific details that are included in each example.

3. Circle the signal words that introduce examples.

Ecocities

Some urban planners are designing ecocities, cities that are built to be environmentally friendly. For example, there is easy access to public transportation, so residents don't need to own cars, and the community is connected by many bicycle and pedestrian paths. In addition, ecocities use sustainable energy by incorporating solar and wind power rather than relying solely on fossil fuels. Ecocities also have green space, including parks and forests that provide a natural habitat for wildlife, and community gardens where residents can grow fruits and vegetables. Furthermore, the buildings in an ecocity are constructed using ecological building materials, such as recycled materials and wood from certified sustainable forestry operations. By incorporating all of these features into ecocities, urban planners believe we will be able to start restoring our environment so there will be something left for our grandchildren.

2 *Work with a partner. Read the general statement. Then choose the FOUR examples that give strongest support to the statement. Discuss why the alternatives are not as effective.*

General Statement: Our university policies help encourage recycling on campus.

1. _____ Recycling is easy and doesn't take much time to do. It's very quick, so it's easy to do.

2. _____ The science department has an ecology research program that investigates better ways to recycle. For example, they are studying how to make plastics that decompose in landfills without polluting the soil.

3. _____ The store in the student center accepts bottles and cans for recycling. Students get a refund of five cents per container when they return them to the store.

4. _____ The university buys recycled paper for use in all academic and administrative offices. In addition, the bookstore sells recycled paper at the same price as regular paper.

5. _____ Most students have used recycling programs at home, although some may not think much about the importance of recycling.

6. _____ The university has several "green" buildings that conserve electricity by using solar energy, including the new earth sciences building.

7. _____ The university strongly supports recycling.

3 *Work in pairs. Look back at your writing for the Independent Task on page 81. Underline the examples you used to explain your main points. Then discuss the following questions with your partner. Choose one example and rewrite it to make it more effective.*

1. Do your examples help prove your main point?

2. Did you include specific details to explain the examples?

3. Did you use signal words to introduce the examples?

Philanthropy

LISTENING	
Campus Conversation	A student talks to an advisor about volunteering.
Academic Listening	Lecture: Philanthropist Andrew Carnegie

READING	
Article	*Some Take the Time Gladly*

WRITING	
Integrated Task: Read, Listen, Write	Summarize reasons for charitable giving.

SPEAKING	
Independent Task	Discuss the ideas of donating money and time to charity.

SKILL FOCUS	
Identifying and Using Rhetorical Structure	Identifying and using rhetorical structure means you understand the relationships among facts and ideas in different parts of a spoken or written passage.

TOEFL® iBT TARGET SKILLS

- Identify and express main ideas
- Identify and express details
- Make inferences
- Take notes in an outline
- Summarize using details and examples
- Organize reasons and details to support an opinion
- Identify the rhetorical structure of a text
- Identify an author's purpose

(ETS) For extra practice of TOEFL iBT skills, go to pages 206–223.

1 Listening

PRE-LISTENING VOCABULARY

Read the sentences. Guess the meaning of the boldfaced words and phrases. Then match each word or phrase with a definition or synonym from the list below. Work with a partner and compare your answers.

_____ 1. They are not answering the doorbell, so I **assume** that they are not home.

_____ 2. I'll do some research on the problem and let you know if I **come up with** a solution.

_____ 3. Our volunteers need to make the **commitment** to work for two hours a week.

_____ 4. Admission to some universities is a **competitive process**. Many students may apply, but only a few are invited to attend the school.

_____ 5. I have **a heavy load** this semester. I'm taking six classes, so I have a lot of work to do.

_____ 6. In my history class, we do the reading for homework, and then the professor **goes over** the important points in his lecture.

_____ 7. Math classes have always been easy for my sister. I think she's just mathematically **inclined**.

_____ 8. There are many different **opportunities** available to volunteer in the community. For example, you can help in a homeless shelter, tutor children in school, or do office work for a non-profit organization.

_____ 9. The students went to an **orientation** before the first week of school during which they learned about the class registration process, housing policies, and other important information.

_____ 10. Student volunteers must complete a short training program before they start work. All students must meet this **requirement** before they begin their volunteer job.

a. a lot of classes

b. chances

c. reviews and explains

d. interested in and good at

e. promise

f. a procedure with winners and losers

g. something you have to do

h. think of

i. think something is true, without proof

j. training for a new activity

Culture Note: Some colleges and universities have community service requirements for graduation, which means that students have to do volunteer work for a campus group or local organization. Other schools do not require volunteer work but encourage students to volunteer in order to gain experience and become involved in the community. To assist students in finding a job, most schools have placement offices that list the volunteer positions available in the community.

FIRST LISTENING

Read the questions. Listen to the conversation between a student and an advisor. Take notes as you listen. Share your notes with a partner. Then use your notes to answer the questions.

1. Why does the student go to see the advisor? _____

_____

2. What advice does the advisor give the student? _____

_____

SECOND LISTENING

Read the questions. Listen to the conversation again. Add details to your notes. Then use your notes to answer the questions. Work with a partner and compare your answers.

1. Why does the student go to see the advisor?
   (A) She is required to get a volunteer job.
   (B) Her advisor wants her to quit her volunteer job.
   (C) She doesn't like her volunteer job with young children.
   (D) She wants to find a volunteer job.

2. Why does the student want to volunteer at a school?
   (A) Because she has past experience working in schools
   (B) Because the job fits in her schedule
   (C) Because she thinks the job will be fun
   (D) Because she is an education major

3. What are the requirements for getting most volunteer jobs?
   (A) The student must apply early in the year.
   (B) The student must be an education major.
   (C) The student must have enough free time.
   (D) The student must have special skills.

Listen to part of the conversation. Then answer question 4.

4. What can you infer about the student when she says, "Uh, not me!"?
   (A) She's not good at music.
   (B) She doesn't want to work in a music program.
   (C) She has changed her mind about volunteering.
   (D) She wants to teach music to kids.

Listen to part of the conversation. Then answer question 5.

5. What does the advisor imply when he says, "Well, that's a consideration."?
   (A) The student has too much homework.
   (B) The student should drop a class so she has more time.
   (C) The student probably shouldn't volunteer.
   (D) The student should think carefully about her schedule.

6. What does the advisor suggest to the student?
   (A) She should look at a listing of volunteer jobs that are available in the community.
   (B) She should make phone calls to different groups asking about volunteer jobs.
   (C) She should fill out an application for a volunteer job and leave it at the office.
   (D) She should make an appointment to go back and talk to the advisor again.

ACADEMIC LISTENING

FIRST LISTENING

Listen to a lecture from a history class. Take notes as you listen. Work with a partner to combine your notes. Then use your notes to answer the questions.

1. Who was Andrew Carnegie?

   _____

   _____

   _____

   _____

2. What philanthropic causes did he support?

   _____

   _____

   _____

SECOND LISTENING

Read the questions. Listen to the lecture again. Add details to your notes. Then use your notes to answer the questions. Work with a partner and compare your answers.

1. What is the lecture mainly about?
   (A) The influence of Andrew Carnegie's philanthropy today
   (B) The reasons for Andrew Carnegie's philanthropy
   (C) The relationship between Andrew Carnegie and other philanthropists
   (D) The story of Andrew Carnegie's life

2. What did Carnegie do to encourage people to educate themselves?
   (A) He built new schools.
   (B) He built public libraries.
   (C) He asked people to read his book.
   (D) He encouraged people to share their books.

3. Why does the professor tell the story about Carnegie and the rich man's library?
   (A) To describe a difficult time in Carnegie's life
   (B) To explain a motivation for Carnegie's philanthropy
   (C) To illustrate the problems of poor children
   (D) To tell the history of philanthropy before Carnegie

4. Why did Carnegie want to simplify English spelling?
   (A) To improve international communication
   (B) To make it easier to learn how to read and write
   (C) To encourage people to read books in English
   (D) To change the way dictionaries are written

Listen again to part of the lecture. Then answer question 5.

5. Why does the professor say, "So, in other words, he thought that it was shameful for wealthy people to keep all their money for themselves, that instead they should use their money to help others."?
   (A) To restate her point in a different way
   (B) To introduce a new topic
   (C) To check whether the students understood her
   (D) To correct an earlier point

Listen again to part of the lecture. Then answer question 6.

6. What does the professor mean when she says, "Realistically, I don't see why he believed that people would ever change something as . . . as . . . central to the language as spelling—most people completely opposed it!"?
   (A) She is surprised that Carnegie thought his plan could succeed.
   (B) She understands why Carnegie proposed his idea.
   (C) She doubts that Carnegie was serious about his plan.
   (D) She regrets that Carnegie's plan did not succeed.

ANALYSIS

It is helpful to know the purpose of a test item. There are three types of questions in the listening section.

1. Basic Comprehension

- main ideas
- details
- the meaning of specific sentences

2. Organization

- the way information is structured
- the way ideas are linked

3. Inference

- ideas are not directly stated
- speaker's intention, purpose, or attitude not explicitly stated

Go back to the listening questions and label each question with 1, 2, or 3. Then work with a partner to see if you agree. Check the Answer Key for the correct answers. Which questions did you get right? Which did you get wrong? What skills do you need to practice?

2 Reading

SOME TAKE THE TIME GLADLY

PRE-READING

Read the first and last paragraph of the article. Work with a partner to predict answers to the questions.

1. What is "mandatory volunteering"?

_____

2. How do Maryland high school students feel about it?

_____

READING

Read the passage on the next page and then answer the questions. Work with a partner and compare your answers. When you disagree, go back to the text to find helpful information.

Some Take the Time Gladly

By Mensah Dean, from the *Washington Times*

1   Mandatory[1] volunteering made many members of Maryland's high school class of '97 grumble with indignation. They didn't like a new requirement that made them take part in the school's community service program.

2   Future seniors, however, probably won't be as resistant now that the program has been broken in. Some, like John Maloney, already have completed their required hours of approved community service. The Bowie High School sophomore earned his hours in eighth grade by volunteering two nights a week at the Larkin-Chase Nursing and Restorative Center in Bowie.

3   He played shuffleboard, cards, and other games with the senior citizens. He also helped plan parties for them and visited their rooms to keep them company.

4   John, fifteen, is not finished volunteering. Once a week he videotapes animals at the Prince George's County animal shelter in Forestville. His footage is shown on the Bowie public access television channel in hopes of finding homes for the animals.

5   "Volunteering is better than just sitting around," says John, "and I like animals; I don't want to see them put to sleep."

6   He's not the only volunteer in his family. His sister, Melissa, an eighth grader, has completed her hours also volunteering at Larkin-Chase.

7   "It is a good idea to have kids go out into the community, but it's frustrating to have to write essays about the work," she said. "It makes you feel like you're doing it for the requirement and not for yourself."

8   The high school's service learning office, run by Beth Ansley, provides information on organizations seeking volunteers so that students will have an easier time fulfilling their hours.

9   "It's ridiculous that people are opposing the requirements," said Amy Rouse, who this summer has worked at the Ronald McDonald House and has helped to rebuild a church in Clinton.

10   "So many people won't do the service unless it's mandatory," Rouse said, "but once they start doing it, they'll really like it and hopefully it will become a part of their lives—like it has become a part of mine."

[1] ***mandatory:*** required

1. What is the article mostly about?
  (**A**) A volunteer program at Bowie High School
  (**B**) Students who earn extra money after school
  (**C**) The high school class of 1997
  (**D**) Students who volunteer to work with senior citizens

2. In paragraph 2, the word *resistant* is closest in meaning to
   (A) disappointed
   (B) nervous
   (C) unhappy
   (D) unwilling

3. In paragraph 4, the word *footage* is closest in meaning to
   (A) volunteers
   (B) animals
   (C) video
   (D) shoes

4. In paragraph 7, Melissa says "It makes you feel . . . " The word *It* refers to
   (A) going out in the community
   (B) writing essays
   (C) doing volunteer work
   (D) completing a requirement

5. From paragraphs 6 and 7, what can you infer about Melissa Maloney?
   (A) She doesn't like to write essays about her volunteer work.
   (B) She volunteers because it's a requirement.
   (C) She is frustrated by her volunteer job.
   (D) She volunteers because it makes her feel good.

6. According to paragraphs 9 and 10, which of the following statements most accurately reflects Amy Rouse's opinion?
   (A) "If they try volunteering, most people will discover that they enjoy it."
   (B) "I don't think the volunteer program should be mandatory."
   (C) "Most people don't like volunteering, so they won't want to do it."
   (D) "I think people should be able to choose whether they want to volunteer."

7. All of the following volunteer activities are mentioned in the article EXCEPT
   (A) visiting elderly people
   (B) videotaping animals in a shelter
   (C) rebuilding a church
   (D) tutoring children

8. Look at the four squares on the next page ☐ that indicate where the following sentence could be added to the passage. Where would the sentence best fit? Circle the letter that shows the point where you would insert this sentence.

   That experience inspired him to continue volunteering in the community.

Mandatory volunteering made many members of Maryland's high school class of '97 grumble with indignation. They didn't like a new requirement that made them take part in the school's community service program.

[A] Future seniors, however, probably won't be as resistant now that the program has been broken in. [B] Some, like John Maloney, already have completed their required hours of approved community service. [C] The Bowie High School sophomore earned his hours in eighth grade by volunteering two nights a week at the Larkin-Chase Nursing and Restorative Center in Bowie. [D]

9. In the passage, the author explains the concept of mandatory volunteer programs by
   (A) arguing in favor of volunteer programs
   (B) comparing two volunteer programs
   (C) describing one volunteer program
   (D) classifying different types of volunteer programs

10. An introductory sentence for a brief summary of the passage is provided below. Complete the summary by circling the THREE answer choices that express the most important ideas in the passage. Some sentences do not belong in the summary because they express ideas that are not presented in the passage or are minor ideas in the passage.

    Bowie High School has a mandatory volunteer program.

    (A) John Maloney works at an animal shelter.
    (B) Many students enjoy their volunteer work.
    (C) Students are required to perform community service jobs.
    (D) Some students can choose not to volunteer.
    (E) Students can volunteer at the high school.
    (F) Students can work for a variety of different organizations.

3 Writing

INTEGRATED TASK: READ, LISTEN, WRITE

In this section, you will read a short text and listen to an excerpt on the same topic. Then you will write about the relationship between the two.

READING

Read the passage on the next page. With a partner, fill in the following outline with the main ideas and examples.

Charitable Giving

What makes people give money to charity? One reason is altruism, the unselfish desire to help other people and make the world a better place. For example, religious institutions receive the highest percentage of donations in the United States. Colleges and universities often receive gifts from successful graduates who want to widen educational opportunities for other students or support research on an issue they feel is important. Hospitals and medical research organizations are often supported by donors who have been affected by a medical problem, either directly or through the experience of family members or friends. Many donors give to causes that have touched them personally in some way.

Charitable gifts can also be made for reasons involving personal interest. Under U.S. tax law, an individual does not have to pay income tax on money that is donated to charity. For extremely wealthy individuals, this can mean millions of dollars they do not have to pay in taxes to the government. In addition to tax benefits, donors often receive favorable publicity for making donations, and they have an opportunity to influence the world around them. For example, new buildings at colleges and universities are often named after important donors, which means that they will be remembered for their generosity for many years to come.

Charitable Giving

Reason: _____

    Examples: _____

    _____

    _____

Reason: _____

    Examples: _____

    _____

LISTENING

Listen to a report on a related topic. Use the outline on the next page to take notes as you listen.

Who was Gladys Holm?

_____retired secretary_____

_____

What did she give to the Children's Memorial Hospital?

_____

Why did she give the gift?

_____

How will her gift be used?

_____

WRITING

Write on the following topic. Follow the steps below to prepare.

Summarize the reasons for charitable giving described in the reading, and explain how the story of Gladys Holm illustrates them. Why did Gladys Holm make her donation? What reasons were not important to her? Explain with details and examples.

Step 1

Work with a partner. Skim the reading and your notes from the reading and listening tasks (pages 95–97). Complete this outline using the following questions to help you.

What are some reasons for charitable giving?

1. _____

2. _____

How did Gladys Holm feel about these reasons?

1. _____

   Supporting Details: _____

   _____

2. _____

   Supporting Details: _____

   _____

Step 2

Write for 20 minutes. Leave the last 5 minutes to edit your work.

> To evaluate a partner's writing, use the Writing Evaluation Form on page 173.

4 Speaking

INDEPENDENT TASK

Speak on the following topic. Follow the steps below to prepare.

I Should people donate money and volunteer time to help others? Why or why not?

Step 1

Work with a partner. Write an outline for your speaking task:

Opinion: _____

    Supporting Reason: _____

      Details: _____

    Supporting Reason: _____

      Details: _____

Step 2

Take turns practicing a one-minute oral response to the topic. Use the information in your outline to help you.

Step 3

Change partners. Take turns giving a one-minute response to the topic again.

> To evaluate your partner's response, use the Speaking Evaluation Form on page 174.

5 Skill Focus

IDENTIFYING AND USING RHETORICAL STRUCTURE

EXAMINATION

1 *Look at the following items from the unit. Which questions ask about the organization of information in the texts, and which questions ask about why the speaker/author mentioned something?*

Item 1 (Academic Listening, p. 91)

What is the lecture mainly about?
(A) The influence of Andrew Carnegie's philanthropy today
(B) The reasons for Andrew Carnegie's philanthropy
(C) The relationship between Andrew Carnegie and other philanthropists
(D) The story of Andrew Carnegie's life

Item 2 (Academic Listening, p. 91)

Why does the professor tell the story about Carnegie and the rich man's library?
(A) To describe a difficult time in Carnegie's life
(B) To explain a motivation for Carnegie's philanthropy
(C) To illustrate the problems of poor children
(D) To tell the history of philanthropy before Carnegie

Item 3 (Reading, p. 95)

In the passage, the author explains the concept of mandatory volunteer programs by
(A) arguing in favor of volunteer programs
(B) comparing two volunteer programs
(C) describing one volunteer program
(D) classifying different types of volunteer programs

2 *How should the writer organize the information to do this writing task?*

Item 4 (Integrated Writing Task, p. 97)

Summarize the reasons for charitable giving described in the reading, and explain how the story of Gladys Holm illustrates them. Why did Gladys Holm make her donation? What reasons were not important to her? Explain with details and examples.

Tips

To do well on the TOEFL, it is important to be able to identify the rhetorical structure of a text. Rhetorical structure refers to the organization of a text and the choices the speaker or writer makes by including a particular piece of information. It is also important to understand the speaker's or writer's purpose in choosing a particular organization.

Whole-Text Organization

While reading and listening, pay attention to the rhetorical structure of a text as a whole, including description, classification (describing types of things in a group), comparison and contrast, narrative (telling a story in chronological order), and persuasion (arguing in favor of or against something).

Purpose of Specific Statements

In some items, you may need to identify the rhetorical purpose of a particular statement. For example, the author or speaker may be trying to give an example, introduce a new topic, make a correction, restate an important point, or express an opinion.

Introduce a new topic	As for the motivations for Carnegie's philanthropy… Well, some say it was based on his life experience.
Make a correction	…that's more than $3 million—I'm sorry, I mean $3 billion in today's dollars!
Restate a point	So, in other words, he thought that it was shameful for wealthy people to keep all their money for themselves, that instead they should use their money to help others.
Express an opinion	Realistically, I don't see why he believed that people would ever change something as … as … central to the language as spelling—most people completely opposed it!

Rhetorical Structure in Speaking or Writing tasks

When you are presenting information in speaking or writing, the rhetorical structure should reflect the type of question you are answering. You must analyze the question to choose which structure is most appropriate.

In the Examination section, Items 1 to 3 ask about rhetorical structure in the lecture about Andrew Carnegie. **Item 1** asks about the main idea of the lecture, but to answer you have to identify the rhetorical structure (telling the story of Carnegie's life). **Item 2** asks about the professor's purpose when she tells a story about Carnegie in the lecture. By listening for how the professor uses the story in her lecture, you can tell that it is to explain the motivation for Carnegie's philanthropy.

Item **3** asks how the author explains a concept in the reading. The article illustrates the concept by describing one mandatory volunteer program.

Item **4** is a writing prompt, so you had to analyze the question to figure out how to structure your answer. You can organize your response as a classification essay, in which you summarize the different reasons for giving to charity and explain whether those reasons were important to Gladys Holms.

PRACTICE

1 *Work with a partner. Read the passage. Make an outline of the information in the paragraph and discuss how it is organized.*

Philanthropists

There are three types of philanthropists: individuals, foundations, and private corporations. Individuals give money or volunteer their time to support causes that are important to them. Foundations are organizations started by very wealthy individuals, such as the Bill and Melinda Gates Foundation, started by Microsoft founder Bill Gates and his wife to improve global health and education. The "business" of these foundations is not to make a profit but to give money away to not-for-profit organizations. Private corporations may also use a portion of their business profits to make donations, or they may give away their products or services free of charge. For example, after the earthquake and tsunami in the Indian Ocean in 2004, pharmaceutical companies donated millions of dollars worth of medicine to the relief effort.

2 *Answer the questions about the paragraph. Then discuss the types of questions. Do they ask about whole-text organization or author purpose? Mark them **WT** (whole text) or **AP** (author purpose).*

_____ **1.** The organization of the paragraph can best be described as
   (**A**) a description of three types of philanthropy
   (**B**) a history of philanthropy
   (**C**) an analysis of the effects of philanthropy
   (**D**) an argument in favor of philanthropy

_____ 2. Why does the author mention Bill Gates?
(A) To encourage other wealthy people to start foundations
(B) To explain why Bill Gates is so wealthy
(C) To give an example of a private foundation
(D) To show the types of charities Bill Gates supports

_____ 3. The author explains the concept of philanthropy by private corporations by
(A) comparing the philanthropy of two corporations
(B) explaining the history of one corporate giving program
(C) giving an example of corporate giving
(D) identifying the benefits of corporate giving

3 _Work with a partner. Read the writing topics and decide which rhetorical structure is best to respond to each prompt. Then choose two prompts and work together to write a short outline of a possible response. Share your outlines with the class and discuss the differences between them._

Writing Topics

_____ 1. Compare the similarities and differences between individual philanthropy and corporate philanthropy.

_____ 2. Describe a time when you practiced philanthropy by donating money or volunteering your time. Who needed your philanthropy, and what did you do to help?

_____ 3. Describe the three types of philanthropists: individual donors, private foundations, and corporate donors.

_____ 4. Some people prefer to donate money to support a charity, whereas other people prefer to volunteer time. Which do you prefer, and why?

_____ 5. Think of a philanthropic cause that you feel is important, such as researching a disease or helping people in need. Why is the cause important and why should people support it?

Rhetorical Structures

a. Opinion   **d.** Persuasion

b. Comparison and contrast   **e.** Classification

c. Narrative

4 _Look back at the writing question for the Integrated Task on page 97. Compare the organization you used with the organization your partner used. Are there any other ways you could have organized the information? Explain._

_____

_____

Education

TOEFL® iBT TARGET SKILLS

- Identify and express main ideas
- Identify and express details
- Make inferences
- Synthesize information
- Recognize comparison in a lecture
- Support a position using examples

(ETS) For extra practice of TOEFL iBT skills, go to pages 206–223.

1 Listening

CAMPUS CONVERSATION

PRE-LISTENING VOCABULARY

Read the passage. Guess the meaning of the boldfaced words and phrases. Then match each word or phrase with a definition or synonym from the list below. Work with a partner and compare your answers.

It can be difficult for college students to decide which classes to take. Some classes are required, such as the classes that make up the (1) **core curriculum**, but the rest are chosen by the student. Some students only want to study subjects that will be (2) **practical**, giving them specific skills for their career or preparing them for graduate school. These students may not like choosing a required class (3) **versus** a class they want to take. On the other hand, many students like to (4) **take advantage** of the opportunity to explore new subjects at college by taking a (5) **broad range** of classes, from art to science, and English to economics. Many experts feel that exploring a variety of subjects is better because students receive a (6) **well-rounded** education. These students may be (7) **better off** in the long run and have more opportunities later in life. For example, students may have a wider ranger of opportunities available once they get a job and join the (8) **workforce**.

_____ **a.** all the people who work

_____ **b.** balanced with a variety of experiences

_____ **c.** basic subjects that must be studied in school

_____ **d.** happier, more successful

_____ **e.** in contrast to

_____ **f.** wide variety

_____ **g.** use a situation to help yourself

_____ **h.** useful

> **Culture Note:** Most undergraduate programs have core curriculum or general education requirements. To meet these requirements, students select a number of courses from disciplines such as the sciences, math, social science, foreign languages, literature, and theater. The purpose of these requirements is to make sure that students receive a foundation of knowledge outside their major.

FIRST LISTENING

Read the questions. Listen to the conversation between a student and an academic advisor. Take notes as you listen. Share your notes with a partner. Then use your notes to answer the questions.

1. Why does the student go to see the academic advisor? _____

_____

2. What advice does the academic advisor give the student? _____

_____

SECOND LISTENING

Read the questions. Listen to the conversation again. Add details to your notes. Then use your notes to answer the questions. Work with a partner and compare your answers.

1. Why does the student go to see her advisor?
   (A) She couldn't get into a class she wants next semester.
   (B) She is having trouble in one of her classes.
   (C) She isn't sure which classes to take next semester.
   (D) She wants to drop a class but isn't sure how.

Listen again to part of the conversation. Then answer question 2.

2. Select the sentence that best expresses how the student probably feels.
   (A) She didn't enjoy the accounting class.
   (B) She felt the accounting class was difficult.
   (C) She liked the teacher in the accounting class.
   (D) She wants to take another accounting class.

Listen again to part of the conversation. Then answer question 3.

3. What does the advisor mean when she says, "Serious?"?
   (A) She thinks the student's parents are wrong.
   (B) She wants the student to talk about her feelings.
   (C) She wants the student to explain what her parents mean.
   (D) She doesn't believe the student.

4. How do the student's parents feel about business and accounting classes?
   (A) Film classes are more interesting than business and accounting classes.
   (B) Film classes are more useful than business and accounting classes.
   (C) Film classes are less difficult than business and accounting classes.
   (D) Film classes are less practical than business and accounting classes.

5. What does the professor say about finding work after college?
   (A) A student needs to have the skills employers want.
   (B) A student's major is the most important factor.
   (C) Employers don't pay attention to a student's grades in school.
   (D) Employers want to hire students right after college.

6. What does the professor suggest the student do about her problem? Check TWO answer choices.
   (A) _____ Ask her parents to come and talk to the professor
   (B) _____ Drop her business and accounting classes
   (C) _____ Find a way to combine film and business
   (D) _____ Stop taking film classes and major in accounting
   (E) _____ Talk to her parents and reach a compromise

ACADEMIC LISTENING

FIRST LISTENING

Listen to a lecture from an education class about home schooling (teaching children at home instead of sending them to school). Take notes using the question and the chart to help you. Work with a partner to combine your notes.

What issue in home schooling does the class discuss? _____

_____

Use this chart to compare the issue of home schools versus traditional schools.

HOME SCHOOL ₀	TRADITIONAL SCHOOL

SECOND LISTENING

Read the questions. Listen to the lecture again. Add details to your notes. Then use your notes to answer the questions. Work with a partner and compare your answers.

1. How is home schooling changing in the United States?
(**A**) Colleges are accepting more home schoolers.
(**B**) Local governments are passing laws to control home schooling.
(**C**) More home-schooled children are returning to traditional schools.
(**D**) The number of home-schooled children is increasing.

2. What does the class do in its discussion of home schooling?
(**A**) Compare socialization in home schools and traditional schools
(**B**) Discuss why children receive better socialization in home schools
(**C**) Explore ways to improve socialization in home schools
(**D**) Study examples of different types of socialization in home schools

3. Put a check (√) to indicate whether each sentence describes a home school, a traditional school, or both, according to the lecture.

	HOME SCHOOL	TRADITIONAL SCHOOL	BOTH
(A) Children learn socialization.			
(B) Children avoid teasing and bullying.			
(C) Children form a closer relationship with parents.			
(D) Children interact with peers.			
(E) Children interact with people in different age groups.			
(F) Children learn to operate in a large group.			

Listen again to part of the lecture. Then answer question 4.

4. Why does the professor say, "Well, not quite . . ."?
   (A) To stop the student from speaking
   (B) To indicate that the student gave the wrong answer
   (C) To repeat the student's point so everyone understands it
   (D) To show that he agrees with the student's point

Listen again to part of the lecture. Then answer question 5.

5. Why does the professor say, "Well, that's a very complex issue, and you can't look at it in isolation."?
   (A) He doesn't want the student to interrupt him.
   (B) He doesn't think it's possible to answer the student's question.
   (C) He doesn't understand the student's question.
   (D) He wants the student to answer the question himself.

2 Reading

EMOTIONAL INTELLIGENCE

PRE-READING

Read the title, headings, and first sentence of each paragraph in the passage. Work with a partner to answer the questions.

1. What is Emotional Intelligence? _____

_____

2. What are some aspects of Emotional Intelligence? _____

_____

READING

Read the passage on the next page and answer the questions. Then work with a partner and compare your answers. When you disagree, go back to the text to find helpful information.

Emotional Intelligence

Adapted from *The World of Psychology* by Samuel E. Wood, Ellen Greenwood, and Denise Boyd

1 Emotional Intelligence is the ability to apply knowledge about emotions to everyday life. This type of intelligence involves an awareness of and an ability to manage one's own emotions, and self-motivation.

Personal Components of Emotional Intelligence

2 The foundation of Emotional Intelligence is said to be self-knowledge, which involves an awareness of emotions, an ability to manage those emotions, and self-motivation.

Awareness and Management of One's Emotions

3 Being aware of one's own emotions—recognizing and acknowledging feelings as they happen—is at the very heart of Emotional Intelligence. And this awareness encompasses not only moods but also thoughts about those moods. People who are able to monitor their feelings as they arise are less likely to be ruled by them and are thus better able to manage their emotions.

4 Managing emotions does not mean suppressing them; nor does it mean giving free rein to every feeling. Psychologist Daniel Goleman (1995), one of several authors who have popularized the notion of Emotional Intelligence, insisted that the goal is balance and that every feeling has value and significance. As Goleman said, "A life without passion would be a dull wasteland of neutrality, cut off and isolated from the richness of life itself" (p. 56). Thus, we manage our emotions by expressing them in an appropriate manner. Emotions can also be managed by engaging in activities that cheer us up, soothe our hurts, or reassure us when we feel anxious.

5 Clearly, awareness and management of emotions are not independent. For instance, you might think that individuals who seem to experience their feelings more intensely than others would be less able to manage them. However, a critical component of awareness of emotions is the ability to assign meaning to them—to know why we are experiencing a particular feeling or mood. Psychologists have found that, among individuals who experience intense emotions, individual differences in the ability to assign meaning to those feelings predict differences in the ability to manage them (Gohm, 2003). In other words, if two individuals are intensely angry, the one who is better able to understand why he or she is angry will also be better able to manage the anger.

Self-Motivation

6 Self-motivation refers to strong emotional self-control, which enables a person to get moving and pursue worthy goals, persist at tasks even when frustrated, and resist the temptation to act on impulse. Resisting impulsive behavior is, according to Goleman (1995), "the root of all emotional self-control" (p. 81).

7 Of all the attributes of Emotional Intelligence, the ability to postpone immediate gratification and to persist in working toward some greater future gain is most closely related to success—whether one is trying to build a business, get a college degree, or even stay on a diet. One researcher examined whether this trait can predict a child's success in school. The study showed that 4-year-old children who can delay instant gratification in order to advance toward some future goal will be "far superior as students" when they graduate from high school than will 4-year-olds who are not able to resist the impulse to satisfy their immediate wishes (Shoda et al., 1990).

1. In paragraph 3, the word *monitor* is closest in meaning to
   (A) discuss
   (B) hide
   (C) ignore
   (D) pay attention to

2. Which of the sentences below best expresses the essential information in the passage excerpt?

   > People who are able to monitor their feelings as they arise are less likely to be ruled by them and are thus better able to manage their emotions.

   (A) If people pay attention to their feelings, they can control their emotions better.
   (B) People who can manage their emotions will not be controlled by them.
   (C) If people pay attention to their feelings when they happen, they will not be able to manage them.
   (D) Some people can understand their feelings better than others.

3. According to paragraphs 3 to 5, why is it important to be aware of our emotions?
   (A) So we can explain them to other people
   (B) So we can experience feelings more intensely
   (C) So we can stop feeling angry
   (D) So we can manage our emotions appropriately

4. According to paragraph 4, what did psychologist Daniel Goleman do?
   (A) He studied how people manage their emotions.
   (B) He trained people to increase their Emotional Intelligence.
   (C) He treated patients who had emotional problems.
   (D) He wrote about Emotional Intelligence.

5. Which of the following is NOT mentioned in paragraph 4 about our emotions?
   (A) Emotions are part of a satisfying life.
   (B) Every feeling is important.
   (C) Some feelings should be ignored.
   (D) Emotions can be managed.

6. In paragraph 5 in the sentence ending "differences in the ability to manage them," the word *them* refers to
   (A) psychologists
   (B) individuals
   (C) intense emotions
   (D) individual differences

7. In paragraph 5, how does the author explain the concept of the awareness and management of emotions?
   (A) By comparing how two people might respond to an intense emotion
   (B) By describing how people learn to control their emotions
   (C) By explaining why some people are not aware of their emotions
   (D) By giving an example of why people get angry

8. In paragraph 6, the word *persist* is closest in meaning to
 (**A**) quit
 (**B**) explain
 (**C**) finish
 (**D**) learn

9. According the paragraph 7, why might children be more successful in school if they can resist impulses?
 (**A**) They are more popular with their teachers.
 (**B**) They can focus on their work and not get distracted.
 (**C**) They easily understand new information.
 (**D**) They have more friends at school.

10. Look at the four squares ☐ that indicate where the following sentence could be added to the passage. Where would the sentence best fit? Circle the letter that shows the point where you can insert this sentence.

> Research like this shows how important Emotional Intelligence can be in a person's life.

 ☐A Of all the attributes of Emotional Intelligence, the ability to postpone immediate gratification and to persist in working toward some greater future gain is most closely related to success—whether one is trying to build a business, get a college degree, or even stay on a diet. ☐B One researcher examined whether this trait can predict a child's success in school. ☐C The study showed that 4-year-old children who can delay instant gratification in order to advance toward some future goal will be "far superior as students" when they graduate from high school than will 4-year-olds who are not able to resist the impulse to satisfy their immediate wishes (Shoda et al., 1990). ☐D

11. Select the appropriate phrases from the answer choices and match them to the personal components of Emotional Intelligence to which they relate. TWO of the answer choices will NOT be used.
 (**A**) communicate with others about our feelings
 (**B**) control our impulses
 (**C**) express our emotions appropriately
 (**D**) recognize our feelings
 (**E**) understand the feelings of others
 (**F**) understand why we feel the way we do
 (**G**) work toward a future goal

Awareness and Management of Emotions

- _____
- _____
- _____

Self-Motivation

- _____
- _____

ANALYSIS

It is helpful to know the purpose of a test item. There are four types of questions in the reading section.

1. Basic Comprehension

- main ideas
- details
- the meaning of specific sentences

2. Organization

- the way information is structured in the text
- the way ideas are linked between sentences or between paragraphs

3. Inference

- ideas are not directly stated in the text
- author's intention, purpose, or attitude not explicitly stated in the text

4. Vocabulary and Reference

- the meaning of words
- the meaning of reference words such as *his, them, this,* or *none*

Go back to the reading questions and label each question with 1, 2, 3, or 4. Then work with a partner to see if you agree. Check the Answer Key for the correct answers. Which questions did you get right? Which did you get wrong? What skills do you need to practice?

3 Speaking

INTEGRATED TASK: READ, LISTEN, SPEAK

In this section, you will read a short passage and listen to an excerpt on the same topic. Then you will speak about the relationship between the two.

READING

Read the excerpt on the next page from a psychology textbook. With a partner, complete the task.

Motivation

Have you ever been in a situation in which you needed to do something, but you just weren't motivated enough to do it? We often talk about "being motivated," but have you ever thought about exactly what that means?

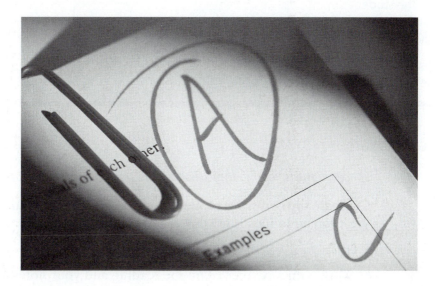

At any given time, your behavior can be explained by one or more motives—needs or desires that direct behavior toward a goal. Motives can arise from an internal source, such as when you keep studying because you find the subject matter interesting. When activities are pursued as ends in themselves—simply because they are enjoyable or satisfying, and not because any external reward is attached—the type of motivation we experience is known as intrinsic motivation. Other motives come from outside sources, when some external incentive influences you to act. For example, when you study because you want to get a good grade or to avoid a bad grade, the grade is serving as an incentive. When we act in order to gain some external reward or to avoid some undesirable consequence, we are pulled by extrinsic motivation.

Define these terms.

1. Motivation: _____

2. Intrinsic Motivation: _____

3. Extrinsic Motivation: _____

LISTENING

Listen to the conversation between two classmates in the library. Use the chart to take notes as you listen.

	STUDENT 1 (MALE)	STUDENT 2 (FEMALE)
How does the student feel about the class?		
How does the student feel about the article on Emotional Intelligence?		
How does the student feel about the class project?		

SPEAKING

Speak on the following topic. Follow the steps below to prepare.

Compare the two types of motivation defined in the reading. Use examples from the listening to illustrate your points.

Step 1

- Work with a partner. Skim the reading and your notes from the listening (pages 112–114).

- Complete the chart with the type of motivation each student shows and examples of how they show their motivation.

TYPE OF MOTIVATION	EXAMPLES
	Student 1 (male)
	Student 2 (female)

Step 2

Take turns practicing a one-minute oral response to the topic. Use the information in your chart to help you.

Step 3

Change partners. Take turns giving a one-minute response to the topic again.

To evaluate your partner's response, use the Speaking Evaluation Form on page 174.

4 Writing

INDEPENDENT TASK

Write on the following topic. Follow the steps below to prepare.

Compare and contrast two classes you had in elementary school. Describe the similarities and differences (e.g., subject matter, teaching style, class activities). Explain the comparison using details and examples.

Step 1

Choose two classes to write about and write the name of the class in the chart. Then use the chart to brainstorm the factors that were similar or different in the two classes.

FACTOR	CLASS 1	CLASS 2
Teacher		
Teaching style		
Subject matter		
Class activities		
Other:		
Other:		
Other:		
Other:		

- Work in groups. Take turns describing your experiences.

- React to what you have heard. What were the biggest differences? What do you want to know more about?

Step 2

Write for 20 minutes. Leave the last 5 minutes to edit your work.

To evaluate a partner's writing, use the Writing Evaluation Form on page 173.

5 Skill Focus

COMPARING AND CONTRASTING

EXAMINATION

Look at the items from the unit. What information is being compared or contrasted in each question? Complete the comparison after each question.

Item 1 (Campus Conversation, p. 105)

How do the student's parents feel about business and accounting classes?
(A) Film classes are more interesting than business and accounting classes.
(B) Film classes are more useful than business and accounting classes.
(C) Film classes are less difficult than business and accounting classes.
(D) Film classes are less practical than business and accounting classes.

Comparison: business and accounting classes versus _____

Item 2 (Academic Listening, p. 107)

What does the class do in its discussion of home schooling?
(A) Compare socialization in home schools and traditional schools
(B) Discuss why children receive better socialization in home schools
(C) Explore ways to improve socialization in home schools
(D) Study examples of different types of socialization in home schools

Comparison: _____ versus _____

Item 3 (Academic Listening, p. 107)

Put a check (√) to indicate whether each sentence describes a home school, a traditional school, or both, according to the lecture.

	HOME SCHOOL	TRADITIONAL SCHOOL	BOTH
a. Children learn socialization.			
b. Children avoid teasing and bullying.			
c. Children form a closer relationship with parents.			
d. Children interact with peers.			
e. Children interact with people in different age groups.			
f. Children learn to operate in a large group.			

Comparison: _____ versus _____

Item 4 (Reading, p. 110)

In paragraph 5, how does the author explain the concept of the awareness and management of emotions?

(A) By comparing how two people might respond to an intense emotion
(B) By describing how people learn to control their emotions
(C) By explaining why some people are not aware of their emotions
(D) By giving an example of why people get angry

Comparison: _____ versus _____

Tips

To do well on the TOEFL, it is essential to learn how to compare and contrast information. You will need to recognize similarities and differences, analyze information for similarities and differences, and distinguish points of view. You will also need to express ideas by categorizing them into different parts.

(continued on next page)

Listening and Reading

Comparisons may be made on the whole-text level, as in the lecture comparing home schooling versus traditional school, or on the sentence level.

- Pay attention to comparative phrases:

    People who are able to monitor their feelings as they arise are *less likely* to be ruled by them and are thus better able to manage their emotions.

    Home schoolers interact with a *much wider* range of people, of different age groups and in different settings, through volunteer work, sports groups, and other activities, and this is *better than* a school setting, where kids only interact with kids in their grade, who are about the same age.

- Pay attention to comparative signal words:

    Introducing similarities: *likewise, similarly, in the same way*

    Introducing difference: *but, on the other hand, conversely, in contrast, however*

Writing and Speaking

The Integrated Tasks require you to summarize and compare the information in the reading and the listening.

- Organize your ideas using a chart or Venn diagram.

Chart

	Home School	Traditional School
Socialization		
Curriculum		
Activities		

Venn Diagram

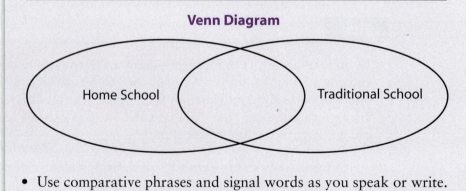

- Use comparative phrases and signal words as you speak or write.

In **Item 1** of the Examination section, the comparison is between business and accounting classes and other classes. You probably listened for the student's description of her parents' preference for business and accounting classes, instead of "not practical" classes like a film class.

In **Item 2**, you had to identify the rhetorical structure of the lecture—a comparison of home schools and traditional schools. You probably listened for comparative phrases such as "home schooling versus traditional schools," "home schoolers interact with a much wider range of people," and "in contrast."

In **Item 3**, you had to fill in details about the comparison between home schools and traditional schools. You probably listened for specific pieces of information from the chart.

In **Item 4**, you had to recognize the author's discussion of the relationship between awareness and response, and that he or she was contrasting assumptions and research results.

PRACTICE

1 *Read the excerpts from the listenings and readings. Underline the comparative phrases or signal words. The first one is done for you.*

1. Because the children spend <u>more</u> time with the family, with their parents and siblings, they actually develop stronger ties and stronger relationships that way.

2. And, in contrast, they also argue that kids at traditional schools get a lot more negative socialization such as teasing, bullying, and so on, that doesn't happen at a home school.

3. For instance, you might think that individuals who seem to experience their feelings more intensely than others would be less able to manage them. However, a critical component of awareness of emotions is the ability to assign meaning to them—to know why we are experiencing a particular feeling or mood.

4. People who are able to monitor their feelings as they arise are less likely to be ruled by them and are thus better able to manage their emotions.

5. The study showed that 4-year-old children who can delay instant gratification in order to advance toward some future goal will be "far superior as

students" when they graduate from high school than will 4-year-olds who are not able to resist the impulse to satisfy their immediate wishes.

2 *Work with a partner to do the following:*

1. Read the information about a lecture class versus a discussion class. Add one idea of your own to the list. Then organize the information using a chart or Venn diagram.

2. Work individually to write comparative sentences about the information.

3. Take turns reading your sentences.

Lecture Class

- The professor stands at the front of the class and talks to the students.
- The class follows a syllabus that outlines course content.
- The students don't discuss the information.
- Students may ask questions after they raise their hands.
- Lecture classes are often very large.
- Students must do homework for the class.
- Students don't get individual interaction with the professor.
- Lecture classes are usually graded by exams.
- _____

Discussion Class

- The professor and students sit in a group.
- The class follows a syllabus that outlines course content.
- The professor introduces a subject, and the students discuss it.
- Students must be prepared to discuss the information in class.
- Discussion classes are usually small.
- Students must do homework for the class.
- Students and professors get to know each other well.
- Discussion classes are graded in part on how much a student participates in class.
- _____

3 *Work with a partner. Look back at your writing from the Independent Task. How did you organize the information? What comparisons or contrasts did you make?*

UNIT 8

Food

TOEFL® iBT TARGET SKILLS	
• Identify and express main ideas • Identify and express details • Make inferences • Recognize a speaker's or writer's attitude • Summarize a text and relate it to a listening	*(ETS)* For extra practice of TOEFL iBT skills, go to pages 206–223.

1 Listening

CAMPUS CONVERSATION

PRE-LISTENING VOCABULARY

Read the conversations. Guess the meaning of the boldfaced words and phrases. Then match each word or phrase with a definition or synonym from the list on the next page. Work with a partner and compare your answers.

_____ 1. **A:** Wow! That's a big plate of food. Are you going to eat it all?

        B: I like to eat a lot so that I **get my money's worth**. I want to get what I pay for!

_____ 2. **A:** What's wrong? You look upset!

        B: Oh, it's my parents. They're **giving me a hard time** because I want to stay here over the winter break, but they want me to come home.

_____ 3. **A:** Which **meal plan** do you have?

        B: The fourteen-meal plan. On most days, I eat lunch and dinner in the dining hall, but I buy breakfast foods to eat in my room.

_____ 4. **A:** What do you think of our economics class? Do you like it?

        B: It's pretty boring, so I'**m not crazy about** it.

_____ 5. **A:** I just bought this and it's the wrong size! What should I do?

        B: Take it back to the store for a **refund**. They'll give you your money back.

_____ 6. **A:** Hey, I'm going over to the **Student Center** to get something to eat. Want to come?[1]

        B: Sure, I need to make some copies over there, too, and then stop by the bookstore.

_____ 7. **A:** Why are you throwing your sandwich away? You hardly ate any of it!

        B: I know. I hate to **waste** food. It's a good sandwich, but I'm really late for lab, and we're not allowed to eat in there.

[1]**Want to come?**: Do you want to come?

a. a central campus building that has student services and offices

b. an amount of money given back to you

c. complaining to or bothering someone

d. dining service purchased from a college or university

e. don't like

f. get full value for something

g. not use something effectively

> **Culture Note:** Colleges and universities provide a variety of meal plans for students who live on campus. Students pay for the meal plan in advance and use their meal card to buy food at campus dining halls, restaurants, and coffee shops on campus.

FIRST LISTENING

Read the questions. Listen to the conversation between a student and a Resident Assistant in the school dining hall. Take notes as you listen. Share your notes with a partner. Then use your notes to answer the questions.

1. What are the student and the Resident Assistant discussing?

_____

2. What does the Resident Assistant suggest the student should do?

_____

SECOND LISTENING

Read the questions. Listen to the conversation again. Add details to your notes. Then use your notes to answer the questions. Work with a partner and compare your answers.

1. What is the conversation mainly about?
 (**A**) The student's ideas for healthy eating
 (**B**) The student's plans for the next semester
 (**C**) The student's problems with her meal plan
 (**D**) The student's questions about the dining hall

2. Why are the student's parents upset with her?
 (**A**) She doesn't like the food in the dining hall.
 (**B**) She is eating too much fast food.
 (**C**) She is wasting money by not eating in the dining hall.
 (**D**) She wants to change meal plans.

3. How does the Resident Assistant suggest the student solve her problem?
(A) Move off campus so she can cook for herself
(B) Sign up for a different meal plan next semester
(C) Talk to her parents and explain her problem to them
(D) Try new dishes at the cafeteria to see if she likes them

Listen again to part of the conversation. Then answer question 4.

4. What does the student mean when she says, "So here I am, trying to get my money's worth."?
(A) She is eating the cafeteria food.
(B) She is offering food to the Resident Assistant.
(C) She is spending her own money on food.
(D) She is trying to save money by eating less.

Listen again to part of the conversation. Then answer question 5.

5. What can you infer about the student?
(A) She likes eating in restaurants.
(B) She has a class at lunchtime.
(C) She doesn't have many friends.
(D) She likes eating with other people.

ACADEMIC LISTENING

FIRST LISTENING

Listen to the report "Food in a Bowl" from the program Satellite Sisters, *a radio show featuring sisters who live in five different places. Take notes using the chart on the next page. Work with a partner to combine your notes.*

SISTER	PLACE	COMMENTS ABOUT THE WAY FOOD IS SERVED
Lian		
Julie		
Liz		

SECOND LISTENING

Read the questions. Listen to the report again. Add details to your notes. Then use your notes to answer the questions. Work with a partner and compare your answers.

1. What is the report mainly about?
  (**A**) The way food is served in restaurants and markets
  (**B**) The best restaurants in cities around the world
  (**C**) The eating habits of people around the world
  (**D**) The Satellite Sisters' food preferences

2. Which of the following best describes the presentation of information in the report?
  (**A**) A description of two contrasting ideas
  (**B**) An analysis of facts
  (**C**) An argument in favor of an idea
  (**D**) An expression of personal opinions

Listen again to part of the report. Then answer question 3.

3. Select the sentence that best expresses how Lian Dolan probably feels.
  (**A**) "Fast food is convenient when I don't have much time."
  (**B**) "I don't have enough time to have a long meal."
  (**C**) "People like to eat quickly because they are busy."
  (**D**) "People should take more time to eat."

Listen again to part of the report. Then answer question 4.

4. What does Julie Dolan imply about Bangkok, Thailand?
  (**A**) Eating food in a bowl is popular.
  (**B**) Restaurants don't serve food in bowls.
  (**C**) The city is a nice place to live.
  (**D**) There are many popular restaurants.

Listen again to part of the report. Then answer question 5.

5. Why does Liz mention lamb kabobs served on skewers?
   (A) To describe why she doesn't like to eat out in restaurants
   (B) To explain what is served at her favorite restaurant
   (C) To give an example of food she has trouble eating
   (D) To illustrate how her eating habits differ from her sisters'

ANALYSIS

It is helpful to know the purpose of a test item. There are three types of questions in the listening section.

1. Basic Comprehension

- main ideas
- details
- the meaning of specific sentences

2. Organization

- the way information is structured
- the way ideas are linked

3. Inference

- ideas are not directly stated
- speaker's intention, purpose, or attitude not explicitly stated

Go back to the listening questions and label each question with 1, 2, or 3. Then work with a partner to see if you agree. Check the Answer Key for the correct answers. Which questions did you get right? Which did you get wrong? What skills do you need to practice?

2 Reading

"SLOW FOOD" MOVEMENT AIMS AT RESTORING THE JOY OF EATING

PRE-READING

Read the title and the first and last paragraphs of the article. Then answer the questions.

1. What is the Slow Food movement? _____

_____

2. How do Slow Food members feel about fast-food restaurants?

_____

READING

Read the passage and answer the questions. Then work with a partner and compare your answers. When you disagree, go back to the text to find helpful information.

"Slow Food" Movement Aims at Restoring the Joy of Eating

By Cathy Heiner (from *USA Today*)

1   "The Slow Food movement is committed to the preservation and restoration of a traditional convivial joy, the joy of the table," says Jonathan White, a member of the Slow Food organization and owner of Egg Farm Dairy in Peekskill, N.Y. "And that's not just about food and wine; it's also about kinship and companionship, which you just don't get going to a drive-through and eating in traffic."

2   Whopper[1] lovers, don't have a meltdown. Slow Food may use a snail as its logo, but it's not anti-fast food. "We're not against anything," White says. "Our agenda is to educate people who don't know about the pleasures of the table and, through education, to help traditional food artisans—bakers, cheesemakers, farmers growing heirloom[2] vegetables—to survive by sustaining demand for their product."

3   Members of Slow Food meet for long, leisurely meals. They talk food, wine, culture and philosophy. They organize wine tastings and cooking classes. But most of all, they work to eradicate the "nuke[3] it and eat it" American lifestyle.

4   "Slow Food is not only about literally eating slowly, but also about savoring and appreciating the pleasures of good food and drink. Slow Food is a way of life," says its Web site (www.slowfood.com).

5   The movement got cooking in the late 1980s when a fast-food burger joint was about to open on Rome's beloved Piazza Spagna. A young Italian organization called Arcigola, dedicated to rediscovering and advocating authentic Italian traditions, protested. From the fray, Slow Food was born.

[1] *Whopper:* a type of hamburger from Burger King
[2] *heirloom:* old-style and usually valuable
[3] *nuke:* to cook or heat something in a microwave oven

6   "It was just a game at first," says founder Carlo Petrini, "a chance to remind people that food is a perishable[4] art, as pleasurable in its way as a sculpture by Michelangelo."

7   Today, Slow Food is 20,000 strong in Italy, where the joy of the table is a matter of national pride. And there are Slow Food organizations in more than 15 countries, from Switzerland to Singapore.

8   Although the movement is new to these shores, adherents say they believe Americans will take to it like pigs to truffles. "Every year Americans are going to more restaurants, asking and learning more about food," says Paul Bartolotta, Slow Foodist and owner of Chicago's Spiaggia restaurant.

9   He says the USA is ripe for Slow Food. "Ten years ago, there were hardly any farmers markets, we were fast-food-driven, and there was less interest in food and wine. It has dramatically changed. Now there are organic supermarkets. There's a cultural awareness of what we're eating and why."

[4] *perishable:* unpreserved and therefore able to decay or spoil quickly

1. Based on the information in paragraph 2, why might traditional food artisans need help to survive?
   (A) Fewer people are eating their products.
   (B) Their products are too expensive for most people.
   (C) People don't like their products.
   (D) They can't make enough of their products.

2. Which of the sentences below best expresses the essential information in the passage excerpt?

   "Slow Food is not only about literally eating slowly, but also about savoring and appreciating the pleasures of good food and drink."

   (A) Eating slowly is more important than enjoying eating and drinking.
   (B) Enjoying eating and drinking is more important than eating slowly.
   (C) Enjoying eating and drinking is equally important to eating slowly.
   (D) Eating slowly is not the same thing as enjoying eating and drinking.

3. In paragraph 3, the word *eradicate* is closest in meaning to
   (A) control
   (B) eliminate
   (C) increase
   (D) understand

4. In paragraph 5, the word *advocating* is closest in meaning to
   (A) encouraging
   (B) explaining
   (C) researching
   (D) trying

5. In paragraph 6, why does Carlo Petrini mention Michelangelo?
   (A) To give an example of a great artist
   (B) To explain about Italian culture
   (C) To describe things he likes in addition to food
   (D) To make a comparison between food and art

6. In paragraph 8, the phrase *these shores* refers to
   (A) the United States
   (B) Switzerland
   (C) Italy
   (D) Singapore

7. Which of the following statements most accurately reflects Paul Bartolotta's opinion in paragraphs 8 and 9?
   (A) The Slow Food movement will soon become popular in the United States.
   (B) The people in the United States are not ready for the Slow Food movement.
   (C) The people in the United States prefer eating at fast-food restaurants.
   (D) Slow Food in only popular at his Chicago restaurant.

8. All of the following are mentioned in the passage as goals of the Slow Food movement EXCEPT
   (A) dining with other people
   (B) enjoying a good meal
   (C) going out to restaurants more often
   (D) learning more about the food we eat

9. An introductory sentence for a brief summary of the passage is provided below. Complete the summary by circling THREE answer choices that best express the most important ideas in the passage.

   > The Slow Food movement encourages people to eat slowly and enjoy their food.

   (A) The movement's founder believes food should be compared to art.
   (B) The movement encourages people to buy food from traditional food producers and organic farmers.
   (C) The movement, which began in Italy in the late 1980s, has grown to include members in more than 15 countries including the United States.
   (D) The movement is trying to prevent more fast-food restaurants from opening.
   (E) The movement supports home cooking and sharing meals with family and friends, instead of eating fast food.

3 Writing

INTEGRATED TASK: READ, LISTEN, WRITE

In this section, you will read a short text and listen to an excerpt on the same topic. Then you will write about the relationship between the two.

READING

Read the passage from a university newspaper. With a partner, complete the outline on the next page.

CHANGES PLANNED FOR FOOD SERVICE ON CAMPUS

The university is planning to change the food-service system on campus, but not everyone is happy about it. University food services, including the three main cafeterias and many small cafés and sandwich shops, are currently run by a variety of different food-service companies, student groups, and independent contractors. The university is proposing to find one or two providers to run all the food outlets on campus.

The assistant director of student services, Joe Lansky, who manages the food-service providers, said that the university's goal is to improve overall service, quality, and choice. "We want to make sure that our students are getting the best-quality food possible and to increase the variety of food offered on campus. Right now, we have many different providers, but they all offer similar food, and we don't have the authority to ask them to make changes." In addition, with fewer food vendors, administrative costs to the university will go down. He explained that they are looking for student input into the plan, on everything from the hours of operation to type of menu offered in each location.

A group of students, staff, and professors has formed to oppose the plan. They want to meet with the administration to discuss the future of the university's dining options.

1. What is the university proposing?

_____

_____

2. What are the reasons for the change?

- _____

- _____

- _____

3. How do people on campus feel about the proposal?

_____

_____

LISTENING

Listen to a conversation about the issue described in the newspaper article. Use the outline to take notes as you listen.

1. What are the students' opinions about the university's proposal?

_____

_____

2. What are the reasons for their opinions?

- _____

- _____

- _____

3. What are the students going to do next?

_____

_____

WRITING

Write on the following topic. Follow the steps below to prepare.

Summarize the university's proposal and explain the students' opinions about the proposal.

Step 1

Work with a partner. Skim the reading and your notes from the reading and listening. Complete the outline on the next page.

University Proposal: _____

University's Reasons
- _____
- _____
- _____

Students' Opinions: _____

Students' Reasons
- _____
- _____
- _____

Step 2

Write for 20 minutes on the topic. Leave the last 5 minutes to edit your work.

> To evaluate a partner's writing, use the Writing Evaluation Form on page 173.

4 Speaking

INDEPENDENT TASK

Speak on the following topic. Follow the steps below to prepare.

What is the most memorable meal you have had? Describe the experience of eating this meal. Use details.

Step 1

Think of a memorable meal you have had. Use the cluster diagram to brainstorm about the place you had the meal, the people who were with you, the tastes and smells, and your feelings at the meal. Add another category to the cluster.

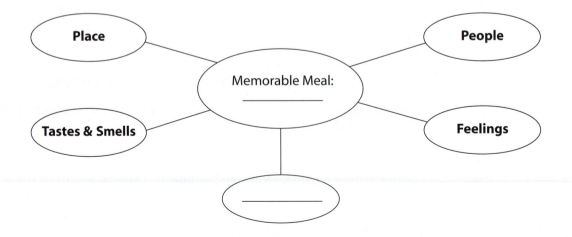

Step 2

Work in pairs. Take turns describing your experience to your partner.

To evaluate your partner's response, use the Speaking Evaluation Form on page 174.

5 Skill Focus

SUMMARIZING

EXAMINATION

Look at the questions from the unit.

- What is the purpose of a summary?
- What kind of information is used in a summary?

Item 1 (Reading, p. 129)

An introductory sentence for a brief summary of the passage is provided below. Complete the summary by circling THREE answer choices that best express the most important ideas in the passage.

The Slow Food movement encourages people to eat slowly and enjoy their food.

(A) The movement's founder believes food should be compared to art.
(B) The movement encourages people to buy food from traditional food producers and organic farmers.
(C) The movement, which began in Italy in the late 1980s, has grown to include members in more than 15 countries including the United States.
(D) The movement is trying to prevent more fast-food restaurants from opening.
(E) The movement supports home cooking and sharing meals with family and friends, instead of eating fast food.

Item 2 (Writing, p. 131)

Summarize the university's proposal and explain the students' opinions about the proposal.

Tips

To do well on the TOEFL, it is essential to learn how to summarize. A summary is a shorter version of a text. In some of the TOEFL Reading sections, you have to choose answers to complete a summary of the reading text. To complete the Integrated Tasks, you have to summarize the information in the reading text and the listening.

Summary

To understand, write, or present a summary, learn its important features:

- the main idea or topic of the text

- the important supporting details of the text. (A supporting detail is a fact or example that helps explain the main idea.)

- any definitions of important words

- information that is <u>not</u> summary writer's opinion

- length that is approximately one-fourth the length of the text

Summary of *"Slow Food" Movement Aims at Restoring the Joy of Eating*

The Slow Food movement encourages people to eat slowly and enjoy their food. The movement, which began in Italy in the late 1980s, has grown to include members in more than 15 countries, including the United States. The movement supports home cooking and sharing meals with family and friends, instead of eating fast food. It also encourages people to buy food from traditional food producers and organic farmers.

In **Item 1** of the Examination section, you had to choose the three statements (B, C, and E) that summarized the most important ideas in the passage. Statement A does not belong in a summary because it is a minor idea that is less important than the others. Statement D does not belong because it contains incorrect information.

In **Item 2**, you had to explain the most important ideas in the university's proposal and the students' opinions.

PRACTICE

1 *Work with a partner. Discuss your Integrated Writing task on page 131. Which parts summarized the article from the reading? Did your summary follow the tips outlined above?*

2 *Use the following sentences to create a summary of the Integrated Reading text on page 130. THREE sentences will not be used in the summary. Rewrite the sentences in a new paragraph below.*

1. Find the sentence that states the main idea of the article. This sentence goes first in the summary.

2. Cross out the sentences that do not belong in the summary. These sentences may contain too much detail or information that is not in the article.

3. Organize the remaining sentences and rewrite them to form a paragraph. Add connecting words and replace repeated nouns with pronouns if necessary.

Summary Sentences
(A) Food service is currently provided by many different companies.
(B) Joe Lansky, Assistant Director of Student Services, manages the university food services.
(C) Some people on campus oppose the idea and want to meet with the university administration.
(D) Some students oppose the change because they think there will be fewer food choices.
(E) I usually eat in the dining hall on campus every day.
(F) The purpose of the change is to improve the quality of the food, give students more choices, and reduce administrative costs.
(G) The university is planning to change the food-service system on campus.
(H) The university wants to replace the companies with one or two providers.

Summary

_____

_____

_____

_____

_____

_____

3 *Work with a partner. Write a summary of the following article. Compare your summary with another pair's summary. How are the summaries similar or different?*

FAST FOOD AT THE STUDENT CENTER

A new fast-food restaurant may be opening soon at the Student Center, serving favorites such as hamburgers, cheeseburgers, and french fries. Fresh salads would also be available. "This is a great opportunity for us to offer inexpensive food that our students want," said Joe Lansky, Assistant Director of Student Services. However, others have voiced concern over the plan. "Everyone knows how unhealthy fast food is," said Professor Elena Vargas, head of the Food Science and Nutrition Department. "We should be teaching our students to eat a healthy diet, not encouraging bad eating habits." The plan, which has not yet been approved by the university administration, will be discussed next week by the Student Council. Administration officials will attend and answer questions.

Immigration

| LISTENING |

Campus Conversation
A student talks to an admissions advisor about requirements for international students applying to law school.

Academic Listening
Excerpt from the novel *Lucy* by Jamaica Kincaid

| READING |

History Article about Immigration
Coming to America

| SPEAKING |

Integrated Task: Read, Listen, Speak
Do a role play about culture shock.

| WRITING |

Independent Task
Discuss opposing views about whether immigrants should hold onto their home culture or adopt the culture of the new country.

| SKILL FOCUS |

Using Context Clues
Using context clues means using surrounding information to understand meaning and details, and make inferences.

| TOEFL® iBT TARGET SKILLS |

- Identify and express main ideas
- Identify and express details
- Make inferences
- Scan for facts
- Outline information
- Express and support an opinion

ETS For extra practice of TOEFL iBT skills, go to pages 206–223.

1 Listening

PRE-LISTENING VOCABULARY

Read the sentences. Guess the meaning of the boldfaced words and phrases. Then match each word or phrase with a definition or synonym from the list below. Work with a partner and compare your answers.

_____ 1. Before I turned in my economics paper, I checked all the facts and data to make sure they were **accurate** and that there weren't any errors.

_____ 2. I wanted to apply for the job, but I didn't have the right **credentials**. I only have a master's degree, but the position required someone with a PhD.

_____ 3. The professor set a **deadline** for finishing the term paper. Students have to turn their papers in by 3:00 P.M. Friday.

_____ 4. A birth certificate is a **document** that shows when and where a person was born.

_____ 5. At the end of the semester, the professor must **evaluate** the students' work and give the students a grade.

_____ 6. When going for a job interview, it's important to dress well and be on time so that you **make a good impression on** the interviewer.

_____ 7. You can still send a university admission application by mail, but these days most students **submit** their applications online.

_____ 8. To apply for graduate school, you need a **transcript** showing the classes you took in college.

a. a date or time by which something must be completed

b. a piece of paper with official information on it

c. an official school report showing a student's classes and grades

d. cause someone to have a positive opinion of you

e. carefully consider something to make a judgment about it

f. someone's education and experience that proves he or she has the ability to do something

g. to give something to someone in authority for approval

h. true and correct

> **Culture Note:** International students can apply for undergraduate admission to colleges and universities in the United States and Canada if they have completed an equivalent secondary school education—about twelve years of schooling starting at age six. However, since educational systems differ around the world, a student may have to meet additional requirements or take additional classes.

FIRST LISTENING

Read the questions. Listen to the conversation between a student and an admissions advisor. Take notes as you listen. Share your notes with a partner. Then use your notes to answer the questions.

1. Why does the student go to the admissions office? _____

_____

_____

2. What does the advisor explain to the student? _____

_____

_____

SECOND LISTENING

Read the questions. Listen to the conversation again. Add details to your notes. Then use your notes to answer the questions. Work with a partner and compare your answers.

1. Why does the student go to the admissions office?
 (A) To get information for his cousin about applying to law school
 (B) To get a copy of his cousin's law school transcript
 (C) To submit his cousin's application to law school
 (D) To help his cousin sign up for law school classes

2. What part of the application do the student and advisor discuss? Choose TWO answers.
 (A) Letters of recommendation
 (B) School transcripts
 (C) Standardized admission tests
 (D) Financial documents
 (E) Employment history

3. What can you infer about the student's cousin?
 (A) He attended law school in Korea.
 (B) He is living in the United States.
 (C) He speaks English well.
 (D) He and the student have a close relationship.

Listen again to part of the conversation. Then answer question 4.

4. Why does the advisor say, "Not that you'd do a bad job . . . "?
   (A) To ask the student for more information
   (B) To emphasize the importance of her point
   (C) To persuade the student not to translate the documents
   (D) To indicate that she doesn't want to offend the student

Listen again to part of the conversation. Then answer question 5.

5. What does the advisor imply about a letter of recommendation from a family member?
   (A) It is less helpful than a letter from someone the student knows professionally.
   (B) It is more effective than other types of recommendation letters.
   (C) It isn't important who writes the letter, as long as it is a positive recommendation.
   (D) It will not be accepted as part of the student's application.

ACADEMIC LISTENING

You will hear an excerpt from the novel *Lucy* by Jamaica Kincaid, the story of a young woman from a small island in the West Indies who comes to North America to work.

FIRST LISTENING

Listen to the story. Take notes using the chart on the next page. Note the things the young woman sees, does, and feels at different moments in the story.

MOMENTS IN THE STORY	WHAT DID SHE SEE?	WHAT DID SHE DO?	HOW DID SHE FEEL?
Leaving the airport			
Arriving at the apartment			
The first morning			

SECOND LISTENING

Read the questions. Listen to the story again. Add details to your notes. Then use your notes to answer the questions. Work with a partner and compare your answers.

1. What season is it when Lucy arrives at her new home?
   (A) Spring
   (B) Summer
   (C) Fall
   (D) Winter

2. How does Lucy feel when she sees her new city for the first time?
   (A) She was happy that her trip was finally over.
   (B) She was excited to see the famous buildings and places.
   (C) She was afraid of being in a new place.
   (D) She was disappointed that it was dirty and ordinary.

Listen again to part of the story. Then answer question 3.

3. What can be inferred about Lucy when she says, "I slept soundly that night, but it wasn't because I was happy and comfortable—quite the opposite; it was because I didn't want to take in anthing else."?
   (A) She had seen too many new things.
   (B) She was afraid of all the new things.
   (C) She wanted to learn more about all the new things.
   (D) She was excited about all the new things.

4. What does Lucy discover after she gets dressed in the morning?
   (A) Her employers have left for the day.
   (B) She has to start working right away.
   (C) The apartment is bigger than she first thought.
   (D) The weather is colder than she expected.

5. How does Lucy feel her first full day in her new home?
   (A) She is excited about exploring the city.
   (B) She is happy to start her new life.
   (C) She is unsure about her decision to come.
   (D) She is worried about her family back home.

 Listen again to part of the story. Then answer question 6.

6. Why does Lucy say, "Something I had always known—the way I knew my skin was the color brown of a nut rubbed repeatedly with a soft cloth, or the way I knew my own name—something I took completely for granted, 'the sun is shining, the air is warm,' was not so."?
   (A) To describe what she looks like
   (B) To explain how she felt about the weather
   (C) To explain how she got her name
   (D) To describe the work she has to do

2 Reading

COMING TO AMERICA

PRE-READING

Scan the article to find the answers to the questions.

1. What countries or continents did immigrants to America come from?

2. What happened during these years?

   1607 _____

   1698 _____

   mid-1800s _____

   1840s _____

   mid-1850s _____

   1882 _____

READING

Read the passage on the next page and answer the questions. Then work with a partner and compare your answers. When you disagree, go back to the text to find helpful information.

COMING TO AMERICA

BY TOD OLSON

1   For more than 300 years, immigrants from every corner of the globe have settled in America, creating the most diverse nation on earth. Though immigrants have given much to the country, their passage here was never easy, nor their welcome always friendly.

1607–1820: The Arrival

2   "What then is the American, this new man? He is either a European or a descendant of a European, hence that strange mixture of blood, which you will find in no other country."—Hector St. John de Crevecoeur, French immigrant and author (1782)

3   "England is swarming," said a British observer in the 1590s, "with valiant youths rusting by lacke of employment." From 1607, when the first ragged band[1] of English settlers arrived in Jamestown, Virginia, to 1820, when a new wave of immigration began, it was these "rusting youths" who colonized America.

4   Six out of 10 immigrants in Colonial times came from England. While the most vocal—Puritans, Pilgrims, and Quakers—came to escape religious persecution, most came for work. Many enjoyed wages triple those found in England. But nearly half came as indentured servants, selling their labor in exchange for free passage to America.

5   By the time of the Revolutionary War, Americans were a diverse lot.[2] In addition to containing some 200 Indian tribes, the country in 1780 had 3.2 million Europeans and nearly 800,000 Africans, forcibly brought to the U.S. as slaves.

The Reception

6   "Why should Pennsylvania, founded by the English, become a colony of aliens?"—Benjamin Franklin, American patriot (1751)

7   Most immigrants in Colonial times were welcomed with open arms. Of course, there were exceptions. Quakers and Jews could not testify in court in New York City. In 1698, South Carolina offered land to all newcomers—except Scot-Irish and Catholics. But in general, the Colonies not only welcomed immigrants but sought them out. William Penn, for one, sent agents to Europe to proclaim the virtues of his Pennsylvania colony. After all, the infant[3] colonies were desperate for that basic resource without which they couldn't survive: people.

---

[1] *ragged band:* poorly dressed group of people
[2] *lot:* group
[3] *infant:* young, new

1821–1890: The Arrival

8   "My dear Father . . . Any man or woman are fools that would not venture[4] and come to this plentyful Country where no man or woman ever hungered or ever will and where you will not be seen naked"— Margaret McCarthy, Irish immigrant (1850)

9   In the mid-1800s, immigration began to soar . As many people arrived in the 1840s (1.7 million) as had come in the 230 preceding years. For the first time, the English were outnumbered at American ports by Germans and Irish, who made up 70 percent of America's foreign-born by 1860.

10   In the 1840s, disease wiped out potato crops in both Germany and Ireland, sending thousands of hungry peasants fleeing for their lives. Most Irish, dirt poor when they arrived, settled in Boston and New York City, working as laborers. The Germans, a little better off, headed for the farmland of the Midwest.

11   On the West Coast, the Chinese became the first non-Europeans to immigrate to the U.S. They were drawn by tales of gold; in fact, the Chinese name for California means "gold mountain." But many Chinese ended up in back-breaking labor on the railroads.

The Reception

12   "Wanted. A Cook or Chambermaid. Must be American, Scotch, Swiss, or African—no Irish." —Help wanted ad, *New York Evening Post* (1830)

13   America in the mid-19th century still welcomed immigrants. Some states even gave immigrants the right to vote before they became citizens. But as the immigrant population grew, the old-guard English became resentful. The newcomers competed for jobs, and many of them practiced Catholicism in a mostly Protestant country. In the mid-1850s, the so-called nativists burned or attacked dozens of Catholic churches.

14   But Chinese immigrants suffered the most. In 1876, a California legislative committee reported, "The Chinese are inferior to any race God ever made." And in 1882, all Chinese laborers were barred from entering the U.S.

[4] *venture:* try

1. In paragraph 1, the word *diverse* is closest in meaning to
   (A) open
   (B) similar
   (C) successful
   (D) varied

2. According to paragraph 4, why did people become indentured servants?
   (A) To be paid higher wages
   (B) To express their opinions about religion
   (C) To have more freedom
   (D) To pay for their trip from Europe

3. In paragraph 7, the word *they* in the phrase "without which they couldn't survive" refers to
   (A) agents
   (B) virtues
   (C) colonies
   (D) people

4. According to paragraph 7, what did William Penn want?
   (A) He didn't want immigrants to use all the basic resources.
   (B) He didn't want to give land to the Scot-Irish or Catholics.
   (C) He wanted more land for his colony in Pennsylvania.
   (D) He wanted more people to come to his colony in Pennsylvania.

5. In paragraph 9, the word *soar* is closest in meaning to
   (A) fly
   (B) open
   (C) rise
   (D) shrink

6. Which of the sentences below best expresses the essential information from the passage excerpt?

   > In the 1840s, disease wiped out potato crops in both Germany and Ireland, sending thousands of hungry peasants fleeing for their lives.

   (A) Many German and Irish immigrants left their homes in the 1840s because they didn't have enough food.
   (B) Many German and Irish immigrants left their homes in the 1840s and became peasants.
   (C) Many people went hungry in Germany and Ireland during the 1840s because the potato crops died.
   (D) Most people in Germany and Ireland relied on potato crops as an important source of food.

7. Paragraphs 9 to 11 mentioned immigrants from all of the following countries EXCEPT
   (A) Germany
   (B) Scotland
   (C) Ireland
   (D) China

8. What does the author want to show by including the quote in paragraph 12?
   (A) The attitude toward Irish immigrants
   (B) The origin of immigrants in the United States
   (C) The topics discussed in newspapers in 1830
   (D) The type of jobs available in New York

9. Based on paragraphs 13 and 14, what can be inferred about nativists?
   (A) They didn't believe in religion.
   (B) They didn't like immigrants.
   (C) They wanted better jobs.
   (D) They wanted to help immigrants.

10. Look at the four squares ☐ that indicate where the following sentence could be added to the passage. Where would the sentence best fit? Circle the letter that shows the point where you would insert this sentence.

    The resentment grew, and then sparked violence.

    America in the mid-19th century still welcomed immigrants. Some states even gave immigrants the right to vote before they became citizens. [A] But as the immigrant population grew, the old-guard English became resentful. [B] The newcomers competed for jobs, and many of them practiced Catholicism in a mostly Protestant country. [C] In the mid-1850s, the so-called nativists burned or attacked dozens of Catholic churches. [D]

11. Select the appropriate phrases from the answer choices on the next page and match them to the period in American history to which they relate. TWO of the answer choices will not be used.

    1607–1820

    • _____

    1821–1890

    • _____

    • _____

    • _____

(**A**) By the end of the century, Chinese immigrants were not allowed to come to the U.S. anymore.

(**B**) Many immigrants helped fight in the Revolutionary War.

(**C**) Most immigrants were from England.

(**D**) Most new immigrants settled in the middle of the country.

(**E**) Mostly German, Irish, and Chinese immigrants came to the United States.

(**F**) Some people of English descent began to oppose immigration.

(**G**) New immigrants were welcomed because the colonies needed more people.

ANALYSIS

It is helpful to know the purpose of a test item. There are four types of questions in the reading section.

1. Basic Comprehension

- main ideas

- details

- the meaning of specific sentences

2. Organization

- the way information is structured in the text

- the way ideas are linked between sentences or between paragraphs

3. Inference

- ideas are not directly stated in the text

- author's intention, purpose, or attitude not explicitly stated in the text

4. Vocabulary and Reference

- the meaning of words

- the meaning of reference words such as *his*, *them*, *this*, or *none*

Go back to the reading questions and label each question with 1, 2, 3, or 4. Then work with a partner to see if you agree. Check the Answer Key for the correct answers. Which questions did you get right? Which did you get wrong? What skills do you need to practice?

3 Speaking

INTEGRATED TASK: READ, LISTEN, SPEAK

In this section, you will read a short passage and listen to an excerpt on the same topic. Then you will speak about the relationship between the two.

READING

Read the passage and then complete the outline on the next page.

What Is Culture Shock?

Culture shock refers to the feelings of discomfort experienced as a person adjusts to a new culture. It is caused by having to cope with many new and unfamiliar situations and traditions. Newcomers feel helpless because they cannot understand all the new things they experience. However, understanding the stages of culture shock—and knowing that it is only temporary—can help newcomers make the transition.

There are four stages of culture shock, although the length of time each stage lasts will differ for each person. The first stage is the honeymoon stage. During this time, when you first enter a new culture, everything is interesting and exciting. You are curious about the new culture and eager to learn. Everything seems interesting, the people are friendly, the food is delicious, and you are eager to explore your new surroundings. However, after some time, the distress stage begins. The newcomer starts to feel uncomfortable and unhappy in the new culture. Everything seems very difficult: shopping, getting around, and making friends all seem confusing. You may begin to feel homesick and want to return home. Feelings of anger and sadness are common, and you may be overwhelmed by small problems. However, these feelings are only temporary. Gradually, the newcomer becomes more comfortable in the culture and enters the recovery stage. The new customs seem clearer, and everyday interactions are easier. You begin to enjoy the new culture once more. Finally, the stability stage begins. Life becomes more normal, and your sense of humor returns. You may not like everything about the new culture, but it doesn't make you so unhappy. You begin to feel at home in the new culture.

Definition of Culture Shock: _____

Stage 1: _____

   Feelings: _____

Stage 2: _____

   Feelings: _____

Stage 3: _____

   Feelings: _____

Stage 4: _____

   Feelings: _____

LISTENING

Listen to the excerpt from Lucy *by Jamaica Kincaid. Use the questions to take notes as you listen.*

   1. How does Lucy feel? _____

   _____

   2. What does she miss from home? _____

   _____

SPEAKING

Work with a partner to create a role play. Follow the steps below to prepare.

One partner plays Lucy and the other partner plays Lucy's friend. Lucy explains her feelings of culture shock, using examples from the listening. Lucy's friend explains how her feelings are an example of culture shock.

Step 1

With your partner, skim the reading and your notes from the reading and listening tasks (pages 148–149). Fill in an outline for your speaking task:

   1. How does Lucy feel? Explain using examples.

EMOTION	EXAMPLES

2. What stage of culture shock is she experiencing? _____

Define the stage.

_____

_____

_____

3. Give examples from Lucy's experience.

_____

_____

_____

Step 2

Take turns practicing a two-minute role play between Lucy and her friend. Use the information in your outline to help you.

Step 3

Work with another pair. Take turns performing your two-minute role play.

> To evaluate your partner's response, use the Speaking Evaluation Form on page 174.

4 Writing

INDEPENDENT TASK

Write on the following topic. Follow the steps below to prepare.

Do you agree or disagree with the following statement?
"Immigrants should try to become part of the culture in their new home, and not hold onto the traditions of their home culture."

Step 1

Outline your response. First write down your opinion in response to the prompt. Then brainstorm reasons for your opinion. Think of specific details or examples to support your reasons.

Opinion: _____

Reason: _____

Details/Examples: _____

Reason: _____

Details/Examples: _____

Reason: _____

Details/Examples: _____

- Work in groups. Take turns describing your opinion.

- React to what you have heard. What were your classmates' opinions? Why do your classmates have those opinions?

Step 2

Write for 20 minutes. Leave the last 5 minutes to edit your work.

> To evaluate a partner's writing, use the Writing Evaluation Form on page 173.

5 Skill Focus

USING CONTEXT CLUES

EXAMINATION

Look at the following items from the unit. What clues helped you choose the answers?

Item 1 (Campus Conversation, p. 139)

What can you infer about the student's cousin?
(A) He attended law school in Korea.
(B) He is living in the United States.
(C) He speaks English well.
(D) He and the student have a close relationship.

Item 2 (Reading, p. 145)

In paragraph 9, the word *soar* is closest in meaning to
(A) fly
(B) open
(C) rise
(D) shrink

Item 3 (Reading, p. 145)

In paragraph 7, the word *they* in the phrase "without which they couldn't survive" refers to
(A) agents
(B) virtues
(C) colonies
(D) people

Item 4 (Reading, p. 146)

Look at the four squares ☐ that indicate where the following sentence could be added to the passage. Where would the sentence best fit? Circle the letter that shows the point where you would insert this sentence.

The resentment grew, and then sparked violence.

America in the mid-19th century still welcomed immigrants. Some states even gave immigrants the right to vote before they became citizens. [A] But as the immigrant population grew, the old-guard English became resentful. [B] The newcomers competed for jobs, and many of them practiced Catholicism in a mostly Protestant country. [C] In the mid-1850s, the so-called nativists burned or attacked dozens of Catholic churches. [D]

Tips

To do well on the TOEFL, it is essential to learn how to use context clues to understand meaning. Context clues may help you to understand words and ideas in a passage. Context clues may be stated directly in the passage or they may be inferred; that is, not directly stated in the passage. Context clues include key ideas, words, and nonverbal clues such as punctuation in writing or intonation that convey meaning or attitude.

Inference Questions

Use context clues to find information that is not stated directly in the text. In **Item 1**, you had to identify details about the student's cousin. While listening to the conversation, you probably noticed the details shown in *italics*.

Student: Graduate. For the Master's in International Law.

Advisor: OK, so then we'd need his transcripts from *the school where he got his law degree*. And we also need an official translation of the document.

Student: My uncle—not Chin's dad but another uncle—*he's a lawyer too* and works with my cousin. Can he write a letter for him?

Advisor: Well, it'd make a better impression to have a letter from someone other than a relative—*someone the student knows professionally or from school.*

Although no one in the conversation directly states that Chin is a lawyer, you can infer the information from the clues in the passage.

Vocabulary Questions

Context clues can provide information about unfamiliar vocabulary. Look for synonyms, details, or examples that give clues to the meaning. In **Item 2**, you had to identify the meaning of the word *soar* in the passage. The second sentence explains that the number of immigrants increased in the mid-1800s, so you can guess that the word *soar* is closest in meaning to the word *rise*.

Reference Questions

Use context clues to help you find the meaning of reference words such as *it, they, those, one,* and *he*. Look before or after the reference word to find the word or phrase it refers to. In **Item 3**, you had to identify the meaning of the word *they* in the passage. Looking at the context of the sentence, you can see that choice (C), *colonies*, is the only one that makes sense in the passage.

Insert Text

Context clues help you identify the place to insert a sentence in a paragraph. Look for clues such as pronouns *(it, he, they)*, synonyms, and signal words *(therefore, however)* that link the ideas in the sentence and the rest of the paragraph. In **Item 4**, you had to place the sentence *The resentment grew, and then sparked violence* in a paragraph. The first part of the sentence refers to "resentments" that are described in the first part of the paragraph (newcomers took more jobs and practiced different religions). The second part of the sentence refers to "violence" described in the last paragraph (nativists attacked and burned Catholic churches). Therefore, the new sentence serves as a transition between the third and fourth paragraphs.

PRACTICE

1 *Read the questions. Label each type of question* Inference, Vocabulary, Reference, *or* Insert Text.

_____ 1. In paragraph 1, the word ***they*** refers to
    (**A**) immigrants from every nation
    (**B**) the five boroughs of New York City
    (**C**) immigrant teenagers
    (**D**) new realities

_____ 2. Look at the four squares ☐ that indicate where the following sentence could be added to paragraph 1. Where would the sentence best fit? Circle the letter that shows the point where you would insert this sentence.

One example can be found in New York City.

_____ 3. In paragraph 2, the word *innovative* is closest in meaning to
(A) difficult
(B) expensive
(C) new
(D) traditional

_____ 4. In paragraph 2, the word *mission* is closest in meaning to
(A) attempt
(B) decision
(C) opinion
(D) purpose

_____ 5. In paragraph 2, the word *eligible* is closest in meaning to
(A) interested
(B) qualified
(C) rejected
(D) trained

_____ 6. In paragraph 2, the phrase *this population* in the last sentence refers to
(A) new immigrant students
(B) educators
(C) politicians
(D) young people

_____ 7. Look at the four squares ☐ that indicate where the following sentence could be added to paragraph 2. Where would the sentence best fit? Circle the letter that shows the point where you would insert this sentence.

Other school districts have started to take notice of this success.

_____ 8. The passage supports the idea that
(A) immigrant and non-immigrant students have different needs in school
(B) non-immigrant students do not like going to school with immigrant students
(C) immigrant students cannot do well in a school with non-immigrant students
(D) immigrant and non-immigrant students do well in the same schools

2 *Read the article and answer the questions in Exercise 1.*

1   [A] The United States has always attracted immigrants from around the world; consequently, some cities are made up of people from every nation imaginable. [B] Queens, one of the five boroughs of New York City, is one of the most ethnically diverse areas of the country. [C] Many of the newcomers are teenagers who have not yet completed their schooling. [D] Unfamiliar with the language and the culture, they face the enormous task of learning to adapt to their new realities.

2   Due to the diverse backgrounds of these immigrants, teachers and school administrators face the complex task of helping these students find their niche in the United States. Consequently, educators have worked to develop innovative programs that address this challenge. One such program in the New York City public school system is the International High School in Long Island City, Queens. [A] Its mission is to help new immigrant students develop not only academic but also cultural skills that are necessary for success in high school, college, and beyond. [B] Only students who have been in the United States for less than four years are eligible for admission. [C] Since it was established in 1985, the school has received a great deal of recognition from educators and politicians for its success in teaching young people. [D] As a result, more programs aimed specifically at this population are being started around the country.

3 *Compare your answers with a partner's. Identify the clues that helped you answer the questions.*

Technology

| LISTENING |

Campus Conversation   A student asks a professor about a term he did not understand during the professor's lecture.

Academic Listening   Radio discussion about technology pet peeves

| READING |

Journal Entry   "Thoreau's Home" from *Walden*

| WRITING |

Integrated Task: Read, Listen, Write   Discuss the impact of the Internet on society using details and examples from a reading and a lecture.

| SPEAKING |

Independent Task   Discuss what you think about new technology.

| SKILL FOCUS |

Identifying and Using Cohesive Devices   Cohesive devices are words and phrases that connect parts of a written or spoken text and signal how ideas are related and organized.

| TOEFL® iBT TARGET SKILLS |

- Identify and express main ideas
- Identify and express details
- Make inferences
- Recognize markers of introductions, conclusion, and topic change
- Use signal words and rhetorical devices to express ideas coherently
- Recognize hypotheses and explain them

(ETS) For extra practice of TOEFL iBT skills, go to pages 206–223.

1 Listening

CAMPUS CONVERSATION

PRE-LISTENING VOCABULARY

Read the sentences. Guess the meaning of the boldfaced words and phrases. Then match each word or phrase with a definition or synonym from the list below. Work with a partner and compare your answers.

_____ 1. It's important for students to keep a **balance** between studying and having fun. They should spend time working hard and relaxing with friends.

_____ 2. After the first home computers were introduced, it took a while for them to **catch on**. It was several years before most people had them.

_____ 3. When giving a presentation, it's better to plan and prepare what you will say, rather than just saying **whatever comes to mind** at the moment.

_____ 4. I carry around a lot of electronic **devices** with me for work, including a cell phone, a pager, and a personal digital assistant.

_____ 5. When camera phones first came out, they were a **novelty**, but now a lot of people have them.

_____ 6. In my computer science class, we are studying technology **on the cutting edge**. It isn't used much yet, but someday it may be in every home computer.

_____ 7. We were talking about the history of home computers, but we got **sidetracked** when someone asked a question about something else.

a. small machines that do special jobs

b. state in which two things have the right amount of importance

c. at the newest stage of something

d. become popular

e. something new and unusual

f. off the main topic

g. something you suddenly think of

Culture Note: Most professors encourage students to ask questions during class if they don't understand something or want further explanation, particularly if it is something that other students may wonder about as well. However, if a student has a specific question that would not be of interest to the whole class, the student usually asks the question after class.

FIRST LISTENING

Read the questions. Listen to the conversation between a student and professor. Take notes as you listen. Share your notes with a partner. Then use your notes to answer the questions.

1. Why does the student want to talk to the professor? _____

_____

_____

2. What do the professor and student discuss? _____

_____

_____

SECOND LISTENING

Read the questions. Listen to the conversation again. Add details to your notes. Then use your notes to answer the questions. Work with a partner and compare your answers.

1. Why does the student talk to the professor?
   (A) To ask the professor about something she mentioned in class
   (B) To explain why he missed a class the previous week
   (C) To find out when the professor has office hours
   (D) To request extra time to hand in his homework

2. According to the professor, what is an "early adopter"?
   (A) A person who always arrives early to events
   (B) A person who is the first to use a new technology
   (C) A person who learns to use new technology from a friend
   (D) A person who works in a high-tech industry

3. Why are early adopters important for industry?
   (A) They have good ideas about what technology to develop next.
   (B) They help companies fix problems with new technology.
   (C) They introduce new technologies to their friends.
   (D) They keep new technological devices for a long time.

Listen again to part of the conversation. Then answer question 4.

4. What can be inferred about the professor when she says, "We did get a bit sidetracked talking about computer disasters."?
   (A) She agrees with the student's comment.
   (B) She disagrees with the student's comment.
   (C) She doesn't understand the student's comment.
   (D) She is insulted by the student's comment.

Listen again to part of the conversation. Then answer question 5.

5. Why does the student say, "Well, I have to get to my next class."?
  (A) To change the subject of the conversation
  (B) To keep the conversation going
  (C) To return to an earlier topic in the conversation
  (D) To signal that he wants to end the conversation

ACADEMIC LISTENING

FIRST LISTENING

Listen to a call-in radio show. Take notes as you listen. Work with a partner to combine your notes. Then use your notes to answer the questions.

1. What is the radio show about? _____

_____

_____

2. What is the first caller's opinion? Why? _____

_____

_____

3. What is the second caller's opinion? Does the host agree? _____

_____

_____

SECOND LISTENING

Read the questions. Listen to the radio show again. Add details to your notes. Then use your notes to answer the questions. Work with a partner and compare your answers.

1. What is the radio show mostly about?
   (A) Complaints about technology
   (B) Technology in the workplace
   (C) Technology of the future
   (D) Useful new technology

2. What is the first caller's opinion about automated phone systems? Choose TWO answers.
   (A) _____ They are expensive to operate.
   (B) _____ They are frustrating to use.
   (C) _____ They can cause companies to lose business.
   (D) _____ They break down frequently.

3. What is the second caller's opinion about cell phones. Choose TWO answers.
   (A) _____ Most people use them in the wrong places.
   (B) _____ The ringing sound is annoying.
   (C) _____ People don't really need them.
   (D) _____ They are difficult to use.

Listen again to part of the conversation. Then answer question 4.

4. Why does the host say, "But that's not your complaint, is it?"?
   (A) To express agreement with the caller's opinion
   (B) To signal that she wants to end the call
   (C) To bring the caller back to his main point
   (D) To stop the caller from talking so much

Listen again to part of the conversation. Then answer question 5.

5. What is the host trying to do when she says, "People might argue that in some cases, people really do need to be reached in an emergency, like a doctor or something."?
   (A) Give an example to support the caller's opinion
   (B) Make sure that she understands the caller's point
   (C) Present an opposing point of view
   (D) Show that she agrees with the caller

ANALYSIS

It is helpful to know the purpose of a test item. There are three types of questions in the listening section.

1. Basic Comprehension

- main ideas
- details
- the meaning of specific sentences

2. Organization

- the way information is structured
- the way ideas are linked

3. Inference

- ideas are not directly stated
- speaker's intention, purpose, or attitude not explicitly stated

Go back to the listening questions and label each question with 1, 2, or 3. Then work with a partner to see if you agree. Check the Answer Key for the correct answers. Which questions did you get right? Which did you get wrong? What skills do you need to practice?

2 Reading

THOREAU'S HOME

PRE-READING

Read the first sentence of each paragraph. Look at the chart in paragraph 6. Then answer the questions.

1. What year does Thoreau write about? _____

2. What did the author do? _____

3. How much did it cost? _____

READING

Read the passage on the next page and answer the questions. Then work with a partner and compare your answers. When you disagree, go back to the text to find helpful information.

THOREAU'S HOME

BY HENRY DAVID THOREAU
(edited, from *Walden*)

1   Near the end of March 1845, I borrowed an axe and went down to the woods by Walden Pond[1] nearest to where I intended to build my house, and began to cut down some tall arrowy white pines, still in their youth, for timber. . . . It was a pleasant hillside where I worked, covered with pine[2] woods, through which I looked out on the pond, and a small open field in the woods where pines and hickories were springing up. The ice on the pond was not yet dissolved, though there were some open spaces, and it was all dark colored and saturated with water . . .

2   So I went on for some days cutting and hewing timber, and also studs and rafters, all with my narrow axe, not having many communicable or scholar-like thoughts, singing to myself,

3   Men say they know many things;
But lo! they have taken wings—
The arts and sciences,
And a thousand appliances;
The wind that blows
Is all anybody knows.

4   My days in the woods were not very long ones; yet I usually carried my dinner of bread and butter, and read the newspaper in which it was wrapped, at noon, sitting amid the green pine boughs which I had cut off, and to my bread was imparted some of their fragrance , for my hands were covered with a thick coat of pitch[3] . . .

5   Before winter I built a chimney, and shingled[4] the sides of my house, which were impervious to rain . . .

(continued on next page)

---

[1] *pond:* a small area of fresh water
[2] *pine:* a type of tree that stays green all winter
[3] *pitch:* a sticky liquid from a pine tree
[4] *shingle:* attach small, flat pieces of wood to the outside of a house

6   I have thus a tight shingled and plastered house, ten feet wide by fifteen feet long, and eight-feet posts, with a garret and a closet, a large window on each side, two trap doors, one door at each end, and a brick fireplace opposite. The exact cost of my house, paying the usual price for such materials as I used, but not counting the work, all of which was done by myself, was as follows; and I give the details because very few are able to tell exactly what their houses cost, and fewer still, if any, the separate cost of the various materials which compose them:

Boards	$8.03½	Mostly shanty boards
Refuse shingles for roof and sides	4.00	
Laths	1.25	
Two second-hand windows with glass	2.43	
One thousand old bricks	4.00	
Two casks of lime	2.40	That was high.
Hair	0.31	More than I needed.
Mantle-tree iron	0.15	
Nails	3.90	
Hinges and screws	0.14	
Latch	0.10	
Chalk	0.01	
Transportation	1.40	I carried a good part on my back.
In all	$28.12½	

1. According to paragraph 1, where does the author build his house?
   (A) In a small field
   (B) In the woods near a pond
   (C) Next to a road
   (D) On a hillside

2. Look at the four squares ☐ that indicate where the following sentence could be added to the passage. Where would the sentence best fit? Circle the letter that shows the point where you would insert this sentence.

   These trees would make fine, strong walls for my new home.

   A Near the end of March 1845, I borrowed an axe and went down to the woods by Walden Pond nearest to where I intended to build my house, and began to cut down some tall arrowy white pines, still in their youth, for timber. . . . B It was a pleasant hillside where I worked, covered with pine woods, through which I looked out on the pond, and a small open field in the woods where pines and hickories were springing up. C The ice on the pond was not yet dissolved, though there were some open spaces, and it was all dark colored and saturated with water. . . . D

3. In paragraph 1, the word *it* in the sentence "and it was all dark colored and saturated with water . . . " refers to
   (A) the pond
   (B) the field
   (C) the ice
   (D) the water

4. The word *fragrance* in paragraph 4 is closest in meaning to
   (A) appearance
   (B) color
   (C) smell
   (D) weight

5. The word *impervious* in paragraph 5 is closest in meaning to
   (A) resistant
   (B) open
   (C) damaged
   (D) weak

6. Based on the passage, what can be inferred about the author's attitude toward building his house?
   (A) He enjoyed the hard work.
   (B) He liked to work quickly.
   (C) He wanted someone to help him.
   (D) He was tired at the end of the day.

7. What is the author's primary purpose in the passage?
   (A) To analyze the reasons for building a house
   (B) To compare different methods for building a house
   (C) To describe the disadvantages of building one's own house
   (D) To tell the story of how he built his house

8. Which of the sentences below best expresses the essential information in the passage excerpt?

   > The exact cost of my house, paying the usual price for such materials as I used, but not counting the work, all of which was done by myself, was as follows; and I give the details because very few are able to tell exactly what their houses cost, and fewer still, if any, the separate cost of the various materials which compose them:

   (A) "It's important to record the cost of building a house."
   (B) "I did all the work on my house, so I didn't have to pay any labor costs."
   (C) "Most people don't know the cost of the materials used to build their houses."
   (D) "The following is a list of materials used to build my house and the price I paid for each one."

9. Put a check (✓) next to the activities the author describes in the passage. TWO of the answer choices will NOT be used.

(A) _____ buying supplies
(B) _____ cutting wood
(C) _____ singing
(D) _____ reading the newspaper
(E) _____ building a chimney
(F) _____ building the roof
(G) _____ shingling the house

3 Writing

INTEGRATED TASK: READ, LISTEN, WRITE

In this section, you will read a short passage and listen to an excerpt on the same topic. Then you will write about the relationship between the two.

READING

Read the passage from the 1995 book The Road Ahead *by Bill Gates, founder of Microsoft. Then discuss the questions that follow.*

> One of the many fears expressed about the information highway is that it will reduce the time people spend socializing. Some worry that homes will become such cozy entertainment providers that we'll never leave them, and that, safe in our private sanctuaries, we'll become isolated. I don't think that's going to happen. As behaviorists keep reminding us, we're social animals. We will have the option of staying home more because the highway will create so many new options for home-based entertainment, for communication—both personal and professional—and for employment. Although the mix of activities will change, I think people will decide to spend almost as much time out of their homes.
>
> The highway will not only make it easier to keep up with distant friends, it will also enable us to find new companions. Friendships formed across the network will lead naturally to getting together in person. This alone will make life more interesting. Suppose you want to reach someone to play bridge with. The information highway will let you find card players with the right skill level and availability in your neighborhood, or in other cities or nations.

1. What did people fear would happen with increased Internet usage? _____

_____

2. What was Gates's opinion about what would happen? _____

_____

LISTENING

Listen to an excerpt from a lecture. Use the questions to take notes as you listen.

1. What do people say is the most important use of the Internet? _____

_____

2. What example does the professor give? _____

_____

3. What is the professor's conclusion about Internet usage? _____

_____

WRITING

Write on the following topic. Follow the steps below to prepare.

> Discuss the impact of the Internet on society. What did people fear would happen because of the Internet? What has happened? Explain with details and examples from the reading and lecture.

Step 1

Work with a partner. Skim the reading and your notes from the reading and listening tasks (pages 166–167). Complete the outline below.

The Internet and Society

1995: Many people feared: _____

_____

Bill Gates thought: _____

_____

Today: _____

_____

Examples: _____

_____

Step 2

Write for 20 minutes. Leave the last 5 minutes to edit your work.

To evaluate a partner's writing, use the Writing Evaluation Form on page 173.

4 Speaking

INDEPENDENT TASK

Take turns leading a group discussion on the following topic. Follow the steps below to prepare.

> When a new technology is released, some people like to try it right away, while others prefer to wait until the technology becomes more established and popular. How do you feel about new technology? Explain your answer with details and examples.

Step 1

- Work in groups of five. Think of some examples of new technology that you have heard about or tried to use, such as a new type of cell phone, computer program, or other electronic device. Make a short list.

- Assign one technology to each person to lead a group discussion.

- Decide who will evaluate each person as they speak.

Step 2

- Take turns leading the discussion about the technology you were assigned in Step 2.

- When you are leading the discussion, ask questions to get the group members to talk about how they felt about the new technology when it came out. Call on people to get their participation and ask follow-up questions to get more information.

Sample Questions

1. Did you try to use _____ right away when it came out or did you wait a while? Why?

2. What do you like or dislike about _____?

- When it is your turn to participate in the discussion, allow the discussion leader to direct the discussion. Observe your evaluation partner to complete the Speaking Evaluation Form later.

To evaluate your partner's response, use the Speaking Evaluation Form on page 174.

5 Skill Focus

IDENTIFYING AND USING COHESIVE DEVICES

EXAMINATION

Read the excerpts from the lecture about the Internet.

What kind of information does the underlined phrases introduce?

1. Um, <u>I'd like to look at</u> Internet usage now . . . a recent study in the United States found that—on a typical day—about 70 million American adults accessed the Internet. But what are people doing online?

2. . . . there were warnings that society was changing, that people would become more isolated. <u>However</u>, what we've found is . . . for the most part, people go online to do many of the *same* type of activities they do offline . . .

3. <u>The important point here is</u> that many of the activities that take place on the Internet involve socializing with other people in some way.

4. <u>In fact</u>, the Internet has allowed us to develop relationships that we could have never imagined a few years ago! <u>For example</u>, people can stay in touch with family members who are living far away. . . . <u>Like</u> my sister and her family, who're living in Japan right now, . . .

5. <u>So we can see that</u>, in many cases, the Internet has actually strengthened the ties between people, not weakened them as some people originally feared.

Tips

To do well on the TOEFL, you need to be able to understand and use cohesive devices such as signal words in speaking and writing. Effective speakers use signal words to help the listener follow what is being said. Good writers also use signal words to help the reader understand connections between the ideas presented in a text.

Listening and Reading

- Signal words can help you understand how information in a lecture or written text is organized and show the relationship between ideas.

- Pay attention to signal words. Listen and look for the important information that signal words introduce.

- Use signal words to help organize your note taking.

(continued on next page)

Speaking and Writing

- Plan and organize your ideas before you speak or write, making note of places where you should include signal words.

- Use signal words to show how you are organizing your ideas.

- Use signal words to connect ideas and make them easy to follow.

Common Signal Words

- show how information is organized
  First I'd like to talk about . . .
  Finally . . .
  There are three reasons for this . . .

- introduce examples
  For example . . .
  One example is . . .

- highlight important information
  Remember that . . .
  The most important point is . . .

- introduce comparison and contrast
  on the other hand . . .
  similarly . . .

- introduce conclusion or summary
  To summarize . . .
  This means that . . .

In the lecture in the Examination section, the speaker used signal words to help the listeners identify the relationship between ideas: "I'd like to look at" introduces the topic of the lecture. "However" and "In fact" both introduce contrasts, whereas "For example" and "Like" introduce examples. "The important point here is" highlights important information, and "So we can see" identifies a conclusion.

PRACTICE

1 *Look at your writing from the Integrated Writing task on page 167. Underline the signal words you used. Did you use the signal words appropriately? Can you add more signal words to make your writing clearer?*

2 *Work with a partner. Take turns giving a one-minute oral response to one of the questions below while your partner keeps track of the signal words you use.*

1. Should cell phones be banned on public transportation such as buses and trains? Why or why not?

2. Which technological device do you like the most? Which do you hate the most? Why?

   - Use signal words as you speak.

   - Listen to your partner speak. Make a list of the signal words you heard.

   - Look at the list of signal words you used. Discuss what other signal words you could have used or whether you could have used more of them.

Evaluation Forms for Integrated and Independent Tasks

WRITING

Exchange papers with a partner. Evaluate each other's writing using the grid below. Discuss strengths and weaknesses. Use the evaluation to revise and edit your writing. Write a second draft and give it to your teacher.

4 = always   **3** = most of the time   **2** = some of the time   **1** = rarely or never

UNIT	1	2	3	4	5	6	7	8	9	10
CONTENT										
The response . . .										
addresses the topic.										
is organized.										
shows connections between ideas.										
LANGUAGE										
The writing incorporates . . .										
effective vocabulary.										
correct grammar.										
correct spelling and punctuation.										
TOTAL:										

SPEAKING

As you and your partner respond to the topic, evaluate each other's speaking using the grid below. Discuss strengths and weaknesses. Use the evaluation to improve your presentation.

4 = always   **3** = most of the time   **2** = some of the time   **1** = rarely or never

UNIT	1	2	3	4	5	6	7	8	9	10
CONTENT										
The response ...										
addresses the topic.										
covers the main points.										
contains good examples.										
has ideas that connect well.										
LANGUAGE										
The response ...										
is free of hesitations.										
exhibits clear pronunciation.										
incorporates effective vocabulary.										
incorporates correct grammar.										
TOTAL:										

Audioscript

UNIT 1: Media

CAMPUS CONVERSATION

PAGE 3, FIRST LISTENING

Professor: Hi, are you waiting to see me for office hours?

Student: Um, yeah, I'm in Journalism 101.

P: Right. ahhh . . . Lisa, isn't it? Come on in. . . . So, what's up?

S: Well, I have a question about the term paper . . . I'm trying to come up with a topic for my paper, but I was wondering if you could help me, you know, narrow it down a bit.

P: OK, well, it should be on one of the general topics we cover in class, but I want you to go into a bit more depth. Is there something that's, um, we discussed in class that you'd like to know more about?

S: There's a lot of things, but I guess, well, what we talked about last week about the influence of Internet news on journalism . . .

P: Yes, Internet news is an important topic these days. That'd be a good focus.

S: So I can look at the Internet news sources, and how, um, how they are affecting news coverage?

P: Yes, like how it allows us to have instant access to news from many different sources, so we can look for news from any part of the world, and from many different points of view.

S: And that's really different from traditional news sources, like newspapers, where you can't choose the type of news you get; you just have to read what they give you.

P: Exactly! Umm . . . did you get a chance to read the article I put on reserve this week in the library?

S: No, I tried to get it, but they couldn't find it.

P: At the reference desk?

S: Yeah, I went to the reference desk, and they had the list for the class, but the article wasn't on it.

P: Really? I left it there last week. Well, I'll have to check on that . . . but . . . let's see, I think I have another copy. Um here . . . I would look at this article and try to get some ideas. It has a good analysis of this "new media" and how it's changing, um, the field of journalism.

S: Yeah, so . . .

P: So there's a couple of directions you can go in, but you'll still need to focus your topic.

S: Can I keep this?

P: Yeah, that's an extra copy.

S: This is great. Thanks a lot, Professor Green.

P: No problem. And come see me if you need some more help!

S: OK, thanks.

PAGE 3, SECOND LISTENING

4. Listen again to part of the conversation. Then answer question 4.

S: Yeah, I went to the reference desk, and they had the list for the class, but the article wasn't on it.

P: Really? I left it there last week. Well, I'll have to check on that.

Why does the professor say, "Really?"?

5. Listen again to part of the conversation. Then answer question 5.

P: Here . . . I would look at this article and try to get some ideas. It has a good analysis of this "new media" and how it's changing, um, the field of journalism.

What can you infer about the professor?

ACADEMIC LISTENING

PAGE 4, FIRST LISTENING

Cheryl Corley: In the Midwest, people say you can drive past a cornfield in the morning, and by the time you drive home in the evening, the corn will seem taller. Watching the corn grow is a beloved and necessary pastime in the Midwest, but its appeal is spreading, thanks to CornCam. In May of last year, editors for Iowa Farmer Today mounted a camera behind one of their tool sheds. They pointed it at the adjacent field and fed the images to the publication's website. Since then, CornCam has gained a loyal audience with more than 600,000 visitors to the site last year. Dan Zinkat is crops editor at Iowa Farmer Today, and one of CornCam's creators. So what exactly is CornCam?

Dan Zinkat: Uh, CornCam is a uh, digital camera that takes an image of a cornfield every fifteen minutes and updates it, in, in its simplest form.

CC: Well, well, who tunes in to watch this?

DZ: Mmmm, people from around the world, literally. We've had, uh, hits from Beijing, Russia, England, South Africa . . . I think most of them are people who live in the cities. We do get a fair number of commercial farmers who are pretty proud to see someone focusing on corn.

CC: Can it be that riveting, really? What's the appeal?

DZ: I, I think it's riveting in kind of a quiet sense. I think many people tell us that watching the, the cornfield reminds them of growing up on a farm or a small town. Or others tell us they live in big cities on the East Coast or the West Coast, and they think the uh, cornfield is somewhat relaxing and soothing.

CC: Mmm hmm. Well, just how fast does corn grow?

DZ: Well, given the right uh, temperatures, enough moisture in the ground, timely rainfall, you could conceivably have corn grow up to six inches a day, but that's in, in a short-lived period—usually in July.

CC: Mmm hmm . . . All right, well thanks so much, Dan.

DZ: You're quite welcome, Cheryl. Thank you.

CC: Dan Zinkat is crops editor for Iowa Farmer Today.

PAGE 5, SECOND LISTENING

3. Listen again to part of the report. Then answer question 3.

DZ: We do get a fair number of commercial farmers who are pretty proud to see someone focusing on corn.

CC: Can it be that riveting, really? What's the appeal?

What can you infer about the woman when she says, "Can it be that riveting, really? What's the appeal?"?

5. Listen again to part of the report. Then answer question 5.

DZ: Well, given the right uh, temperatures, enough moisture in the ground, timely rainfall, you could conceivably have corn grow up to six inches a day, but that's in, in a short-lived period—usually in July.

What does the man mean when he says this?

INTEGRATED TASK

PAGE 10, LISTENING

Professor: So we can see that modern technology, such as satellite communication and the Internet, has changed the way news is reported. Now you may assume that all this instant information makes us better informed, but John Somerville, a professor of history at the University of Florida, has an interesting perspective on that. He wrote a book called "How the News Makes Us Dumb: The Death of Wisdom in an Information Society," As the title implies, he argues that modern news reporting actually makes us . . . well, dumber! Somerville feels that dailiness of the news—the news updates every day, every hour—is the problem. He says that the daily news reports on unconnected events, and does not go into enough depth—um, we don't learn the often complicated history behind the reports we see. So we may learn a lot of facts, learn about events, but we don't have the tools or background to really understand what those events mean. Somerville also criticizes the way that some media, like, say, the local newspapers, try to report on everything, but as a result, report on nothing very well. In particular, he mentions the coverage of international news. He gives the example of a local paper having four short articles about international news—four for the entire world. Now the person reading that may feel like they're getting updated on important world events, but really, in four stories, that does not cover international news in any depth.

UNIT 2: Overcoming Obstacles

CAMPUS CONVERSATION

PAGE 17, FIRST LISTENING

Professor: Hi, Steven, come on in. How're you feeling?

Student: Better, you know, but still not totally one hundred percent. But I went back to class today . . .

P: Yes, I was sorry to hear you were sick. What was it, flu?

S: Yeah, flu, but really bad. I couldn't get out of bed for, like, five days. I felt awful.

P: Oh, dear. Well, I'm glad you're feeling better . . .

S: But I missed, um, more than a week of class . . .

P: Four classes, I think . . .

S: . . . so I'm worried about catching up on the work.

P: Yeah, last week was pretty important. We started a new topic, on disability rights. Have you gotten any notes from your classmates?

S: Yeah, I'm working on that. My friend Tom said he'd copy his notes for me, and we can go over them together. But I have a question about that . . .

P: Yeah?

S: He said we'd be breaking into groups to research one aspect of disability rights . . .

P: That's right . . .

S: But I wasn't sure what he meant, I mean, what are the different options?

P: Well, there are several things I'm asking the students to look at. And each group'll be making a presentation on this at the end of the term.

S: Right.

P: So there are four aspects to research, and that's disability rights in Healthcare, Education, Housing and Transportation, and Employment . . . I have the handouts here . . . somewhere . . .

S: Oh, Tom picked those up for me . . .

P: Oh? Good! You're on top of things!

S: So, looking at this, I think I'm interested in the group on Education . . . .

P: OK.

S: Yeah, because I don't know if I mentioned it in class, but my sister's paralyzed, she's in a wheelchair . . .

P: Ah!

S: . . . and when she was in school, she did really well, but I know it was hard sometimes . . .

P: Uh-huh.

S: . . . with the other kids' attitudes and things, or the teachers sometimes not knowing how to deal with her disability, so I'm pretty interested in that issue.

P: Well, I think you'll make a good contribution to the group, then.

S: Thanks. Boy, I have a lot of reading to catch up on, with my other classes and all . . .

P: But you've done pretty well in this class up to this point . . .

S: Mh-huh.

P: . . . so I think if you just do your best, you'll be OK.

S: Right.

P: I mean, if you really have a problem, you could get an extension to finish your work during the winter break . . .

S: Oh Yeah? How do I . . .

P: But let's see how it goes. Just keep me updated, OK? Let me know if you're having any problems.

S: Sure, thanks.

P: And take care of yourself! Don't get sick again.

S: I hope not! Thanks, Professor Rogers. Bye.

P: Bye, see you tomorrow.

3. Listen again to part of the conversation. Then answer question 3.

P: . . . I have the handouts here . . . somewhere . . .

S: Oh, Tom picked those up for me . . .

P: Oh? Good! You're on top of things!

Select the sentence that best expresses how the professor probably feels.

5. Listen again to part of the conversation. Then answer question 5.

P: I mean, if you really have a problem, you could get an **extension** to finish your work during the winter break . . .

What does the professor imply?

ACADEMIC LISTENING

PAGE 18, FIRST LISTENING

Reporter: They climbed one of the world's tallest mountains— a group of disabled climbers from the New York area. It's a story of reaching new heights, and overcoming great odds. Monica Pellegrini introduces us to those inspirational athletes.

Climber 1: I thought a few times going up that I wouldn't make it. Um, I almost turned back around twice.

Monica Pellegrini: Mount Kilimanjaro, in the northern part of the African nation of Tanzania. Scaling it is no small task for your average climber, but for a group of seven from New York's Achilles Track Club, it was a much greater challenge. They are all disabled in some way. Five are blind. One is deaf and asthmatic. The other, a cancer survivor and amputee.

Climber 2: It was a lot more difficult than I had expected. Uh, a difficult climb, and the altitude really did affect a lot of us. But we persevered, and the majority of the athletes were able to make it.

MP: The accomplishment makes the group the largest of disabled athletes ever to climb Mount Kilimanjaro, an expedition they call a testament to the human spirit, and a chance to empower themselves and others.

Climber 3: I just wanted to reach deep down, and grab all the energy I had, and keep on going. Because behind accomplishing this physical challenge for myself, I knew there was a greater message we were all carrying.

MP: The group kept a diary of their travels online, and even when the going got tough, they buckled down, turning to each other for inspiration as they continued on the trail to the peak.

Climber 4: I heard it was going to be hard, I just didn't imagine it was going to be so tough.

MP: Tough, yes, but an experience that will not be forgotten any time soon.

C1: When you're experiencing this wide open space, wind, and sunshine, the strength of the sun like you've never felt before . . .

MP: The adventure began on August 28th, and ended this past Sunday, when the group, along with their eighteen volunteer guides from the Achilles Track Club, reached the summit.

C1: Getting to the top was definitely the high point.

MP: Monica Pellegrini, UPN 9 news.

PAGE 19, SECOND LISTENING

2. Listen again to part of the report. Then answer question 2.

C3: I just wanted to reach deep down, and grab all the energy I had, and keep on going. Because behind accomplishing this physical challenge for myself, I knew there was a greater message we were all carrying.

What does the woman mean when she says, "Because behind accomplishing this physical challenge for myself, I knew there was a greater message we were all carrying."?

4. Listen again to part of the report. Then answer question 4.

MP: The adventure began on August 28th, and ended this past Sunday, when the group, along with their eighteen volunteer guides from the Achilles Track Club, reached the summit.

C1: Getting to the top was definitely the high point.

What does the woman mean when she says, "Getting to the top was definitely the high point."?

INTEGRATED TASK

PAGE 25, LISTENING

Professor: Since the Americans with Disabilities Act—the ADA—was passed in 1990, thousands of Americans have benefited from it. Brian Wong is one example. Brian became paralyzed from the waist down in a car accident, and he badly injured his left hand. But despite his disability, he is able to lead a full and productive life, thanks in large part to the provisions of the ADA.

Brian works as a manager for a computer service company just outside of Baltimore, Maryland. His employers have made special accommodations so that he can work there. One important one is accessibility. The building he works in is wheelchair accessible, so he can use the parking garage, elevators, bathrooms and cafeteria just as any other employee can. They have also arranged the furniture inside the office so that he can use his wheelchair in any of the rooms, including conference rooms, copy rooms, and the offices of his co-workers.

The company has also provided special equipment for his office. The shelves and filing cabinets in his office are low so that he can reach things without help. He also has some special devices that help him work with his injured hand.

Because of his special needs, the company also allows Brian to work a flexible schedule, so, arrive at work later or leave early if he needs to. He can make the work up on the weekends, or stay later at the office on some days. They also allow him to use his sick time if he needs to visit the doctor.

Brian has worked at the company for seven years, and he appreciates everything that his company has done for him. In return, the company gets a dedicated and productive employee.

UNIT 3: Medicine

CAMPUS CONVERSATION

PAGE 35, FIRST LISTENING

Student: Hi, I talked to you the other day—about joining intramural basketball?

Coach: Chris, right? Yeah, I remember.

S: Well, my friend said practices start today so I was wondering if I could start.

C: Did you get your health clearance?

S: My what?

C: The health clearance. You know, from Student Health Services. You need that before you can start playing.

S: Oh, that. The thing is, I just saw my own doctor this summer, and got a physical and everything, and he said I was fine. So I thought maybe I could skip it.

C: Sorry, but I really can't let you play unless I have the clearance. It's university policy.

S: Can't I just ask my doctor to send his report or something? Instead of going through another physical?

C: Umm, sorry . . .

S: I was really hoping to start playing today! Can't I play just for today. And then I'll get the clearance, I promise.

C: I wish I could help you, but I really need that clearance before you can join a team. If I let you play without it, *I'll* get in trouble.

S: . . . But I was hoping . . . .

C: Yeah, I know. I can see you're anxious to get started. But do you know the reason they do this? Do you remember a few years back? There was a basketball player, and he collapsed and died during a game.

S: No, I didn't hear about that.

C: Well, that was a real tragedy, and it turned out that the kid had some kind of undiagnosed problem, a heart problem, that no one knew about.

S: And he died?

C: Yeah, and that's why the university has this policy now. We just want to be careful, so you don't end up getting hurt.

S: I guess that makes sense . . . I'm just . . . So what do I have to do?

C: Just go over to Health Services and make an appointment. There's a form you have to fill out with your, uh, medical history. And then you'll see the doctor. It's really no big deal.

S: So when can I start playing?

C: Well, that depends on health services . . . . when they have an appointment for you. But they're usually pretty good about it.

S: And then I bring it back here?

C: Right, give it to me or one of the other coaches, and then you're all set and you can start practicing. But in the meantime—since you're here, your team's over on that court. Why don't you come and meet them, and you can hang out for a while and watch the practice.

S: Ok, that'd be great. Then I'll go to Health Services first thing tomorrow.

C: Good. Sounds like a plan!

PAGE 36, SECOND LISTENING

2. *Listen again to part of the conversation. Then answer question 2.*

S: Can't I just ask my doctor to send his report or something? Instead of going through another physical?

C: Umm, sorry . . .

S: I was really hoping to start playing today!

Select the sentence that best expresses how the student probably feels.

3. *Listen again to part of the conversation. Then answer question 3.*

C: I wish I could help you, but I really need that clearance before you can join a team. If I let you play without it, I'll get in trouble.

S: . . . But I was hoping . . .

C: Yeah, I know. I can see you're anxious to get started.

Why does the coach say, "Yeah, I know. I can see you're anxious to get started."?

4. *Listen again to part of the conversation. Then answer question 4.*

C: Just go over to Health Services and make an appointment. There's a form you have to fill out with your, uh, medical history. And then you'll see the doctor. It's really no big deal.

What does the coach imply about getting a health clearance?

ACADEMIC LISTENING

PAGE 37, FIRST LISTENING

Lian: This is Lian, and, like many of our listeners out there, I'm tired. I'm tired in the morning, I'm tired in the afternoon, and I'm really tired at night. And frankly, I'm tired of being tired. My excuse is that I have two small children who sleep a little, and wake up a lot. Dr. Walsleben, why are we all so tired?

Dr. Walsleben: We're probably tired because we don't make sleep a priority. And I think as a young mother and a career woman, your days are pretty well filled, and I would suspect that you probably think you can do without sleep or at least cut your sleep short, and one of the things that happens is that we forget that sleep loss accumulates, so even one bad night, teamed with another will make an effect on our performance the following day. The other aspect, which you did touch on, is that even though we may sleep long periods of time, the sleep may not be really of good quality.

L: How serious of a problem is sleep deprivation?

DW: Well, it can be very serious, because lack of sleep can affect our performance. It's not . . . . we can get cranky and all that, but if our performance is poor, and we are in a very critical job, we can have a major incident. And there have been many across society in which sleep and fatigue were issues.

The Exxon Valdez was one in which the captain got a lot of attention, but the mate who was driving the ship had been on duty for 36 hours . . . But you can read your local papers; every weekend, you'll see a car crash with probably a single driver at around 2 or 3 am, no reason why they would happen to drive off the road, and we all believe that that's probably a short sleep event that occurred when they weren't looking for it.

L: Dr. Walsleben, I know how this sleep deprivation affects me. By the end of the day, with my children, I'm tired and cranky, I'm not making good parenting decisions, I don't have a lot to give my husband when he comes home, and then I just feel too tired to exercise. So I think, "Oh, I'll eat or I'll have a big cup of coffee, and that will give me the energy that I don't have naturally. Are these pretty common effects of sleep deprivation amongst your patients?

DW: They're very common, and so many people accept them.

L: I would even say that by Friday afternoon, I'm afraid to get behind the wheel of a car, because I just feel like I am not a safe driver on the road. That's how tired I am by Fridays.

DW: I think it's great of you to have recognized that . . . . and that's a real, major concern for most of America's workers. By Friday, everyone seems to be missing, probably, 5 hours of sleep . . .

PAGE 38, SECOND LISTENING

4. Listen again to part of the conversation. Then answer question 4.

L: I would even say that by Friday afternoon, I'm afraid to get behind the wheel of a car, because I just feel like I am not a safe driver on the road. That's how tired I am by Fridays.

DW: I think it's great of you to have recognized that . . . .

What does Dr. Walsleben imply when she says , "I think it's great of you to have recognized that . . . ."?

INTEGRATED TASK

PAGE 44, LISTENING

Student 1: Did you see the announcement about the Late-Night Study Center? I think it's great. You can stay there all night and study.

Student 2: I dunno, I don't think it's such a good idea.

S1: Why?

S2: You know, I'm taking a class now in cognitive science . . .

S1: Really? I didn't know . . .

S2: Yeah, it's really interesting. And right now we're looking at these studies about sleep and learning, and they show that people really don't learn well when they don't sleep.

S1: Really?

S2: Yeah. And it's not just being tired. Sleep actually helps your brain turn new information into long-term memories. It's like . . . like, if you learn something, and then go to sleep, you actually remember it better. And if you don't sleep, you forget the information.

S1: Huh. I never heard that.

S2: But it's not just that. Also I think that . . . well, having the center just encourages bad sleep habits.

S1: What do you mean?

S2: Sleep deprivation is a big problem, especially for students who have so much to do. But the university should be teaching us how to take care of ourselves, not encouraging us to stay up late and try to function without enough sleep!

S1: Huh. I never thought of it that way.

UNIT 4: Natural Disasters

CAMPUS CONVERSATION

PAGE 53, FIRST LISTENING

Student: Hi, I hope you can help me.

Computer Technician: I'll see what I can do . . .

S: I'm really in trouble, because I was working on my laptop . . .

CT: Yeah?

S: . . . you know, during the storm last night. And then all of a sudden, the power went off, and I lost all my work!

CT: It didn't stay on with the battery power?

S: Well, I think there's something wrong with the battery, because it hasn't been working for a few weeks. So I just plug it in and don't use the battery.

CT: OK, and what happened when you turned the laptop on today?

S: It started up, but I can't find the paper I was working on. I mean, I found it, but not with all the changes I made. So can you help me find it somewhere on my disc?

CT: Well, I hate to tell you this, but chances are . . . it's probably lost forever . . .

S: Oh, no . . .

CT: Yeah. That's why it's so important to back up your data as you work.

S: This is great . . .

CT: . . . That was some storm, huh?

S: Tell me about it. First this, and then with all the rain, we had a leak from the window, and my roommate's stuff got all wet.

CT: Really?

S: Yeah, we woke up and there was a big flood on his desk, and all his books and everything were wet.

CT: When I came in this morning, there was a big puddle in front of this building too.

S: Oh yeah?

CT: But fortunately the water didn't get inside.

S: The whole campus is in bad shape. There's water everywhere . . .

CT: I've never seen it rain so hard.

S: Yeah, and the wind!

CT: The wind was intense . . . But about your computer, is there anything else I can help you with?

S: Oh, um, yeah . . . How can I fix the battery?

CT: Well, unfortunately, you can't really fix it. You have to buy a new one.

S: Really? Can I get one here on campus?

CT: Well, the bookstore has some computer stuff . . . you can try looking there . . .

S: Well, I'll deal with that later. Right now, I have to finish my paper. At least I have my notes, but I'll have to write a whole section all over again.

CT: Sometimes you have to learn the hard way, right? This time, don't forget to back it up!

S: Yeah, I don't think I'll forget that again!

CT: Take care!

S: Thanks! Bye.

PAGE 53, SECOND LISTENING

2. Listen again to part of the conversation. Then answer question 2.

S: So can you help me find it somewhere on my disc?

CT: Well, I hate to tell you this, but chances are, it's probably lost forever . . .

S: Oh, no . . .

CT: Yeah. That's why it's so important to back up your data as you work.

S: This is great . . .

2. *When the student says, "This is great . . ." he probably feels*

4. *Listen again to part of the conversation. Then answer question 4.*

CT: I've never seen it rain so hard.

S: Yeah, and the wind!

CT: The wind was intense . . . . But about your computer, is there anything else I can help you with?

4. *Why does the student consultant say, "But about your computer . . ."?*

5. *Listen again to part of the conversation. Then answer question 5.*

S: Oh, um, yeah . . . How can I fix the battery?

CT: Well, unfortunately, you can't really fix it. You have to buy a new one.

S: Really? Can I get one here on campus?

CT: Well, the bookstore has some computer stuff . . . you can try looking there . . .

5. *What does the student consultant mean when she says, "Well the bookstore has some computer stuff . . . you can try looking there . . ."?*

ACADEMIC LISTENING

PAGE 54, FIRST LISTENING

Alex Zhao: This is Alex Zhao reporting live from aboard a reconnaissance squadron, known as the Hurricane Hunters. The sun is shining in South Florida as the aircraft gets ready. It's carrying six officers from the postcard-like weather here directly into the eye of Hurricane Haley, as the big storm turns northward. They'll fly through the hurricane and relay vital information back to the mainland—information on wind speed, pressure, and organization of the storm.

Today I get to go with them . . . into the eye of the storm. Two of the crew members, Andrea Davis and Miguel Rios are with me now. Andrea, look how dark it is over there. Where are we headed?

Andrea Davis: We're heading right into the storm's eye, Alex. It's about twelve miles wide.

AZ: Now the plane is becoming dark as we enter the eye wall, which is what we call the thick clouds around the center of the storm. The ends of the wings seem to have disappeared in the clouds and the rain. Inside the eye wall, you can't see anything at all. But wait . . . it's suddenly so bright! In fact, the sun is shining so intensely it's almost blinding.

AD: Yes, we've broken into the eye. Now we're going to drop the equipment from the plane to record data.

AZ: Miguel, can I ask you something? Isn't this job dangerous?

Miguel Ríos: Well yes, but it's necessary. Machines can't do what we do. Technology tells you where the storm is located, but it's not as accurate as having people on board. For instance, we can tell certain things about the speed and direction of the

storm by looking down onto the ocean surface. It's pretty exciting.

AZ: Really? I'm amazed you don't panic. I think you are all very brave. I wouldn't want to do this every day!

AD: Well, it can get intense, but when we get this information back to the mainland, who knows? We could end up saving some lives.

AZ: And how do you use the information when you get back?

AD: We give it to the weather forecasters, who look at information such as wind speed and pressure, and use it to predict where the hurricane'll go, and how strong it'll be. That helps authorities decide what areas on the coastline are in danger and need to be evacuated.

AZ: It's heartening to know you're risking your lives to keep the rest of us safe. Thank you so much for taking me on your trip—into the eye of the storm! I'm Alex Zhao, reporting.

PAGE 55, SECOND LISTENING

2. *Listen again to part of the conversation. Then answer question 2.*

AZ: The ends of the wings seem to have disappeared in the clouds and the rain. Inside the eye wall, you can't see anything at all. But wait . . . it's suddenly so bright! In fact, the sun is shining so intensely it's almost blinding.

Why does the reporter Alex Zhao say, "But wait . . ."?

4. *Listen again to a part of the conversation. Then answer question 4.*

AZ: . . . I'm amazed you don't panic. I think you are all very brave. I wouldn't want to do this every day!

AD: Well, it can get intense, but when we get this information back to the mainland, who knows? We could end up saving some lives.

Select the sentence that best expresses Andrea Davis's reply to the reporter.

INTEGRATED TASK

PAGE 62, LISTENING

Professor: OK, today I want to talk about another weather phenomenon—hurricanes. Hurricanes—um, also called typhoons or tropical cyclones, depending on where they form— hurricanes are very large storms. The winds of a hurricane circle around a central "eye," an area in the middle about 16 to 64 kilometers—(or 10 to 40 miles) wide—an area that's normally very calm, with no rain or clouds.

Now—hurricanes form over water, over the Atlantic, Pacific, or Indian oceans near the equator, usually in summer or late fall when the ocean water is warm. After forming they then move south or north, toward the poles.

But what about hurricane prediction? Well, fortunately for us, it's gotten much better over the past fifty years. Hurricanes take from three to fourteen days to form, so they can be effectively tracked with modern technology, like, ah, satellite and radar. So we can watch hurricanes as they form over the ocean, and see where they're going. But, the problem is, that it's still difficult to predict the exact path of a long-lasting hurricane—it may travel up to about 6400 kilometers (or 4,000 miles) and also change directions several times. So even when there's a hurricane warning, the predicted path often changes as the storm gets closer to shore.

As far as the damage, um, the destructive power of hurricanes, I think we've all seen how devastating they can be. But fortunately, most hurricanes die out slowly as they move over cooler water, and never hit land, so they never really cause any problems, except maybe to boats in the area. But the hurricanes that do come to shore can be extremely destructive—with winds reaching up to 320 kilometers (or 200 miles) per hour just around the eye, and a damage path that extends about 400 kilometers (or 250 miles) out from the center of the eye. So when it hits land, a hurricane can cause extensive wind damage and flooding. I'm sure you've seen on TV the aftermath of a hurricane, with vast areas damaged or destroyed. I mean it can be just devastating. But hurricanes can't move very far inland. So after hitting large areas, they quickly lose strength over land, although there can still be a lot of wind damage and flooding from the rain.

SKILL FOCUS

PAGE 64, EXAMINATION

Item 1

Listen again to part of the conversation. Then answer the question.

S: So can you help me find it somewhere on my disc?

CT: Well, I hate to tell you this, but chances are, it's probably lost forever . . .

S: Oh, no . . .

CT: Yeah. That's why it's so important to back up your data as you work.

S: This is great . . .

When the student says, "This is great . . . " he probably feels

Item 2

Listen again to part of the conversation. Then answer the question.

S: Oh, um, yeah . . . How can I fix the battery?

CT: Well, unfortunately, you can't really fix it. You have to buy a new one.

S: Really? Can I get one here on campus?

CT: Well, the bookstore has some computer stuff . . . you can try looking there . . .

What does the student consultant mean when she says "Well, the bookstore has some computer stuff . . . you can try looking there . . . "

Item 3

Listen again to a part of the conversation. Then answer the question.

AZ: The ends of the wings seem to have disappeared in the clouds and the rain. Inside the eye wall, you can't see anything at all. But wait . . . it's suddenly so bright! In fact, the sun is shining so intensely it's almost blinding.

Why does the reporter Alex Zhao say, "But wait . . . "

PRACTICE: LISTENING

PAGE 67, LISTENING 1

Student 1: How's it going? Are you ready for the hurricane?

Student 2: Well, I think so . . . I just went to the store to get some supplies.

S1: Yeah, me too! Look at this great flashlight! I got two of them, just in case . . .

S2: Wow, that's nice. They were all out of flashlights when I went . . . I could *really* use one of those. You said you got *two*?

S1: You know, I'd like to help you out, but unfortunately I promised I'd give this one to my roommate. Sorry about that!

EXERCISE 2, LISTENING 2

Professor: Planning for earthquakes is difficult because there is no way to predict when one will occur. Well, some people think that in the future, we'll be able to predict earthquakes, but there are many factors that would make this difficult. If you read the article in the last issue of *Science Review*, by Brown, umm, Rosalyn Brown? um, anyway, it's in the last issue . . . It's really an important article because it addresses a lot of the problems with earthquake prediction, a lot of the difficulties we have, so it's really worth reading.

UNIT 5: Conservation

CAMPUS CONVERSATION

PAGE 71, FIRST LISTENING

Resident Assistant: So, now you've seen most of the dormitory, let's go down here a minute. I want to show you our . . . our favorite room over here . . . the garbage room! This is where you can empty your trash cans and stuff. And you'll notice over here, we have our recycling area.

Student: Over there?

RA: Yeah, those big blue plastic bins over there. So we have one for paper, metal, and glass . . .

S: Do we have to sort everything ourselves?

RA: Well, yeah. But it's pretty simple. You just put the different material in the right bin.

S: I mean, do we have to do it? We don't recycle where I live.

RA: Well, keep in mind that the university has a strong commitment to conservation. Recently, they built some new "green" buildings that are really energy efficient. And this year, they're really pushing us to do recycling campus-wide.

S: I know, but, like, what's a few cans here or there. It doesn't make that big a difference.

RA: Well, for one person, sure. But it's like, everyone has to do their part. I mean, look at the big picture—if everyone does it, it will make a difference!

S: I guess. It's just, I know I'm going to be really busy with studying and all, and I might not remember to sort through everything each week.

RA: Well, no one's forcing you to do it. But really, it's not that much work. And a lot of people just keep some separate containers for each type of trash, like paper, and bottles and cans.

S: The dorm rooms are kind of small! Where am I going to find room for all that?

RA: Well, talk to your roommate about it. Or you can even set up some sorting bins in the lounge.

S: The lounge?

RA: Oh, that's over here. Here . . . It's for everyone to use, to like . . . last year, we used to have pizza parties here every week, or we'd watch TV together.

S: What about cleaning in here? Do we have to clean it too?

RA: Yeah, that's the responsibility of the people in the hall. A lot of times people work out a cleaning schedule, so that way it's fair. But you have to work it out with the people in your hall.

S: I didn't expect to have all this responsibility for cleaning! I'm going to be really busy this semester, I just know it!

RA: Hey—I don't want you to get all stressed out about this. It's really not a big deal! Come on! I'll take you over to see where the dining hall is. At least you don't have to cook!

PAGE 71, SECOND LISTENING

2. *Listen again to part of the conversation. Then answer question 2.*

RA: Well, keep in mind that the university has a strong commitment to conservation. Recently, they built some new "green" buildings that are really energy efficient. And this year, they're really pushing us to do recycling campus-wide.

2. *Why does the Resident Assistant say, "Recently, they built some new "green" buildings that are really energy efficient. And this year, they're really pushing us to do recycling campus-wide."?*

3. *Listen again to part of the conversation. Then answer question 3.*

RA: Well, for one person, sure. But if each person recycles one or two cans, that adds up to a lot of cans for the whole campus.

S: I guess. It's just, I know I'm going to be really busy with studying and all, and I might not remember to sort through everything each week.

RA: Well, no one's forcing you to do it. But really, it's not that much work . . .

What can be inferred about the Resident Assistant when he says, "Well, no one's forcing you to do it. But really, it's not that much work . . . "?

ACADEMIC LISTENING

PAGE 72, FIRST LISTENING

Professor: So, we've talked a bit about "green" buildings—buildings that are designed to consume less energy, to conserve heat, and so on. But today I want to look at some examples, examples of real buildings, and how these concepts are being applied today.

So my first slide, this is called an "Earthship" home, and it's something that . . . there's quite a few . . . um, this one here is from . . . let's see . . . I believe it's in Bristish Columbia, Canada. But they've been built all over the world . . . the United States, Japan, Australia, Europe, and South America . . . all over.

So what makes these Earthship homes so unusual? Well, they don't use brick and concrete, or wood, or any of the traditional materials we think of. The primary materials are recycled tires—like the tires on your car—and dirt, regular dirt from the ground! And how they're made is . . . the tires are piled up on their sides, and tightly packed with dirt . . . completely filled . . . So the walls are quite wide—A tire is what? Three feet wide? So the walls are a bit wider than that. And then, the walls are finished inside and out, so the house looks nice and you don't see the tires.

The great thing about this type of construction is the energy efficiency. See, the dirt and the rubber from the tires trap heat—just hold that heat inside! And if you look here, you'll also notice that the house also has great, long windows on the front of the building. These windows face south—to get the maximum amount of sunlight, so they help heat the home. And believe it or not, you don't even need a furnace or stove to heat the building! Even in cold climates like in, er, way up, um, way up north in Canada.

Another advantage of these homes is the low cost, both to build them and to live in them. So they're attractive to people with low incomes, since they can be built relatively cheaply with recycled materials, and there are no heating bills . . . Yes? Michael?

Student: Um, yeah, I was wondering, it seems like a great idea, but is anyone really building them? I mean, they're kind of funny-looking, don't you think?

P: Well, I don't know about that! But to answer your question, yes, people are building them . . . In fact, some communities are actively encouraging this kind of development, not only because it generates new low-cost housing, but also because it is a way to dispose of old tires, which is a big problem in many places. In Alberta, Canada, for example, the government started a recycling program that encourages people to recycle tires in innovative ways. They do this by paying people to use the tires—two dollars per tire! So it's a great incentive, because you can get the materials you need, and be paid for it. . . . basically, you make money instead of spending money to build your home!

PAGE 73, SECOND LISTENING

2. *Listen again to part of the lecture. Then answer question 2.*

P: But they've been built all over the world . . . the United States, Japan, Australia, Europe, and South America . . . all over. So what makes these Earthship homes so unusual? Well, the most unusual thing is the material used to build them: recycled tires—like the tires on your car!

Why does the professor ask, "So what makes these Earthship homes so unusual?"?

3. *Listen again to part of the lecture. Then answer question 3.*

S: Um, yeah, I was wondering, it seems like a great idea, but is anyone really building them? I mean, they're kind of funny-looking, don't you think?

P: Well, I don't know about that!

What does the professor mean when she says, "Well I don't know about that!"?

INTEGRATED TASK

PAGE 79, LISTENING

Student 1: Did you read the article about ecocities?

Student 2: Yeah, I just finished it.

S1: Don't you think it'd be great to live in one of those?

S2: Really? How so?

S1: Well, it'd be a lot better to live and work in energy efficient buildings. Think about all the cost savings you'd get in utility bills, because you wouldn't use as much energy! Where I live, we have to pay a lot for electricity and heating each month. And with solar and wind energy, the air'd be cleaner too.

S2: I see your point, but don't you think the buildings would be more expensive to buy? Because they're . . . Putting in solar and wind power is so expensive. The article says it adds several thousand dollars to the cost. I'm not sure you'd get that back in energy savings.

S1: Eventually, you might . . . But another advantage is transportation. A big problem living here is that you really need a car, because you have to drive everywhere. But in an ecocity, everything's planned for public transportation. So you can take public transportation, or walk where ever you need to go, or take your bike. You probably wouldn't even need a car!

S2: I don't know. I don't think I'd like to live where you have to wait for a bus, or walk and bike everywhere. My roommates always tease me because, if I have to go two blocks to the store, I'll get in my car and drive there!

S1: Maybe ecocities aren't for you then. But I still think they're a good idea.

S2: OK, when you move to one, I'll drive out to visit you and see what it's like. How about that?

SKILL FOCUS

PAGE 82, EXAMINATION

Item 1

Listen again to part of the conversation. Then answer the question.

RA: Well, keep in mind that the university has a strong commitment to conservation. Recently, they built some new "green" buildings that are really energy efficient. And this year, they're really pushing us to do recycling campus-wide.

Why does the resident assistant say, "Recently, they built some new green buildings that are really energy efficient. And this year, they're really pushing us to do recycling campus-wide."?

UNIT 6: Philanthropy

CAMPUS CONVERSATION

PAGE 89, FIRST LISTENING

A: Can I help you?

S: Yeah, I have an appointment . . . I want to sign up for the ah, Volunteer Service Program?

A: OK, Susan, right?

S: Yeah . . Sorry I'm late . . .

A: That's OK. So, do you know about the program?

S: A little. I mean, just what I heard about it in orientation last year. But my advisor recommended I look into it.

A: Well, I'll just go over how it works for you. This is a volunteer program where you volunteer to work for an organization either on- or off-campus. We'll help you find the opportunity that's right for you, and check in with you during the year to make sure there are no problems. Do you know what kind of job you're looking for?

S: Umm, I'm an education major, so I'd really like to work with kids.

A: Good, good . . . We have a lot good opportunities. Do you know what age you'd like to work with?

S: Um, I don't know. I've worked with younger kids before, but I don't really have a preference.

A: Well, there's a lot of choice, depending on what you're interested in—there are jobs working in schools, tutoring kids . . . um, there's a great music program for kids, if you're musically inclined . . .

S: Uh, Not me!

A: And, um, there's a children's theater project.

S: I was hoping—since I'm studying education—that I could get a job that'll give me some teaching experience.

A: Sure, there are lots of possibilities . . . There are tutoring positions in several schools and afterschool programs in the community . . .

S: Oh yeah? What are they like?

A: You can find out more here—these binders here list the different positions. It's um, divided into, you know, different sections, so you would want to go here . . . to the education section, and take a look at the opportunities there. Each page describes a different job, with the hours and what your responsibilities would be, and any requirements they have for the job . . .

S: Is applying to these jobs a competitive process?

A: No, not really. A few programs have special requirements, like teaching music. And there are a few that are pretty popular, so sometimes there aren't enough positions for everyone who applies, but usually, you won't have a problem getting a position.

S: That's good to know.

A: It's just that . . . you need to have enough free time to volunteer. Most organizations want someone who can work two to four hours a week. I assume this will fit in with your schedule . . .

S: I've got a pretty heavy load this semester . . .

A: Well, that's a consideration. If you're going to get too busy down the road, and you feel you won't be able to make the commitment . . . .

S: But I really want to do this. I'm sure I can find the time somewhere in my schedule.

A: Great! I think what you should do now is sit down and look through some of the listings in this binder, and then you'll have a better idea of what's available.

S: OK.

A: And I'll check back with you in a little while and see what you've come up with, and if you have any questions.

S: Great! Thanks.

PAGE 89, SECOND LISTENING

4. *Listen again to part of the conversation. Then answer question 4.*

A: . . . there's a great music program for kids, if you're musically inclined . . .

S: Uh, not me!

What can you infer about the student when she says, "Uh, not me!"?

5. *Listen again to part of the conversation. Then answer question 5.*

A: It's just that… you need to have enough free time to volunteer. Most organizations want someone who can work two to four hours a week. I assume this will fit in with your schedule . . .

S: I've got a pretty heavy load this semester . . .

A: Well, that's a consideration.

What does the advisor imply when he says, "Well, that's a consideration."?

ACADEMIC LISTENING

PAGE 90, FIRST LISTENING

Professor: So, you've been reading about the beginning of modern philanthropy in the late 19th and early 20th centuries—a time of great expansion and progress in the United States—this was during the industrial revolution—and that lead to great wealth for some individuals. Well, today, I want to talk for a moment about Andrew Carnegie, a businessman and investor who rose from a modest background to great wealth, and became one of the most influential philanthropists of the time. He was also the richest man in the world in 1901, when at age 65, he sold his steel business for $480 million dollars! However, Carnegie had a long-standing interest in philanthropy and was one of the first wealthy individuals to say publicly that wealthy people had a responsibility to the community—a responsibility to give away their wealth for the benefit of the community.

Now, in 1889, Carnegie published a book—*The Gospel of Wealth*—and he discussed his ideas about the responsibility of the rich. Carnegie believed that people should only use the money they need to support themselves and their family, and then, beyond that, they . . . they should give the rest away to help the community. He said, "The man who dies rich dies disgraced." . . . "The man who dies rich dies disgraced." So, in other words, he thought that it was shameful for wealthy people to keep all their money for themselves, that instead they should use their money to help others. In fact, he even disapproved of wealthy people leaving money to charity after they died, instead of giving it away while they were alive. He thought that these people didn't really want to give their money away, that they only made these donations because they couldn't take the money with them after death! So he had some very strong views about this.

And he followed through on his beliefs! Because by the time he died in 1911, he had given away ninety percent of his fortune—about $350 million dollars—that's more than $3 million—I'm sorry, I mean $3 billion in today's dollars!

As for the motivations for Carnegie's philanthropy . . . Well, some say it was based on his life experience. For example, take one of his most famous causes: public libraries. During his lifetime, he built more than twenty-five hundred (2,500) public libraries around the world, sixteen hundred (1,600) of them in the United States. And it goes back to when he was a boy, only 13, and he had to go to work to help support his family. So he couldn't go to school. He loved to read, but there was no place for him to get books, because at the time, there were no public libraries open for anyone to use. However, a rich man lived nearby, and he had a library, and he let Carnegie borrow his books for free! So, that's how Carnegie educated himself, by reading these books. And he never forgot that. He believed that anyone—no matter their background—anyone, with the right

inclination and desire, could educate him or herself, and he saw public libraries as an important resource for this.

Now another cause that was very important to Carnegie was that of world peace and the end of war. In 1907, he wrote, "I am drawn more to this cause than to any." He believed that war could be eliminated . . . it could be ended by building stronger international laws and organizations. So, to that end, he established the Carnegie Endowment for World Peace in Washington D.C., with a gift of $10 million dollars. But he had another, more controversial idea for promoting world peace— and that was to simplify English spelling. He believed by making English spelling more sensible and regular, it could become a "lingua franca," a common language spoken around the world. And this, in turn, would help international communication. So, he established the Simplified Spelling Board, which he funded with $25,000 per year. Realistically, I don't see why he believed that people would ever change something as . . as . . . central to the language as spelling—most people completely opposed it! So his ideas never caught on, and twelve years later, after spending $300,000, he gave up and stopped funding it.

Well, it looks like that's all the time we have today. We'll continue next time discussing more about these early philanthropists like Carnegie, and their influence . . . .

PAGE 91, SECOND LISTENING

5. *Listen again to part of the lecture. Then answer question 5.*

P: Carnegie believed that people should only use the money they need to support themselves and their family, and, ah, then beyond that, they . . . they should give the rest away to help the community. He said, "The man who dies rich dies disgraced . . . The man who dies rich dies disgraced." So, in other words, he thought that it was shameful for wealthy people to keep all their money for themselves, that instead they should use their money to help others.

Why does the professor say, "So, in other words, he thought that it was shameful for wealthy people to keep all their money for themselves, that instead they should use their money to help others."?

6. *Listen again to part of the lecture. Then answer question 6.*

P: So, he established the Simplified Spelling Board, which he funded with $25,000 per year. Realistically, I don't see why he believed that people would ever change something as . . . as . . . central to the language as spelling—most people completely opposed it!

What does the professor mean when she says, "Realistically, I don't see why he believed that people would ever change something as . . . as . . . central to the language as spelling— most people completely opposed it."?

INTEGRATED TASK

PAGE 96, LISTENING

Reporter: Chicago's Children's Memorial Hospital is the lucky recipient of a surprise $18 million gift. Gladys Holm was a retired secretary who never earned more than $15,000 a year and never married. She lived alone in a tiny apartment in Evanston, Illinois, and was a volunteer at Children's Memorial Hospital in Chicago. She was called the "Teddy Bear Lady" because she brought stuffed animals to sick children on her regular visits. But Miss Holm, who died in 1996 at the age of

86, was also a long-time buyer of stocks. Over the years, she tucked away money that grew into an impressive nest egg of $18 million, which she left to Children's Memorial. It was the largest single donation in the hospital's 115-year history.

Why did Gladys Holm feel so strongly about Children's Memorial? Jennings says the hospital first touched Miss Holm's heart nearly 50 years ago, when doctors there saved the life of her friend's daughter. She never forgot the relief she felt all those years ago.

Holm's gift will fund heart disease research. People at the hospital said they regretted that they couldn't thank their benefactor for the generous gift.

UNIT 7: Education

CAMPUS CONVERSATION

PAGE 105, FIRST LISTENING

Advisor: Hi, come on in. Mira, right? Right, we talked last fall when you were choosing your classes for this semester. How's everything going? How are your classes?

Student: I'm doing fine, but . . . well . . . the thing is, like, my parents really want me to do this major, accounting.

A: Uh-huh.

S: And it's OK. I mean, I took an accounting class, and I—it was alright. I mean, I got an OK grade in it.

A: Uh-huh.

S: But I took a class, this film and video class, you know, just for fun . . But the thing is, I just love it! It's the greatest class! So I want to sign up for another film class next semester. But I just, I just know my parents won't approve. You know, they want me to take classes like accounting, or business, so I can get a good job, make money, and all that . . .

A: Hmm. So your parents want you to take certain classes, but you want to do something else. What year are you in?

S: I'm a freshman. But my parents think I'll be better off if I take classes that are, you know, serious.

A: Serious?

S: Not like film. They don't think a film class is serious. Not practical.

A: Hmmm . . .Well, I guess my response is . . . First, the purpose of an undergraduate education is to become a well-rounded person, to learn about a broad range of subjects—that's why a variety of classes are required as part of the core curriculum. And secondly, you're only in your freshman year, so you should take advantage of this time, and use it to explore, to try new things.

S: I don't know.

A: You know, my daughter, she majored in Comparative Literature.

S: Uh-huh.

A: But she works in advertising now, which she didn't study at all in college, but I think that employers are looking for, looking for . . ."Did you go to a good college? Were you successful?" So when she got out in the workforce, she found that her major wasn't so important, it was her skills like being able to write well and what she could do . . .

S: Well, my parents say . . . they just see it a different way.

A: I can understand their concern. But there are a lot of ways to be successful, so the question of what's "practical" versus "impractical" isn't always so clear. Like, your interest in film and video. . . . well, there's a lot of ways you could use those skills in a business setting, like doing corporate training, or advertising, or developing web content, so I think there are a lot of possibilities there for practical applications.

S: Hmm, I never thought of it that way.

A: Actually, that's something you might explore—ways to combine your interests with something like a business major. You know, you might be able to come out of school with some unique skills, something that employers will really want. And maybe if you sit down with your parents, and, you know, talk to them, you can reach some sort of compromise, so you can both be happy.

S: Yeah, maybe I'll do that.

PAGE 105, SECOND LISTENING

2. *Listen again to part of the conversation. Then answer question 2.*

S: I'm doing fine, but . . . well . . . the thing is, like, my parents really want me to do this major, accounting.

A: Uh-huh.

S: And it's OK. I mean, I took an accounting class, and I—it was alright. I mean, I got an OK grade in it.

Select the sentence that best expresses how the student probably feels.

3. *Listen again to part of the conversation. Then answer question 3.*

S: I'm a freshman. But my parents think I'll be better off if I take classes that are, you know, serious.

P: Serious?

What does the advisor mean when she says, "Serious?"?

ACADEMIC LISTENING

PAGE 106, FIRST LISTENING

Professor: Today, I want to talk about a recent trend in schooling, ah, homeschooling—parents who educate their children at home. The most recent survey by the U.S. Department of Education estimated that just over one million children in the United States were being home schooled—that's, ah, only 2.2 percent of American children, but a number that has been growing rapidly in recent years up from 1.7 percent just four years ago. So it's an important trend in education . . .

Now, in the reading you've been doing, what are some of the issues that have come up regarding homeschooling versus traditional schools?

Student 1: Um, I'd say . . . one of the big ones I keep reading about is the issue of socialization. That homeschooled kids don't get an opportunity for socialization like kids who go to school.

P: Yes. Right. Let's look at that a moment—socialization, um, the process of learning how to behave in society . . . how to interact with other people. And naturally, for most children, going to school is one of the important ways they develop these skills. They have a classroom full of peers, so they learn how to get along with other children. They also learn to interact with different adults, the different teachers in the school. And in addition, they also have to learn to operate in a large organization—the school—and learn their role in that organization. And that type of skill is very important for people later in life, like when you have to go to work. But what about homeschoolers?

S1: Um, critics of homeschooling say that—because children stay home, aren't in a classroom with a range of peers—that they don't learn how to interact as well with other people.

Student 2: But that's not necessarily true, because homeschoolers argue that they *do* get socialization, just that it's different than the type kids get at school.

P: And how is it different? Yes . . . ?

S2: Um, if they sometimes see other homeschooled kids, like maybe at the playground . . .

P: Well, not quite . . .

S1: I think they mean the relationship between members of the family.

P: Exactly. Many supporters of homeschooling stress that the most important relationships children can have are with their parents and family, that this relationship is the foundation of all other relationships in a child's life. And because the children spend more time with the family, with their parents and siblings, they actually develop stronger ties and stronger relationships that way.

Many homeschoolers also dispute the idea that they never get to interact with people outside their family—they say that in fact, homeschoolers interact with a much wider range of people, of different age groups and in different settings, through the volunteer work, sports groups, and other activities, and that this is better than a school setting, where kids only interact with kids in their grade, who are about the same age. So they have a lot of positive, social relationships. And, in contrast, kids at traditional schools get a lot more negative socialization, such as teasing, bullying, and so on, that doesn't happen at a homeschool.

S2: So, which type of education is better, as far as socialization goes?

P: Well, that's a very complex issue, and you can't look at it in isolation. There are many other aspects of homeschooling that we still have to discuss. So! Let's move onto those now . . . What are some other issues that came up in the reading?

PAGE 107, SECOND LISTENING

4. *Listen again to part of the lecture. Then answer question 4.*

S2: But that's not necessarily true, because homeschoolers argue that they do get socialization, just that it's different than the type kids get at school.

P: And what type is that. Yes . . . ?

S2: Um, if they sometimes see other homeschooled kids, like maybe at the playground . . .

P: Well, not quite . . .

Why does the professor say, "Well, not quite . . ."?

5. *Listen again to part of the lecture. Then answer question 5.*

S2: So, which type of education is better, as far as socialization goes?

P: Well, that's a very complex issue, and you can't look at it in isolation. There are many other aspects of homeschooling that we still have to discuss.

Why does the professor say, "Well, that's a very complex issue, and you can't look at it in isolation."?

INTEGRATED TASK

PAGE 114, LISTENING

Student 1: Hi, what're you doing?

Student 2: Oh, hi. I'm looking for the article about emotional intelligence that Professor Hudson mentioned in class today.

S1: Oh, no—Are we supposed to read that this week? I didn't see it on the syllabus!

S2: Huh? No, I'm just interested, that's all. I just wanted to find out more about it.

S1: Yeah?

S2: It just makes so much sense to me! I've always felt that an education was much more than just getting good grades in academic subjects. This really shows that intelligence is complicated—it's not something you can measure with a simple test.

S1: Uh-huh. Umm . . . let me ask you, how do you like the class, overall?

S2: I think it's great. I'm getting a lot out of it. What about you?

S1: It's OK, I guess. It's a lot of work, with the weekly assignments and all. I'm putting in a lot of time because I really need to get a good grade.

S2: Oh, yeah?

S1: Yeah, I want to get at least a B, or it'll affect my grade point average.

S2: What are you going to do your project on?

S1: Oh, I don't know. Probably one of the topics Professor Hudson suggested. I can't really think of anything else. How about you?

S2: I have a great topic! I'm really excited about it! Professor Hudson didn't suggest it, but I talked to her and she OK'd it. So I'm going to go to a local school and do classroom observations, looking at how kids handle their emotions in class!

S1: That sounds like a lot of work. But interesting, though! But I'm going stick with one of the ideas we got in class.

S2: OK, Oh! Here's the article! Do you want a copy? I'll print you one!

S1: Uh, no . . . no, thanks. That's OK.

S2: OK, I've got to go to the printer. See you later!

S1: See you.

UNIT 8: FOOD

CAMPUS CONVERSATION

PAGE 123, FIRST LISTENING

Resident Assistant: Hi, mind if I sit here?

Student: Sure, have a seat. How's it going?

RA: Pretty good. How about you?

S: I'm OK. Busy, but my classes are going well.

RA: That's good. I don't see you here at the dining hall too much.

S: To tell you the truth, I don't eat here too often.

RA: Not crazy about the food huh?

S: I usually pick something up at the student center, or—I have some friends who live off campus, and I go over there a couple times a week and we cook something and eat together.

RA: Oh, that's nice. Do you like to cook?

S: Yeah. And I like being able to cook what I want.

RA: Right.

S: But actually, my parents are giving me a hard time about it.

RA: Really?

S: Yeah, because last semester—I didn't eat in the dining hall all the time, so I had a bunch of meals left over. So they were kind of mad. Because they paid for it and all.

RA: Oh, I can see their point. They don't want you to waste money because the meals are paid for.

S: Right. So here I am, trying to get my money's worth.

RA: Well, don't make it sound so bad. They have some good food here.

S: Yeah, but I don't like eating it every day!

RA: Well, have you tried going to the dining hall on the other side of campus? They have some different . . . you know, a different menu there.

S: Yeah, I've been there a few times. But it's so far. . . . and none of my friends go there.

RA: Which meal plan are you on?

S: Um, the twenty-one meal plan.

RA: Wow. But that's the most expensive plan!

S: It is? I didn't realize that.

RA: Yeah, there some other plans that are cheaper—you don't get as many meals. I think there's even a plan where you can get a partial refund at the end of the semester, so you don't lose all your money.

S: Really? It sounds like I should look into that. I didn't think too much about it when I signed up last year. I didn't realize there were so many choices.

RA: And actually, the school web site has all this information, and a form you can use to change your meal plan.

S: So I can change it right away?

RA: No, I think you have to wait and sign up for a different plan next semester.

S: OK, I'll take a look anyway, and see what I can do.

RA: Great. And let me know if you need any help with it.

S: Thanks.

PAGE 123, SECOND LISTENING

4. *Listen again to part of the conversation. Then answer question 4.*

S: Yeah, because last semester—I didn't eat in the dining hall all the time, so I had a bunch of meals left over. So they were kind of mad. Because they paid for it and all.

RA: Oh, I can see their point. They don't want you to waste the meals they've paid for.

S: Right. So here I am, trying to get my money's worth.

What does the student mean when she says, " . . . So here I am, trying to get my money's worth."?

5. *Listen again to part of the conversation. Then answer question 5.*

RA: Well, have you tried going to the cafeteria on the other side of campus? They have some different . . . you know, a different menu there.

S: Yeah, I've been there a few times. But it's so far. . . . and none of my friends go there.

What can you infer about the student?

ACADEMIC LISTENING

PAGE 124, FIRST LISTENING

Lian Dolan: A couple of years ago, I started noticing a food trend. And it started at Teryaki Hut. And I noticed a big sign in the window that said: Teryaki Bowl. And I thought: Ah, Teryaki Bowl, OK.

And then I saw at Pollo Loco, which is kind of a fast food Mexican chain—more bowls, more food in bowls. Big bowls, chicken bowls, rice bowls, and I thought: Well rice, that makes sense, that's a cultural thing. You've got to eat rice in a bowl, that makes sense.

But the other day, I was wandering through the frozen food aisle, and I looked up, and there's a whole "Food In Bowl" section. And this has nothing to do with cultural food. I just . . . I don't think lasagna needs to be in a bowl. I don't know. Are we just eating too much food, too fast, that we can't eat on a plate anymore, or we need a bowl because we can get that closer to our mouths for more shoveling in?

What is the next trend, hands free eating, like hands free cell phones? Just forget it. Forget the utensils, just get yourself a nice trough, and put the lasagna in there.

I'm Lian Dolan in Pasadena, and I feel it's my duty as a mother to educate my children to eat on a plate with a knife and a fork.

Julie Dolan: I'm Julie Dolan in Bangkok. And we've got rice bowls, monk bowls. It's pretty much a bowls city, here.

Liz Dolan: I'm Liz Dolan in New York. And of all the challenging methods of presenting food, I've actually been having the most trouble lately wrestling with things on skewers. Last week I actually beaned someone with a lamb kebab!

PAGE 125, SECOND LISTENING

3. *Listen again to part of the report. Then answer question 3.*

Lian: I don't think lasagna needs to be in a bowl. I don't know. Are we just eating too much food, too fast, that we can't eat on a plate anymore, or that we need a bowl because we can get that closer to our mouths for more shoveling in?

Select the sentence that best expresses how Lian Dolan probably feels.

4. *Listen again to part of the report. Then answer question 4.*

Julie: I'm Julie Dolan in Bangkok. And we've got rice bowls, monk bowls, etc. It's pretty much a bowls city, here.

What does Julie Dolan imply about Bangkok, Thailand?

5. *Listen again to part of the report. Then answer question 5.*

Liz: I'm Liz Dolan in New York. And of all the challenging methods of presenting food, I've actually been having the most trouble lately wrestling with things on skewers. Last week I actually beaned someone with a lamb kebab!

Why does Liz mention lamb kabobs served on skewers?

INTEGRATED TASK

PAGE 131, LISTENING

Student 1: OK, so let's talk about our agenda for the meeting with the food service manager. What are the issues we want to talk about?

Student 2: Well, I think a big one is this idea of choice. I don't understand it. Now we have many different people and companies selling food on campus. So there's lots of choice. But they want to get rid of all those people, and replace them with one or two vendors? That will mean less choice, not more.

S1: Right. Another issue is the cost. With so many different businesses, there's some competition on campus to keep prices low. I'm afraid that if just one or two companies are providing all the food, they will raise the prices. I mean, why should they keep them low when they don't have any competition?

S2: Yeah, cost is important. But also, we're going to lose some of the small businesses that have been here forever, and that really contribute to the quality of life on campus. For instance, take that great little café in the law building. Have you been there?

S1: Oh, yeah! The one owned by . . . what's his name? Sam?

S2: Sam, yeah. Everyone knows Sam. He's a great guy. And his food is great. Did you know that's his mom who works with him? The older woman in the back? She's a great cook—especially her soups.

S1: Yeah, the soups are great there.

S2: Plus, Sam's a great example of what we'll lose with the new system. I mean, one reason people love him is that he really listens to his customers, and makes changes they want. Like he'll change his hours during exam time, and he'll even deliver food on campus for parties or other special occasions!

S1: OK, great. We have a lot of good issues here. The meeting's next Monday, so now we can work on our presentation . . . .

UNIT 9: Immigration

CAMPUS CONVERSATION

PAGE 139, FIRST LISTENING

Admissions Advisor: Hi, can I help you?

Student: Yeah, I need some information. My cousin Yong-Min, he's from Korea. And he's interested in coming here to study next year.

A: OK. Has he applied to the university yet?

S: Well, he's looking into it. But we want to find out more about getting a visa. Does he have to get that approved before he applies?

A: No, he applies for the visa after he's accepted for admission to the university.

S: I see. Now, what about transcripts and things like that? What does he need to submit?

A: Well, we do need the transcripts of his high school or undergraduate schools—is he applying as an undergraduate or graduate student?

S: Graduate. For the Masters in International Law.

A: OK, so then we'd need his transcript from the school where he got his law degree. And we also need an official translation of the document.

S: A translation? How do I get that?

A: Here—I'll give you this list of companies that will evaluate a student's credentials from another country.

S: Well, I have a copy of his transcript, so can I translate it for him? I can get my aunt to help me—she's fluent in English and Korean.

A: No, I'm sorry. It's our policy to have the translations done by one of these companies—that way, we know that the translation is accurate. Not that you'd do a bad job, but there's no way we can look at a transcript from Korea and tell if it's translated correctly, right?

S: Oh, I see. What else does he need?

A: Well, the letters of recommendation are very important for admission to the law program.

S: And who should write those?

A: A professor from the law program he attended, or—if he's working as a lawyer now—from his employer. It needs to be someone who can evaluate his performance in school or at work.

S: My uncle—not Yong-Min's dad but another uncle—he's a lawyer too and works with my cousin. Can he write a letter for him?

A: Well, it'd make a better impression to have a letter from someone other than a relative—someone the student knows professionally or from school.

S: OK. Now, when is the admission deadline?

A: It's on March first.

S: So everything has to be in by then?

A: No, just the application form. He has another month to get all the supporting documentation in—his transcripts, letters of recommendation, and so on . . . Um, has your cousin gotten an admissions packet from us?

S: Uh, I'm not sure.

A: Why don't you take one—it explains everything. And we can mail him one in Korea, if he needs it. But also let him know that all the information he needs is available online, with the application form, so he can get it that way as well.

S: I see. OK, thanks a lot!

A: No problem.

PAGE 139, SECOND LISTENING

4. *Listen again to part of the conversation. Then answer question 4.*

A: It's our policy to have the translations done by one of these companies—that way, we know that the translation is accurate. Not that you'd do a bad job, but there's no way we can look at a transcript from Korea and tell if it's translated correctly, right?

Why does the advisor say, "Not that you'd do a bad job. . . ."?

5. *Listen again to part of the conversation. Then answer question 5.*

S: My uncle—not Yong-Min's dad but another uncle—he's a lawyer too and works with my cousin. Can he write a letter for him?

A: Well, it'd make a better impression to have a letter from someone other than a relative—someone the student knows professionally or from school.

What does the advisor imply about a letter of recommendation from a family member?

ACADEMIC LISTENING

PAGE 140, FIRST LISTENING

It was my first day. I had come the night before, a gray-black and cold night before—as it was to be in the middle of January, though I didn't know that at the time—and I could not see anything clearly on the way in from the airport, even though there were lights everywhere. As we drove along, someone would single out to me a famous building, an important street, a park, a bridge, that when built was thought to be a spectacle. In a daydream I used to have, all these places were points of happiness to me; all these places were lifeboats to my small drowning soul, for I would imagine myself entering and leaving them, and just that—entering and leaving over and over again—would see me through a bad feeling I did not have a name for. I only knew it felt a little like sadness but heavier than that. Now that I saw these places, they looked ordinary, dirty, worn down by so many people entering and leaving them in real life, and it occurred to me that I could not be the only person in the world for whom they were a fixture of fantasy. It was not my first bout with the disappointment of reality and it would not be my last. The undergarments that I wore were all new, bought for my journey, and as I sat in the car, twisting this way and that to get a good view of the sights before me, I was reminded of how uncomfortable the new can make you feel.

I got in an elevator, something I had never done before, and then I was in an apartment and seated at a table eating food just taken from a refrigerator. In the place I had just come from, I always lived in a house, and my house did not have a refrigerator in it. Everything I was experiencing—the ride in the elevator, being in an apartment, eating day-old food that had been stored in a refrigerator—was such a good idea that I could imagine I would grow used to it and like it very much, but at first it was all so new that I had to smile with my mouth turned down at the corners. I slept soundly that night, but it wasn't because I was happy and comfortable—quite the opposite; it was because I didn't want to take in anything else.

That morning, the morning of my first day, the morning that followed my first night, was a sunny morning. It was not the sort of bright-yellow sun making everything curl at the edges, almost in fright, that I was used to, but a pale-yellow sun, as if the sun had grown weak from trying too hard to shine; but still it was sunny, and that was nice and made me miss my home less. And so, seeing the sun, I got up and put on a dress, a gay dress made out of madras cloth—the same sort of dress that I would wear if I were at home and setting out for a day in the country. It was all wrong. The sun was shining but the air was cold. It was the middle of January, after all. But I did not know that the sun could shine and the air remain cold; no one had ever told me. What a feeling that was! How can I explain? Something I had always known—the way I knew my skin was

the color brown of a nut rubbed repeatedly with a soft cloth, or the way I knew my own name—something I took completely for granted, "the sun is shining, the air is warm," was not so. I was no longer in a tropical zone, and this realization now entered my life like a flow of water dividing formerly dry and solid ground, creating two banks, one of which was my past—so familiar and predictable that even my unhappiness then made me happy now just to think of it—the other my future, a gray blank, an overcast seascape on which rain was falling and no boats were in sight. I was no longer in a tropical zone and I felt cold inside and out, the first time such a sensation had come over me.

PAGE 141, SECOND LISTENING

3. *Listen again to part of the story. Then answer question 3.*

Everything I was experiencing—the ride in the elevator, being in an apartment, eating day-old food that had been stored in a refrigerator—was such a good idea that I could imagine I would grow used to it and like it very much, but at first it was all so new that I had to smile with my mouth turned down at the corners. I slept soundly that night, but it wasn't because I was happy and comfortable—quite the opposite; it was because I didn't want to take in anything else.

What can be inferred about Lucy when she says, "I slept soundly that night, but it wasn't because I was happy and comfortable—quite the opposite; it was because I didn't want to take in anything else."?

6. *Listen again to part of the story. Then answer question 6.*

But I did not know that the sun could shine and the air remain cold; no one had ever told me. What a feeling that was! How can I explain? Something I had always known—the way I knew my skin was the color brown of a nut rubbed repeatedly with a soft cloth, or the way I knew my own name—something I took completely for granted, "the sun is shining, the air is warm," was not so.

Why does Lucy say, "Something I had always known—the way I knew my skin was the color brown of a nut rubbed repeatedly with a soft cloth, or the way I knew my own name—something I took completely for granted, 'the sun is shining, the air is warm,' was not so."?

INTEGRATED TASK

PAGE 149, LISTENING

In books I had read—from time to time, when the plot called for it—someone would suffer from homesickness. A person would leave a not so very nice situation and go somewhere else, somewhere a lot better, and then long to go back where it was not very nice. How impatient I would become with such a person, for I would feel that I was in a not so nice situation myself, and how I wanted to go somewhere else. But now I, too, felt that I wanted to be back where I came from. I understood it, I knew where I stood there. If I had had to draw a picture of my future then, it would have been a large gray patch surrounded by black, blacker, blackest.

What a surprise this was to me, that I longed to be back in the place that I came from, that I longed to sleep in a bed I had outgrown, that I longed to be with the people whose smallest, most natural gesture would call up in me such a rage that I longed to see them all dead at my feet. Oh, I had imagined that with my one swift act—leaving home and coming to this new place—I could leave behind me, as if it were an old garment never to be worn again, my sad thoughts, my sad feelings, and my discontent with life in general as it presented itself to me. In the past, the thought of being in my present situation had been a comfort, but now I did not even have this to look forward to, and so I lay down on my bed and dreamt I was eating a bowl of pink mullet and green figs cooked in coconut milk, and it had been cooked by my grandmother, which was why the taste of it pleased me so, for she was the person I liked best in the world and those were the things I liked best to eat also.

UNIT 10: Technology

CAMPUS CONVERSATION

PAGE 159, FIRST LISTENING

Student: Um, Professor Wilson?

Professor: Yeah? Can I help you with something?

S: I just have a question about something you mentioned in class.

P: Yeah?

S: I thought the discussion today was really interesting, about the role of technology in society . . .

P: Yeah, it got pretty lively!

S: But I would've liked to have talked more about the positive role that technology plays . . . we ended up focusing a lot on the negative.

P: We did get a bit sidetracked talking about computer disasters. I think some of your classmates have been having a rough time with their computers recently (laughs) . . . but that was really the point I was trying to make, about the balance between the positive and negative when you introduce any new technology. Some people love it, and some people hate it.

S: But, what I wanted to ask you about was . . . the term you mentioned, um . . . "early adopters" . . . . what is that exactly?

P: Well, an early adopter is someone who is the first to use a technology. Like, in your group of friends, there might be someone who's always first to try out the newest high-tech cell phone, or whatever . . .

S: That's what I thought—sort of like me. It's a kind of a joke with my friends. I'm always the first one to get a new device and try it out. I learn how to use it, and then I teach them.

P: Oh, so maybe you're an early adopter!

S: I guess.

P: Well, that's interesting. And you can see how people like you are so important to businesses that introduce new technology. You, ah, introduce your friends to something new, get them to try it out. . . .

S: I just like trying new things, I mean, it's fun to figure them out.

P: And then those people . . . your friends . . . are much more likely to go out and buy the technology themselves. 'Cause you've taught them how to use it!

S: Yeah?

P: . . . In fact, there's a whole industry that's been created to study people just like you, to find out what early adoptors think and what they're interested in. 'Cause you're really on the cutting edge here, of technology.

S: Really? So, is that something we're going to talk more about?

P: Umm . . . I'm not . . . Yeah, I guess in a few weeks we'll be talking about at what point a new technology really catches on. Like, the personal computer comes to mind. When did the home computer turn from a novelty item that only a few people had, to something that many people feel they *must* have . . . ?

S: Oh, good. Well, um thanks, that's what I wanted to find out . . . Well, I have to get to my next class.

P: Right, you'd better get going, then. I'll see you next time.

S: OK, bye.

PAGE 159, SECOND LISTENING

4. *Listen again to part of the conversation. Then answer question 4.*

S: I thought the discussion today was really interesting, about the role of technology in society . . .

P: Yeah, it got pretty lively!

S: But I would've liked to have talked more about the positive role that technology plays . . . we ended up focusing a lot on the negative.

P: We did get a bit sidetracked talking about computer disasters.

What can be inferred about the professor when she says, "We did get a bit sidetracked talking about computer disasters."?

5. *Listen again to part of the conversation. Then answer question 5.*

S: Oh, good. Well, um thanks, that's what I wanted to find out . . . Well, I have to get to my next class.

P: Right, you'd better get going, then. I'll see you next time.

Why does the student say "Well, I have to get to my next class."?

ACADEMIC LISTENING

PAGE 160, FIRST LISTENING

Host: Welcome to Technology Talk. Our topic today is "Technological Pet Peeves." What's one thing about modern technology that really drives you crazy? Our lines are open. Give us a call. . . . Hello. You're on the line with Technology Talk.

Caller 1: Hi. I'm Stanley from Chicago.

H: Welcome, Stanley. Now, as you know, we're taking complaints about technology today. What's one thing that drives you crazy?

C1: Well, what I really hate are automated phone systems. Everyone has them these days, but I . . . um . . . think they're a mixed blessing. They can be convenient sometimes, you know, when you have to leave a message for someone . . .

H: But that's not your complaint, is it?

C1: No, my complaint is that it's awful to try calling somewhere, like your bank or something, and you get this annoying recorded voice saying, ah "If you're calling from a touch-tone phone, press one." Then you get lost in the system and never get to talk to a real person! It's a waste of time, and you never get the information you want anyway.

H: Uh-huh . . . I tend to agree with you, Stanley. But what effect do you think this has on us, beyond being annoying?

C1: Um, it really de-personalizes things. We lose the human contact. I suppose it saves money for companies—'cause they don't have to hire people to answer the phone—but, I don't know, I think they lose a lot of business because of it, too.

H: Good point. Thanks, Stanley. Let's move on to Carol from Houston. Hi, Carol.

Caller 2: Hello?

H: So, Carol, what's the one thing that really makes you frustrated with modern technology?

C2: I'm happy to have a chance to speak out! I know that a lot of people like the convenience of cellular phones, but I find them truly irritating. People don't seem to know when to leave them at home. I hate it when people use their cell phones in a restaurant or a store. One night in the movie theater, some cell phone began to ring and a guy behind me began to have a conversation right there in the movie!

H: Right, I think we've all had that experience. But Carol, many public places have rules now about where you can and can't use your phone—do those help at all?

C2: Some, I'm sure, but there's always someone who doesn't pay attention to the rules. And usually, those people don't care if they're being considerate or not, so they aren't going to follow the rules anyway!

H: So, what do we do about that?

C2: Well, I've heard of a device that kills cell phone signals, so if you're in the area near it, your phone just won't work. I'd like to see more of those around, so people really can't use their phones.

H: That's pretty serious—blocking everyone's calls. People might argue that in some cases, people really do need to be reached in an emergency, like a doctor or something.

C2: True, there might be exceptions, but people got along for thousands of years without cell phones at all, so why can't they turn them off for a couple of hours? I don't get it.

H: Yes, well, it's hard to get people to give up a technology like that. Thanks, Carol, for your comments. Let's move on now to another call . . . .

PAGE 161, SECOND LISTENING

4. *Listen again to part of the conversation. Then answer question 4.*

C1: Well, what I really hate are automated phone systems. Everyone has them these days, but I . . . um . . . think they're a mixed blessing. They can be convenient sometimes, you know, when you have to leave a message for someone . . .

H: But that's not your complaint is it?

Why does the host say "But that's not your complaint, is it?"

5. *Listen again to part of the conversation. Then answer question 5.*

C2: Well, I've heard of a device that kills cell phone signals, so if you're in the area near it, your phone just won't work. I'd like to see more of those around, so people really can't use their phones.

H: That's pretty serious—blocking everyone's calls. People might argue that in some cases, people really do need to be reached in an emergency, like a doctor or something.

What is the host trying to do when she says, "People might argue that in some cases, people really do need to be reached in an emergency, like a doctor or something."?

INTEGRATED TASK

PAGE 167, LISTENING

Professor: Um, I'd like to look at Internet usage now . . . a recent study in the United States found that—on a typical day—about seventy (70) million American adults accessed the Internet. But what are people doing online? When the Internet first started to become more popular . . . when more households got access, there were warnings that society was changing, that people would become more isolated. However, what we've found is . . . for the most part, people go online to do many of the same type of activities they do offline, it's just the way they do things that is different. The important point here is that many of the activities that take place on the Internet involve socializing with other people in some way. The study . . . um . . . showed . . . when asked about their Internet use, people said the most important thing they do is communicate with family and friends, by sending email, instant messaging, sharing photos, and so on . . . In fact, the Internet has allowed us to develop relationships that we could never have imagined a few years ago! For example, people can stay in touch with family members who are living far away. . . . Like my sister and her family, they're living in Japan right now, but because of the Internet, our families have been able to maintain a very close relationship. We send each other email and instant messages on a daily basis . . . Um, and digital photos . . . We even have a web cam hooked up, so my kids and their cousins see each other while they talk. And since we have a big family, my brother-in-law has his own web log for the family where he writes about their experiences in Japan, and posts photos, and so on. So we can see that, in many cases, the Internet has actually strengthened the ties between people, not weakened them as some people originally feared.

Answer Key

UNIT 1

CAMPUS CONVERSATION

Pre-Listening Vocabulary, page 2

1. b   3. b   5. b
2. a   4. b   6. c

First Listening, page 3

1. The student needs help choosing a topic for her paper, and she couldn't find an article on reserve at the library.
2. The professor helps the student narrow her topic and gives her a copy of the article.

Second Listening, page 3

1. D   3. A   5. D
2. C   4. D

ACADEMIC LISTENING

First Listening, page 4

1. CornCam is an Internet website that shows corn growing.
2. It's located in the Midwest state of Iowa, in the United States.
3. People from around the world watch CornCam.

Second Listening, page 5

1. D
2. Yes: A, C, D
3. C
4. A
5. D

FOCUS ON BOMB SUSPECT

Pre-Reading, page 6

1. Richard Jewell was the person accused of the Centennial Olympic Park bombing.
2. Barbara Jewell is Richard Jewell's mother.

Reading, page 6

1. B   4. A   7. D
2. D   5. B   8. D
3. C   6. D   9. A, D, B, C

Analysis, page 9

Basic Comprehension: 1, 3, 7

Organization: 8, 9

Inference: 2

Vocabulary and Reference: 4, 5, 6

INTEGRATED TASK

Reading, page 9

Main Idea: Modern technology allows people to learn more about world events.

Detail: We can get instant updates on the latest news through cable TV, the Internet, email or cell phones.

Detail: News reports and video can travel quickly around the world.

Listening, page 10

Detail: Daily and hourly updates do not report on events in enough depth, so they don't provide history and background to understand the stories.

Detail: Local news sources try to report on everything, such as international news, but can't do it well.

Speaking, page 11

Step 1

	READING	LISTENING
Frequent news updates	Keep people better informed about world events.	Don't have enough depth to help people understand background and history of events.
International news	We can learn instantly about events around the world.	Local news sources can't report on international events well.

SKILL FOCUS: SKIMMING AND SCANNING

Practice, page 13

1

1. Skim
2. Scan for "more than two hours a day"
3. Scan for "the tabloid media"
4. Scan for "news resistors"
5. Skim

2

1. news in the United States
2. 20 percent
3. Tabloid media focuses on negative stories of violence, crime, and scandal.
4. News resistors are people who choose not to watch news on TV or read newspapers everyday.
5. news resistors

UNIT 2

CAMPUS CONVERSATION

Pre-listening Vocabulary, page 16

1. g	4. d	7. h
2. b	5. f	8. i
3. e	6. a	9. c

First Listening, page 17

1. The student goes to see the professor because he was sick and missed several classes.

2. The professor explains the research project for the class.

Second Listening, page 17

1. D	3. C	5. A
2. A	4. C	

ACADEMIC LISTENING

First Listening, page 18

1. blind, deaf, amputee

2. They kept an online diary about the climb.

3. It was difficult, but they were happy to reach the top.

Second Listening, page 19

1. B	3. A	5. C
2. B	4. C	

Analysis, page 20

Basic Comprehension: 1, 3

Organization: none

Inference: 2, 4, 5

THE MIRACLE

Reading, page 21

1. A	5. C	9. A
2. D	6. A	10. B
3. B	7. A	11. Helen Keller: A, G, H;
4. C	8. C	Diane Schuur: B, C, F

INTEGRATED TASK

Reading, page 25

Main Idea: The Americans with Disabilities Act protects people with disabilities from discrimination.

Detail: An employer can't discriminate against a disabled person in hiring, promotion, or firing.

Detail: An employer must make "reasonable accommodations" so the workplace is accessible to disabled people.

Listening, page 25

1. Brian Wong is paralyzed from the waist down. He works for a computer service company.

2. **accessibility:** The building, including the parking garage, elevators, bathrooms, cafeteria, offices, conference rooms and copy room, is accessible by wheelchair.

   equipment: Low shelves and filing cabinets, devices to help him work with his injured hand

   work schedule: Flexible schedule to take sick time if he needs it

3. The company benefits because Brian is a good employee and has worked there for seven years.

SKILL FOCUS: PARAPHRASING

Practice, page 30

1

Sentence 1: A

Sentence 2: B

Sentences 3 and 4: B

Sentence 5: A

Sentence 6: A

2

Answers may vary.

3

2. McCourt loved teaching at Stuyvesant High School.

3. Students read their writing out loud every week.

4. After he turned fifty, McCourt worried about getting older.

5. The book *Angela's Ashes* was available in bookstores in September, 1996.

6. Although he was unhappy with his own writing, he always liked his students' writing.

UNIT 3

CAMPUS CONVERSATION

Pre-listening Vocabulary, page 34

1. k	4. j	7. b	10. h
2. i	5. f	8. c	11. a
3. g	6. e	9. d	

First Listening, page 35

1. The student wants to join the basketball team.

2. The coach tells him that he needs to get a health clearance form.

Second Listening, page 36

1. A	3. C	5. A
2. C	4. D	

ACADEMIC LISTENING

First Listening, page 37

- Lian is tired all day.
- Sleep deprivation is very serious. We get cranky and our job performance is poor. We might have an incident.
  - Exxon Valdez
  - car crashes
- Lian feels tired and cranky, and doesn't make good decisions about parenting or her health.
- By Friday, she is not a safe driver.

Second Listening, page 38

1. B	3. A, C, D	5. A
2. D	4. C	

NORMAN COUSINS' LAUGH THERAPY

Pre-Reading, page 39

Norman Cousins used positive emotions to cure his illness.

Reading, page 39

1. B	4. A	7. B	10. B, C, F
2. B	5. B	8. C	
3. D	6. C	9. A	

Analysis, page 42

Basic Comprehension: 1, 3, 5, 10

Organization: 6, 9

Inference: 8

Vocabulary and Reference: 2, 4, 7

INTEGRATED TASK

Reading, page 43

Purpose: a place for students to study at night after the library closes

Location: In the library on the first floor

Hours: 11:00 pm to 8:00 am on Sunday through Thursday, with extra hours during study periods and exam weeks

Services available: reserves desk, group study rooms, photocopier, public computers, eat-in lounge

Listening, page 44

Opinion: The woman **does not** support the creation of a Late-Night Study Center.

Reasons:

1. People don't learn well when they are tired because sleep helps the brain form long-term memories. If you don't sleep, you don't remember new information well.

2. The university should encourage students to develop good sleep habits, not to try and function without enough sleep.

SKILL FOCUS: IDENTIFYING AND USING MAIN IDEAS AND DETAILS

Practice, page 48

1

1. MI	3. D	5. MI (of paragraph 3)
2. D	4. D	6. MI

2

(Answers to questions in Exercise 1)

1. The article is about the effects of sleep deprivation in doctors and nurses.

2. He went to the hospital to have routine surgery.

3. b

4. The intern had worked 8 days in a row.

5. Hospitals are limiting the number of hours a doctor or nurse can work per week, instituting new rules about giving medication.

6. Sleep deprivation in hospital staff is discussed.

UNIT 4

CAMPUS CONVERSATION

Pre-listening Vocabulary, page 52

1. f	4. g	7. i
2. e	5. a	8. d
3. h	6. b	9. c

First Listening, page 53

1. The battery in the student's laptop doesn't work, and he lost all his work.

2. The student consultant tells the student that he needs a new battery, and that he should back up his work.

Second Listening, page 53

1. C	3. D	5. A
2. A	4. D	6. B

ACADEMIC LISTENING

First Listening, page 54

1. • flying through a hurricane
   • sending info back—wind pressure, speed
2. • eye wall: dark, thick clouds, can't see anything
   • inside the eye: sun shining
3. • drop equipment, look at the ocean surface
4. • machines can't do everything

Second Listening, page 55

1. B	3. B	5. B
2. C	4. A	

Analysis, page 56

Basic Comprehension: 1, 3, 5

Organization: none

Inference: 2, 4

MONOLOGUE OF ISABEL

Reading, page 57

1. D	5. C	9. D
2. B	6. A	10. B
3. C	7. B	11. The narrator's father:
4. C	8. A	B, C, F
		The narrator's
		stepmother: A, G, H

INTEGRATED TASK

Reading, page 60

1. • violent storm (twister)
   • column of rapidly circling air formed under a thunderstorm, extends to ground
2. • winds = 480 km (or 300 mi.) an hour
   • lasting an hour
   • damage path = 1.5 x 97 km (or 1 x 60 miles)
   • lift trees, cars; destroy buildings & neighborhoods.
3. • not well—form quickly w/o warning.
   • tornado watch: tornadoes possible—thunderstorms in area
   • tornado warning: tornadoes seen in area
4. • U.S.—highest # in world—Midwest & southern states.
   • Spring/early summer, esp. afternoon & early evening
   • Also—Australia & Bangladesh.

Listening, page 62

1. • large storm—forms over ocean
     = typhoon, tropical cyclone

   • winds circle around the eye
   • eye = about 16–64 km (or 10–40 mi.) wide, calm, no rain/clouds
2. • over water, Atlantic, Pacific, Indian oceans
   • near equator
   • summer/late fall—water is warm
   • then move north/south
3. • better in past 50 years.
   • 3–14 days to form
   • tracked w/ satellite & radar
   • difficult—predict path
   • travel = 6400 km (or 4000 mi.), change direction
4. • most die over water.
   • winds = 320 km (or 200 mph) near eye
   • 400 km (or 250 mi.) damage path
   • very destructive near shore
   • rain/flooding inland

SKILL FOCUS: MAKING INFERENCES

Practice, page 67

Listening

1

Listening 1

1. F
2. T
3. F

Listening 2

1. T
2. F
3. T

Reading

2

Answers will vary.

Excerpt 1

1. The author lived through **several sand storms**.
2. The author thought that dusts storms were **horrible**.

Excerpt 2

1. The Conway family lived **far away** from doctors and hospitals.

2

Answers will vary.

UNIT 5

CAMPUS CONVERSATION
Pre-listening Vocabulary, page 70

1. g
2. e
3. f
4. a
5. d
6. c
7. h
8. b

First Listening, page 71

1. The student and Resident Assistant are discussing the school's recycling policy and how to recycle in the student's new dormitory.
2. They don't agree about recycling because the student thinks she won't have enough time to do it.

Second Listening, page 71

1. C   3. B   5. A
2. D   4. D

ACADEMIC LISTENING
First Listening, page 72

1. • British Columbia
   • Around the world
   • U.S., Japan, Australia, Europe, S. America
2. • Tires and dirt
   • Tires—piled up on sides, filled with dirt
   • walls 1 meter (about 3 ft.) wide
3. a. energy efficient—hold heat inside, no heat needed
   b. low cost = recycled materials
   c. disposes of old tires

Second Listening, page 73

1. C   3. A   5. A
2. B   4. D   6. A, C, E

INTERVIEW WITH A MEDICINE PRIEST
Pre-Reading, page 74

1. David Winston talks about Cherokee beliefs about the environment and conservation.
2. (1) Don't take any life without a real reason.
   (2) Everything should serve the Great Life.
   (3) Don't pollute where we live.
3. The Great Life is a spirit that fills all things.

Reading, page 74

1. D   6. A   11. First Law of Nature: E, F;
2. A   7. C   Second Law of Nature:
3. B   8. C   D, H;
4. D   9. D   Third Law of Nature: C, B
5. A   10. B

Analysis, page 78

Factual Information: 1, 6, 7

Organization: 9, 11

Inference: 5, 10

Vocabulary and Reference: 2, 3, 4, 8

INTEGRATED TASK
Reading, page 79

1. • Environmentally friendly cities
2. • have public transportation, bike & walking paths
   • use sustainable energy: solar & wind power
   • have green space: parks & gardens
   • are built with recycled/sustainable materials

Listening, page 79

WOULD THE STUDENTS LIKE TO LIVE IN AN ECOCITY?	STUDENT 1	STUDENT 2
Opinion:	• would like to live in an ecocity	• would not like to live in an ecocity
Point:	• cheaper	• more expensive to buy a house
Example:	• lower utility bills	• solar & wind power is more expensive to install, a few thousand more per house
Point:	• better public transportation	• doesn't like taking transportation
Example:	• don't need car. • can take public transportation, bike, or walk.	• drives car two blocks to the store

SKILLS FOCUS: USING DETAILED EXAMPLES

Examination, page 82

Item 1: Examples: They built new "green" buildings; pushing students to recycle

Item 2: Point: Communities are encouraging earthship homes. Example: Alberta, Canada pays people to use old tires.

Item 3: Point: The Second Law of Nature. Example: David Winston's toothbrush.

Practice, page 85

☐1

Ecocities

Some urban planners are designing ecocities, cities that are built to be environmentally friendly. For example, there is easy access to public transportation, so residents don't need to own cars, and the community is connected by many bicycle and pedestrian paths. In addition, ecocities use sustainable energy by incorporating solar and windpower rather than relying solely on fossil fuels. Ecocities also have green space, including parks and forests that provide a natural habitat for wildlife, and community gardens where residents can grow fruits and vegetables. Furthermore, the buildings in an ecocity are constructed using ecological building materials, such as recycled materials and wood from certified sustainable forestry operations. By incorporating all of these features into ecocities, urban planners believe we will be able to start restoring our environment so there will be something left for our grandchildren.

☐2

Examples 2, 3, 4, 6, provide the strongest support for the main point. Examples 1 and 5 as not effective because they do not discuss the university's policies, and Example 7 is a restatement of the main idea.

UNIT 6

CAMPUS CONVERSATION

Pre-listening Vocabulary, page 88

1. i	4. f	7. d	10. g
2. h	5. a	8. b	
3. e	6. c	9. j	

First Listening, page 89

1. The student is talking to the advisor about getting a volunteer job.

2. The advisor tells the student that she should make sure she has enough time to volunteer.

Second Listening, page 89

1. D	3. C	5. D
2. D	4. A	6. A

ACADEMIC LISTENING

First Listening, page 90

1. Andrew Carnegie was a wealthy businessman, investor and philanthropist.

2. He started many charities and gave away most of his fortune.

Second Listening, page 91

1. D	3. B	5. A
2. B	4. A	6. A

Analysis, page 92

Basic Comprehension: 1, 2, 4

Organization: 3

Inference: 5, 6

SOME TAKE THE TIME GLADLY

Reading, page 92

1. A	4. B	7. D	10. B, C, F
2. D	5. A	8. A	
3. C	6. A	9. C	

INTEGRATED TASK

Reading, page 95

Reason: altruism/to make the world a better place

Examples: gifts to religious institutions, colleges/universities, hospitals, medical reseach

Reason: Personal interest

Examples: In U.S., no income tax on money donated to charity; Good publicity for donor, buildings named for donor.

Listening, page 96

Answers will vary, and can include:

Who was Gladys Holm?

- retired secretary
- never married
- volunteer at hospital
- bought stocks
- died at 86

What did she give Children's Memorial Hospital?

- $18 million

Why did she give the gift?

- saved the life of a friend's daughter

How will her gift be used?

- for heart research

SKILL FOCUS: IDENTIFYING AND USING RHETORICAL STRUCTURE

Practice, page 101

1

The paragraph classifies different types of philanthropy.

Outline

A. individuals
- give money or time

B. foundations
- started by wealth individuals
  e.g. Bill & Melinda Gates
- give money to charity

C. private corporations
- donate money, products, services
  e.g. donation of medicine for tsunami relief

2

1. Whole text: The question asks about the organization of the entire paragraph.
2. Author purpose: The question asks about why the author included a piece of information.
3. Author purpose: The question asks how the author chose to explain something.

3

1. b   3. e   5. d
2. c   4. a

UNIT 7

CAMPUS CONVERSATION

Pre-listening Vocabulary, page 104

1. c   3. e   5. f   7. d
2. h   4. g   6. b   8. a

First Listening, page 105

1. The student is trying to decide which courses to take next semester. Her parents want her to study business, but she wants to take a film class.
2. The academic advisor tells the student to take classes she likes, and try to combine her interests with business classes.

Second Listening, page 105

1. C   3. C   5. A
2. A   4. D   6. C, E

ACADEMIC LISTENING

First Listening, page 106

The class discusses socialization in homeschooling.

HOME SCHOOL	TRADITIONAL SCHOOL
2.2% (going up) socialization— close relationship w/ family people outside family: • volunteer work • sports • other different ages less teasing	socialization— class full of peers teachers learn roles in an organization (school) negative: teasing, bullying

Second Listening, page 107

1. D
2. A
3. Homeschool: B, C, E
   Traditional School: F
   Both: A, D
4. B
5. B

EMOTIONAL INTELLIGENCE

Reading, page 108

1. D
2. A
3. D
4. D
5. C
6. C
7. A
8. C
9. B
10. D
11. Awareness and management of emotions: C, D, F; Self-motivation: B, G

Analysis, page 112

Basic Comprehension: 2, 3, 4, 5, 11

Organization: 7, 10

Inference: 9

Vocabulary and Reference: 1, 6, 8

INTEGRATED TASK

Reading, page 112

Answers will vary.

1. Motivation: The desire to do something

2. Intrinsic Motivation: The desire to do something because it is enjoyable or satisfying.

3. Extrinsic Motivation: The desire to do something because of an outside force or reward.

Listening, page 114

TYPE OF MOTIVATION	EXAMPLES
Extrinsic	Student 1 (male) • Doesn't want to read an article that isn't assigned • Doesn't seem interested in the class • Is working hard to get a good grade. • Wants to use the professor's suggestion for the project
Intrinsic	Student 2 (female) • Is looking for an article the professor mentioned in class • Is excited about the class • Thought of her own topic for the project • Wants to do extra research

SKILL FOCUS: COMPARING AND CONTRASTING

Examination, page 116

Item 1: business and accounting classes vs. other classes

Items 2-3: home school vs. traditional school

Item 4: awareness vs. management of emotions

PRACTICE

1

2. in contrast, a lot more
3. more intensely, less able to, however
4. less likely, better able to
5. far superior…than

2

Answers will vary.

	LECTURE	DISCUSSION CLASS
Professor	• stands in front, talks to students	• sits in group with students • introduces topics for discussion
Students	• don't discuss information • raise hands to ask questions • must do homework • don't interact much w/professor	• must be prepared to discuss information • must do homework • get to know professor well
Class	• follows syllabus • often very large • graded by exams	• follows syllabus • usually small • graded partly on participation

UNIT 8

CAMPUS CONVERSATION

Pre-listening Vocabulary, page 122

1. f   3. d   5. b   7. g
2. c   4. e   6. a

First Listening, page 123

1. The student and resident assistant are talking about the food in the cafeteria and the school meal plans.

2. The resident assistant suggests that the student look into changing her meal plan.

Second Listening, page 123

1. C   3. B   5. D
2. C   4. A

OR

VENN DIAGRAM

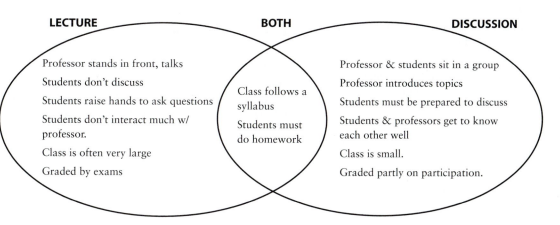

LECTURE

Professor stands in front, talks

Students don't discuss

Students raise hands to ask questions

Students don't interact much w/ professor.

Class is often very large

Graded by exams

BOTH

Class follows a syllabus

Students must do homework

DISCUSSION

Professor & students sit in a group

Professor introduces topics

Students must be prepared to discuss

Students & professors get to know each other well

Class is small.

Graded partly on participation.

ACADEMIC LISTENING

First Listening, page 124

Answers will vary.

SISTER	PLACE	COMMENTS ABOUT THE WAY FOOD IS SERVED
Lian	Pasadena	new food trend—food in a bowl • restaurants • supermarket frozen food Why can't we eat on a plate? Is hands-fee eating next? Wants children to eat on plate with knife & fork
Julie	Bangkok	There's lots of bowls there Bowls city
Liz	New York	Have trouble with skewers/lamb kebab

Second Listening, page 125

1. A 3. D 5. C
2. D 4. A

Analysis, page 126

Basic Comprehension: 1

Organization: 2

Inference: 3, 4, 5

"SLOW FOOD" MOVEMENT

Pre-Reading, page 126

1. The Slow Food movement is a movement to encourage people to slow down and take time to enjoy cooking and eating.
2. Slow Food members think their way of eating is better than going to fast food restaurants.

Reading, page 127

1. A 4. A 7. A
2. C 5. D 8. C
3. B 6. A 9. B, C, E

INTEGRATED TASK

Reading, page 130

Answers will vary.

1. The university is proposing a change to the food service system so there are only one or two providers, instead of many.
2. • The university wants to improve the service and quality of food.
   • The university can't ask food providers to change the food they make.
   • Administrative costs are high.
3. Some people are opposed to the plan.

Listening, page 131

1. They are opposed to the proposal.
2. • There won't be enough choice of where and what to eat.
   • The cost may go up.
   • They will loose small business owners like Sam in the café at the law building.
3. They are going to have another meeting.

SKILL FOCUS: SUMMARIZING

Practice, page 134

2

The university is planning to change the food service system on campus. A. Food service is currently provided by many different companies. F. The purpose of the change is to improve the quality of the food, give students more choices, and reduce administrative costs. C. Some people on campus oppose the idea and want to meet with the university administration.

(Sentences B, D an E are not used)

3

Answers will vary.

A new fast food restaurant may open on campus. It will serve a variety of inexpensive food. However, some people are concerned that the food won't be healthy for students. There will be a meeting to discuss the plan.

UNIT 9

CAMPUS CONVERSATION

Pre-listening Vocabulary, page 138

1. h	3. a	5. e	7. g
2. f	4. b	6. d	8. c

First Listening, page 139

1. The student goes to the international student office to get information for his cousin, who wants to apply to the school.
2. The advisor explains what documents the cousin needs for his application.

Second Listening, page 139

1. D	3. A	5. A
2. A, B	4. D	

ACADEMIC LISTENING

First Listening, page 140

Answers will vary.

WHAT DID SHE SEE?	WHAT DID SHE DO?	HOW DID SHE FEEL?
famous buildings, an important street, a park, a bridge	looked out the window	disappointed
an elevator, a refrigerator	rode up in the elevator	Amazed/ overwhelmed by the new things
pale-yellow sun	got dressed	surprised by the cold air, homesick

Second Listening, page 141

1. D	3. A	5. C
2. D	4. D	6. B

COMING TO AMERICA

Reading, page 142

1. D
2. D
3. C
4. D
5. C
6. A
7. B
8. A
9. B
10. C
11. 1607–1820: C, G. 1821–1890: A, E, F.

Analysis, page 147

Basic Comprehension: 2, 4, 6, 7, 11

Organization: 10

Inference: 8, 9

Vocabulary and Reference: 1, 3, 7, 5

INTEGRATED TASK

Reading, page 148

Answers will vary.

Definition of Culture Shock: The feeling of discomfort as a person adjusts to a new culture.

Stage 1: Honeymoon stage

Feelings: Happy, excited, interested in everything; Wants to explore.

Stage 2: Distress stage

Feelings: Uncomfortable, unhappy, homesick, overwhelmed; Everything is difficult, confusing.

Stage 3: Recovery stage

Feelings: More comfortable; Customs seem clear, everything is easier.

Stage 4: Stability stage

Feelings: Like normal, humor returns, feeling at home.

Listening, page 149

1. • wants to go back home
   • depressed
   • black future—nothing to look forward to
2. • her old bed
   • people that used to annoy her
   • her grandmother's food
   • her grandmother

Speaking, page 149, Step 1

1.

EMOTION	EXAMPLE
Sad, depressed	She sees a black future. She feels she has nothing to look forward to.
Homesick	She misses her old bed, people from home, her grandmother, her grandmother's cooking.

2. She is experiencing the distress stage of culture shock. She feels depressed, wants to go home, and doesn't like the new culture.

3. Lucy is depressed because she sees a black future and feels she has nothing to look forward to. She misses her old bed, the people from home, her grandmother, and her grandmother's cooking.

SKILL FOCUS: USING CONTEXT CLUES

Practice, page 153

1

1. Reference
2. Insert Text
3. Vocabulary
4. Vocabulary
5. Vocabulary
6. Reference
7. Insert Text
8. Inference

2

1. C
2. B
3. C
4. D
5. B
6. A
7. D
8. A

UNIT 10

CAMPUS CONVERSATION

Pre-listening Vocabulary, page 158

1. b
2. d
3. g
4. a
5. e
6. c
7. f

First Listening, page 159

1. The student talks to the professor about the term "early adopter" that was mentioned in class.
2. The professor and student talk about the meaning of the term and why it is important.

Second Listening, page 159

1. A
2. B
3. C
4. A
5. D

ACADEMIC LISTENING

First Listening, page 160

1. The show is about things that people don't like about technology.
2. The first caller dislikes voicemail systems because they are hard to use.
3. The second caller dislikes cell phones because people use them in the wrong places.

Second Listening, page 161

1. A
2. B, C
3. A, C
4. C
5. C

Analysis, page 162

Basic Comprehension: 1, 2, 3

Organization: none

Inference: 4, 5

THOREAU'S HOME

Pre-Reading, page 162

1. 1845
2. He built a house in the woods.
3. $28.12 ½

Reading, page 162

1. B
2. B
3. C
4. C
5. A
6. A
7. D
8. C
9. A, B, C, E, F

INTEGRATED TASK

Reading, page 166

1. It was feared that people using the Internet wouldn't socialize as much and would become isolated.
2. Gates thought that people would use the Internet to socialize and participate in activities in a new way.

Listening, page 167

1. People say the most important use of the Internet is to communicate with family and friends.
2. The professor gives the example of his sister's family in Japan. They communicate by e-mail, instant messaging, digital photos, web cams, web logs.
3. The professor concludes that the Internet has helped strengthen relationships between people.

Writing, page 167

1995: Many people feared:	Many people thought that people would socialize less because of the Internet and become isolated.
Bill Gates thought:	People would continue to socialize and participate in activities, but in new ways using the Internet.
Today:	People are still involved in the same activities.
	The Internet has helped build relationships and communication between people.
Examples:	• the professor's sister in Japan
	• email, instant messaging, digital photos, web cams, web logs

PART TWO

ETS Practice Sets
for the TOEFL® iBT

LISTENING

Listen to the conversations and lectures. Answer the questions based on what is stated or implied by the speakers. You may take notes while you listen. Use your notes to help you answer the questions. (Check the Answer Key on page 229.)

CONVERSATION 1

1. Why does the student visit the professor?
   (**A**) To ask for advice on an assignment
   (**B**) To find out which newspaper the professor reads
   (**C**) To inquire about the professor's opinion of a politician
   (**D**) To discuss a newspaper story the student has written

2. What does the professor imply about the newspapers the student usually reads?
   (**A**) They are mainly for entertainment.
   (**B**) They often contain factual errors.
   (**C**) They are probably not neutral.
   (**D**) They do not cover political stories.

3. What does the professor mean when she tells the student to pay close attention to the words in a news story?
   (**A**) Words may give impressions different from their dictionary meaning.
   (**B**) The student should compare stories from different newspapers.
   (**C**) The student should work harder to improve his vocabulary.
   (**D**) Journalists are often inaccurate when they report what politicians say.

4. Why does the professor recommend that the student read the same newspaper over an extended period of time?
   (**A**) To gain knowledge of what is happening in politics
   (**B**) To understand how reporting can often be subjective
   (**C**) To see if the newspaper's reporters have similar writing styles
   (**D**) To be able to compare his writing with professional reporters' writing

Listen again to part of the conversation. Then answer question 5.

5. Why does the professor ask this?
- (**A**) To show how easy it is for reporters to make mistakes
- (**B**) To point out that it is easy for readers to misunderstand a news story
- (**C**) To see if the student understands the meaning of a word
- (**D**) To show how reporters can put their opinions in news stories

CONVERSATION 2

1. What matters do the speakers mainly discuss? **Choose TWO answers.**
- (**A**) What bookstore work has to be done
- (**B**) How the student enjoyed his trip to Florida
- (**C**) Why the student missed a day of work
- (**D**) Which books the student needs for his classes

2. What does the student imply about his father's business?
- (**A**) It will remain open all year.
- (**B**) It is probably going to be sold.
- (**C**) It requires extra work during May.
- (**D**) It is going to be moved to a new location.

3. What does the manager ask the student to do?
- (**A**) Check that a book order is complete
- (**B**) Make a list of damaged books
- (**C**) Put price tags on new books
- (**D**) Get an order ready for shipment

4. What is the manager's attitude toward the student's absence from work?
- (**A**) She thinks the student is not being truthful.
- (**B**) She is sympathetic to the student's problem.
- (**C**) She is concerned about the student's health.
- (**D**) She warns the student that she may have to hire a replacement.

Listen again to part of the conversation. Then answer question 5.

5. Why does the manager of the bookstore say this?
- (**A**) She wants to change the subject.
- (**B**) She regrets talking to the student about his family.
- (**C**) She wants to imply that the student has missed too much work.
- (**D**) She wants to know if the student can work in the store today.

LECTURE 1

1. What does the class mainly discuss?
   (**A**) How students face challenges in the workplace
   (**B**) How students handle family problems
   (**C**) Experiences of being a first-year college student
   (**D**) Study habits than can help college students succeed

2. What does the professor imply about his first year as a college student?
   (**A**) He did not know how to study for his courses.
   (**B**) He did not want to pay for the required course books.
   (**C**) He had to work in the university bookstore to pay his tuition.
   (**D**) He was not well prepared for his college experience.

3. In what way are the professor and the female student similar?
   (**A**) They both showed up for class without textbooks.
   (**B**) They both have other family members attending the university.
   (**C**) They are both first-generation college students.
   (**D**) They have never had to work to pay for college.

4. What does the female student imply about living at her parents' home?
   (**A**) It is making it harder for her to enjoy college life.
   (**B**) It is not helping her save much money for college.
   (**C**) It is better than living on campus.
   (**D**) It has helped improve her grades.

5. According to the professor, what are two ways to ensure success as a first-generation college student? **Choose TWO answers.**
   (**A**) Enroll in fewer college courses
   (**B**) Have open discussion with peers
   (**C**) Seek support from the university
   (**D**) Talk with one's parents

Listen again to part of the discussion. Then answer question 6.

6. Why does the professor ask this?
  (**A**) To encourage the students to discuss their experiences
  (**B**) To respond to a student's question about his experiences
  (**C**) To show that his first year of college was more difficult than the students' first year
  (**D**) To help the students avoid the mistakes he made

LECTURE 2

1. What is the lecture mainly about?
  (**A**) Dolphins' need for sleep
  (**B**) Similarities between dolphin and human brains
  (**C**) How dolphins sleep
  (**D**) How brain activity is measured in dolphins

2. What advantages do dolphins get by sleeping the way they do? **Choose TWO answers.**
  (**A**) While sleeping, they can rise to the surface.
  (**B**) While sleeping, they can remain observant of their surroundings.
  (**C**) While sleeping, they can communicate with other members of their group.
  (**D**) While sleeping, they can look for food.

3. Why does the professor mention seals and sea lions?
  (**A**) To point out that dolphin sleep behavior is not unique
  (**B**) To give an example of sleep behavior that has been well researched
  (**C**) To show that all aquatic mammals face difficulties sleeping
  (**D**) To show the similarities in brain wave patterns of all aquatic mammals

4. What have researchers concluded about human sleep by studying dolphins?
    (A) It is possible for the human brain to be half awake and half asleep.
    (B) Human and dolphin sleep is remarkably similar.
    (C) Sleep is more important for the brain than for the body.
    (D) Only one small area in the brain requires sleep.

Listen again to part of the lecture. Then answer question 5.

5. What does the professor imply when she says this?
    (A) Some aspects of dolphin sleep are easier to study than human sleep.
    (B) It is hard to know if a dolphin is asleep by looking at its behavior and physiology.
    (C) Researchers prefer to study dolphin communication.
    (D) Researchers have not made much progress studying dolphin sleep.

Listen again to part of the lecture. Then answer question 6.

6. What does the professor imply when she says this?
    (A) She wants to stress a point she made previously.
    (B) She regrets mentioning a subject that is not related to the topic.
    (C) Some students may have reached the wrong conclusion about her point.
    (D) Imitating dolphin sleep can be dangerous for humans.

READING

Read the passages and answer the reading comprehension questions. (Check the Answer Key on page 229.)

READING 1

Positive Illusions

1   Research into self-awareness consistently shows that most people think and speak highly of themselves. Time and again, subjects see positive traits as more self-descriptive than negative ones, they rate themselves more highly than they rate others, they rate themselves more highly than they are rated by others, they overestimate their contribution to team efforts, and they exaggerate their control over life events. It's not that we consciously flatter ourselves, either. The response is more like a mindless reflex. In fact, when subjects are busy or distracted as they make self-ratings, the judgments they come up with are quicker and even more favorable.

2   Most people also exhibit "unrealistic optimism," a tendency to predict a uniquely bright and rosy future for themselves. College students asked to predict their own future compared to that of their classmates believed, on average, that they were more likely to graduate higher in their class, get a better job, earn a higher salary, have a happier marriage, and bear a gifted child. They also believed that they were less likely to get fired, become depressed, become involved in a car accident, or suffer from a heart attack. Many other examples illustrate this point—as when voters predict that their favored candidate will prevail and sports fans bet on their favorite teams to win.

3   Psychologists used to agree that an accurate perception of reality is vital to mental health. More and more, however, this view is being challenged by research on positive illusions. Are these illusions a sign of well-being or symptoms of disorder?

4   In 1988 two psychologists reviewed the relevant research and noticed that people who are mildly depressed or low in self-esteem have less inflated and sometimes more realistic views of themselves than do others who are better adjusted. Their self-appraisals are more likely to match appraisals of them made by neutral others, they are less likely to exaggerate their control over uncontrollable events, and they make more balanced predictions about the future. Based on these results, psychologists arrived at the provocative conclusion that when it comes to the self, positive illusions—not accurate perceptions of reality—promote health and well-being. In their words, "these illusions help make each individual's world a warmer and more active and beneficent place in which to live." In fact, research involving people under stress—such as people with serious illnesses—shows that perceived control, optimism, and other positive beliefs are "health protective" psychological resources that help people cope with adversity.

5   Others are not so sure that eternal optimists are better off than hard realists. They argue that positive illusions can give rise to chronic patterns of self-destruction—as when people escape from self-awareness through the use of drugs and deny health-related problems until it's too late for treatment. In studies of interpersonal relations, people with inflated rather than realistic views of themselves were rated less favorably on certain dimensions by their own friends. In these studies, self-enhancing men were seen as assertive and ambitious, which are OK, but also as boastful, condescending, hostile, and inconsiderate. Self-enhancing women were seen as more hostile, more defensive and sensitive to criticism, more likely to overreact to minor setbacks, and less well liked by others. Consistent with these findings, other research shows that people filled with high self-esteem are more likely to lash out angrily in response to criticism, rejection, and other bruises to the ego. The result: People with inflated self-images may make a good first impression on others, but they are liked less and less as time wears on.

6   Realism or illusion, which orientation is more adaptive? As psychologists debate the short-term and long-term consequences of positive illusions, it's clear that there is no simple answer. For now, it seems that people who harbor positive illusions about themselves are likely to enjoy the benefits and achievements of high self-esteem but may suffer in their relations with others. So what are we to conclude? Is it possible that positive illusions motivate us to personal achievement but alienate us socially from others? Could it be that it's adaptive to see oneself in ways that are slightly inflated, but not too much? It will be interesting to see what researchers find in the years to come.

1. Paragraph 1 mentions all of the following as evidence that people think highly of themselves EXCEPT
  (**A**) People consider themselves to be better than others.
  (**B**) People think they have more control of their lives than they really do.
  (**C**) People think about themselves as often when they are busy as when they are not busy.
  (**D**) People believe that their participation on a team is more important than the participation of others.

2. In paragraph 2, the author provides a list of possible negative events in the future lives of college students as examples of
  (**A**) what happens when people have unrealistic optimism
  (**B**) situations that college students believe may face others but will not happen to them
  (**C**) situations that can occur when people lack confidence in themselves
  (**D**) how optimism about the future can help people deal with problems

3. In paragraph 2, the word *prevail* is closest in meaning to
  (**A**) impress
  (**B**) appear
  (**C**) accept
  (**D**) succeed

4. In paragraph 2, the author mentions *college students*, *voters*, and *sports fans* to support the point that
  (**A**) most people tend to be optimistic
  (**B**) certain people lose their optimism quickly
  (**C**) education plays a role in how people view the future
  (**D**) college students differ from people in the general population

5. In paragraph 3, the word *vital* is closest in meaning to
  (**A**) related
  (**B**) unusual
  (**C**) essential
  (**D**) familiar

6. Which of the following statements about mental health can be inferred from paragraph 3?
  (**A**) Many psychologists have challenged the idea that mental health is related to positive illusions.
  (**B**) Psychologists have only recently begun to consider positive illusions as symptoms of mental disorder.
  (**C**) Psychologists now agree that more mental health research is needed to learn how people can gain an accurate perception of reality.
  (**D**) Some psychologists now believe that people who lack a realistic self-perception may actually be mentally healthy.

7. In paragraph 4, the word **adversity** is closest in meaning to
   (**A**) confidence
   (**B**) misfortune
   (**C**) opportunity
   (**D**) confusion

8. The word **Others** in paragraph 5 refers to
   (**A**) psychologists
   (**B**) people under stress
   (**C**) eternal optimists
   (**D**) hard realists

9. The word **favorably** in paragraph 5 is closest in meaning to
   (**A**) frequently
   (**B**) positively
   (**C**) clearly
   (**D**) carefully

10. According to paragraph 5, what is the relationship between positive illusions and the way men and women are viewed in social situations?
    (**A**) Both men and women with unrealistic views of themselves are often disliked by others and seen as having negative characteristics.
    (**B**) Men who have positive illusions about themselves are considered less socially accepted than women with the same positive illusions about themselves.
    (**C**) Women with positive illusions are seen as likely to handle minor setbacks in social situations better than men are.
    (**D**) It is believed that men with positive illusions about themselves show more anger in social situations than women with positive illusions do.

11. In what ways are paragraphs 4 and 5 related to each other?
    (**A**) Paragraph 4 describes the characteristics of eternal optimists, and paragraph 5 describes the characteristics of hard realists.
    (**B**) Paragraph 4 introduces a concept about positive illusions, and paragraph 5 provides specific examples.
    (**C**) Paragraph 4 indicates an older view of positive illusions, and paragraph 5 provides a more recent understanding of positive illusions.
    (**D**) Paragraph 4 shows the advantages of positive illusions, and paragraph 5 shows the disadvantages of positive illusions.

12. Which of the sentences on the next page best expresses the essential information in the following sentence from the passage? Incorrect choices change the meaning in important ways or leave out essential information.

    For now, it seems that people who harbor positive illusions about themselves are likely to enjoy the benefits and achievements of high self-esteem but may suffer in their relations with others.

(**A**) In modern times, people who have positive illusions often suffer more than people with realistic views about themselves.

(**B**) The current thinking is that high self-esteem can be positive in some ways but a disadvantage in social interactions.

(**C**) It only appears that there are benefits to high self-esteem, whereas in reality positive illusions create problems.

(**D**) People who lack self-esteem often believe that those with positive illusions now suffer in their relationships.

13. Look at the four squares ☐ that indicate where the following sentence could be added to the selection from the passage. Where would the sentence best fit in the selection below?

The pattern that clearly emerged from this study was that the students typically rated themselves above average for positive events and below average for negative events.

Most people also exhibit "unrealistic optimism," a tendency to predict a uniquely bright and rosy future for themselves. **A** College students asked to predict their own future compared to that of their classmates believed, on average, that they were more likely to graduate higher in their class, get a better job, earn a higher salary, have a happier marriage, and bear a gifted child. **B** They also believed that they were less likely to get fired, become depressed, become involved in a car accident, or suffer from a heart attack. **C** Many other examples illustrate this point—as when voters predict that their favored candidate will prevail and sports fans bet on their favorite teams to win. **D**

14. Read the first sentence of a summary of the passage. Then complete the summary by circling the THREE answer choices that express the most important ideas in the passage. Some sentences do not belong in the summary because they express ideas that are not presented in the passage or are minor ideas in the passage.

Psychologists who study self-awareness have found that most people have a positive image of themselves.

(**A**) People tend to be optimistic about their future and to believe they will be successful.

(**B**) College students are often more realistic about what their lives will be like than other people are.

(**C**) Many psychologists who once believed that completely realistic views of ourselves are important for mental health now believe that this is not necessarily true.

(**D**) The research done by psychologists in 1988 showed that the way others see us can make us feel mildly depressed or contribute to our low self-esteem.

(**E**) Research shows that men are more likely to suffer from health-related problems and to become angry due to lower self-esteem than women are.

(**F**) Unrealistic optimism can benefit health, well-being, and the ability to handle difficulties, but it may also damage social relations and lead people to act in self-destructive ways.

READING 2

What Is an Earthquake?

1   An earthquake is the vibration of Earth produced by the rapid release of energy. Most often, earthquakes are caused by slippage along a fault in Earth's crust. The energy released radiates in all directions from it source, called the focus, in the form of waves. These waves are analogous to those produced when a stone is dropped into a calm pond. Just as the impact of the stone sets water waves in motion, an earthquake generates seismic waves that radiate throughout Earth. Even though the energy dissipates rapidly with increasing distance from the focus, sensitive instruments located around the world record the event. Over 30,000 earthquakes that are strong enough to be felt occur worldwide annually. Fortunately, most are minor tremors and do very little damage. Generally, only about 75 significant earthquakes take place each year, and many of these occur in remote regions. However, occasionally a large earthquake occurs near a large population center.

2   The tremendous energy released by atomic explosions or by volcanic eruptions can produce an earthquake, but these events are relatively weak and infrequent. What mechanism produces a destructive earthquake? Ample evidence exists that Earth is not a static planet. We know that Earth's crust has been uplifted at times, because we have found numerous ancient wave-cut benches many meters above the level of the highest tides. Other regions exhibit evidence of extensive subsidence. In addition, we also have evidence that indicates horizontal movement. These movements are usually associated with large fractures in Earth's crust called faults. Typically, earthquakes occur along preexisting faults that formed in the distant past along zones of weakness in Earth's crust. Some are very large and can generate major earthquakes. One example is the San Andreas Fault that separates two great sections of Earth's lithosphere: the North American plate and the Pacific plate. It trends in a northwesterly direction for nearly 1,300 kilometers through much of western California.

3   Other faults are small and produce only minor and infrequent earthquakes. However, the vast majority of faults are inactive and do not generate earthquakes at all. Nevertheless, even faults that have been inactive for years can rupture again if the stresses acting on the region increase sufficiently. In addition, most faults are not perfectly straight or continuous; instead, they consist of numerous branches and smaller fractures that display kinks and offsets. The San Andreas Fault is actually a system that consists of several large faults and innumerable small fractures. Most of the motion along faults can be satisfactorily explained by the plate tectonics theory, which states that large slabs of Earth's lithosphere are in continual slow motion. These mobile plates interact with neighboring plates, straining and deforming the rocks at their margins. In fact, it is along faults associated with plate boundaries that most earthquakes occur. Furthermore, earthquakes are repetitive: As soon as one is over, the continuous motion of the plates adds strain to the rocks until they fail again.

4   The actual mechanism of earthquake generation eluded geologists until H. F. Reid conducted a study following the great 1906 San Francisco earthquake. This enormous earthquake was accompanied by horizontal surface displacements of several meters along the northern portion of the San Andreas Fault. Field investigations determined that during this single earthquake, the Pacific plate lurched as much as 4.7 meters northward past the adjacent North American plate. The mechanism for earthquake formation that Reid deduced from this information is called elastic rebound. First there is an existing fault, or break in the rock. Then tectonic forces ever so slowly deform the crustal rocks on both sides of the fault. Under these conditions, rocks bend and store elastic energy, much like a wooden stick does if bent. Eventually, the frictional resistance holding the rocks in place is overcome. As slippage occurs at the weakest point, the focus, displacement will exert stress farther along the fault, where additional slippage will occur until most of the built-up strain is released. This slippage allows the deformed rock to "snap back." The vibrations known as an earthquake occur as the rock elastically returns to its original shape. The springing back of the rock was termed "elastic rebound" by Reid, because the rock behaves elastically, much like a stretched rubber band does when it is released.

1. Why does the author mention ***a stone dropped in a calm pond*** in paragraph 1?
   (**A**) To prove that seismic waves can travel through water
   (**B**) To explain why most earthquakes are relatively small
   (**C**) To illustrate how an earthquake differs from intense wave activity
   (**D**) To help the reader visualize how energy spreads out from the focus of an earthquake

2. The word ***remote*** in paragraph 1 is closest in meaning to
   (**A**) isolated
   (**B**) foreign
   (**C**) mountainous
   (**D**) sheltered

3. Which of the sentences below best expresses the essential information in the following sentence from the passage? Incorrect choices change the meaning in important ways or leave out essential information.

   Even though the energy dissipates rapidly with increasing distance from the focus, sensitive instruments located around the world record the event.

   (**A**) The energy released by an earthquake disappears quickly, though it can travel around the world.
   (**B**) The focus of an earthquake is sensitive to movement, and the released energy can be detected around the world.
   (**C**) The instruments that detect earthquakes are sensitive enough to detect small seismic waves far away from the earthquake's focus.
   (**D**) Instruments that can sense the energy released in an earthquake are located around the world.

4. According to paragraph 2, which of the following best describes the origin of earthquakes?
   (**A**) They are produced by a shrinking of Earth's crust.
   (**B**) They may begin with cracks in Earth that formed long ago.
   (**C**) They can originate in any region of Earth.
   (**D**) They usually begin in the thickest part of Earth's crust.

5. The highlighted word *It* in paragraph 2 refers to
   (**A**) the Pacific plate
   (**B**) the North American plate
   (**C**) Earth's lithosphere
   (**D**) the San Andreas Fault

6. The word *rupture* in paragraph 3 is closest in meaning to
   (**A**) vibrate
   (**B**) return
   (**C**) disappear
   (**D**) break

7. The word *kinks* in paragraph 3 is closest in meaning to
   (**A**) twists
   (**B**) cracks
   (**C**) weaknesses
   (**D**) rocks

8. It can be inferred from paragraphs 2 and 3 that all of the following are true of the relationship between volcanic eruptions and earthquakes EXCEPT
   (**A**) Both events occur at unpredictable intervals.
   (**B**) Volcanic eruptions can sometimes cause earthquakes.
   (**C**) A large earthquake can set off a volcanic eruption in a nearby mountain.
   (**D**) Earthquakes usually occur on faults, but volcanoes do not.

9. Why does the author mention H. F. Reid in paragraph 4?
   (**A**) He was a famous geologist in the early 1900s.
   (**B**) He was the first person to propose the theory of elastic rebound.
   (**C**) He was in San Francisco at the time of the 1906 earthquake.
   (**D**) He was one of the first people to participate in geological fieldwork.

10. What can be inferred from paragraph 4 about the 1906 San Francisco earthquake?
    (**A**) It affected all portions of the San Andreas Fault.
    (**B**) It affected water levels in the Pacific Ocean.
    (**C**) It was unusually large.
    (**D**) Geologists have not yet determined what caused it to occur.

11. The word *lurched* in paragraph 4 is closest in meaning to
    (**A**) moved suddenly
    (**B**) changed direction
    (**C**) became deeper
    (**D**) grew wider

12. According to the passage, what is the significance of the focus of an earthquake?
   (**A**) Its size determines the strength of an earthquake.
   (**B**) It is the central point from which seismic waves originate.
   (**C**) It is usually located deep in the lithosphere.
   (**D**) It represents the end result of tectonic forces.

13. Look at the four squares ☐ that indicate where the following sentence could be added to the selection from the passage. Where would the sentence best fit in the selection below?

When this happens, an earthquake is among the most destructive natural forces on Earth.

Over 30,000 earthquakes that are strong enough to be felt occur worldwide annually. **A** Fortunately, most are minor tremors and do very little damage. **B** Generally, only about 75 significant earthquakes take place each year, and many of these occur in remote regions. **C** However, occasionally a large earthquake occurs near a large population center. **D**

14. Read the first sentence of a summary of the passage. Then complete the summary by circling the THREE answer choices that express the most important ideas in the passage. Some sentences do not belong in the summary because they express ideas that are not presented in the passage or are minor ideas in the passage.

Earthquakes are natural events that occur all over the world every year.

   (**A**) Most earthquakes do not cause much damage.
   (**B**) Earthquakes are produced by a release of energy.
   (**C**) Volcanic eruptions can sometimes produce earthquakes.
   (**D**) The San Andreas fault is quite small in comparison to other faults.
   (**E**) Earthquakes often occur on faults.
   (**F**) The type of rock deformation called elastic rebound causes most earthquakes.

WRITING

For this task, you will read a passage about an academic topic and you will listen to a lecture about the same topic. Then you will write a response to a question that asks you about the relationship between the lecture you heard and the reading passage. You should allow 3 minutes to read the passage. Then listen to the lecture. Then allow 20 minutes to plan and write your response.

INTEGRATED WRITING TASK 1

READING

Read the passage.

Changes in Charitable Giving

1   Donating part of one's income to public causes, known as charitable giving, used to be a common practice. But, in the United States charitable giving has declined substantially in recent years, and, for several reasons, it is unlikely to increase in the future.

2   One reason that charitable giving has fallen is simply that there is less need for charitable giving, because the United States government now provides most of the important public services. The government assumes much of the responsibility for feeding the poor, providing health care, and taking care of the victims of natural disasters—functions that charities used to perform. These government institutions of social welfare are permanent, and so the diminished need for private charitable giving will also be permanent.

3   Another reason people are, and will be, giving less to charities is that in the past few years there have been highly publicized disclosures that the managers of some prominent national charities were receiving huge salaries and other benefits as large or larger than salaries of heads of major for-profit corporations. These salaries and expenses for travel, fancy offices, and advertising significantly reduced the percentage of donated money that went to charitable purposes. Naturally people have been turned off by these excesses and inefficiencies.

4   Finally, beyond the shortcomings of legitimate charities, there has been an increasing number of fraudulent solicitations by organizations or individuals who merely pose as charities. As a result, people are now becoming skeptical even about what are in fact legitimate appeals for support. So potential donors are starting to give less and give less frequently. And since the incidence of charity fraud seems to be increasing, we can expect further declines in charitable giving as people become more concerned that they are being taken advantage of.

LISTENING

Now listen to part of a lecture on the topic you just read about.

WRITING

Summarize the points made in the lecture, being sure to specifically explain how they cast doubt on points made in the reading passage.

INTEGRATED WRITING TASK 2

READING

Read the passage.

School-year Vacations

1   It used to be that parents took their children on vacation during the summer, when school was out of session. But today, much more often than in the past, many parents take their children on vacation during the school year. Although these children are away from school, sometimes for several weeks, traveling itself serves a valuable educational function.

2   The most important educational benefit of taking children on vacation is that traveling exposes children to new places and cultures. It is good for children to read about distant countries, but it is even better to take them there. What students learn by meeting the people and absorbing the culture of these places is something they could not learn in their classrooms.

3   Moreover, the benefits to the children who have been away from the classroom for several weeks traveling continue after they have returned to their classes. Students who are in school every day of the school year can easily lose enthusiasm for their studies. But students invigorated by time away return with heightened excitement.

4   The trend of students taking vacations during the school year also has benefits for teachers. When these students return to school, their knowledge and enthusiasm contribute positively to the entire class. Teachers can ask the children to share stories of their travels with their peers and can incorporate what they have learned from traveling into writing and reading projects. This makes lesson development easier for teachers because the returning students' experiences provide a ready basis for classroom discussions and projects.

LISTENING

Now listen to part of a lecture on the topic you just read about.

WRITING

Summarize the points made in the lecture, being sure to specifically explain how they oppose points made in the reading passage.

SPEAKING

INTEGRATED SPEAKING TASK 1

You will read a short passage and then listen to a conversation on the same topic. You will then be asked a question about them. After you hear the question, you should take 30 seconds to prepare your response and then speak for 60 seconds.

READING

The administration of Centerville University has announced a new policy. Read the following announcement in the university newspaper about the policy. You will have 45 seconds to read the announcement. Begin reading now.

The university administration has announced a new, campus-wide policy on cell phones. The policy states that all students must turn off their cell phones before entering the classroom or face disciplinary action. The decision to implement this policy was based on an increasing number of complaints from both faculty and students about the disruption cell phones cause in the classroom. The disciplinary actions are as follows: If students' phones ring in class, they may be asked to leave. Upon repeated offenses, a faculty member may penalize students by lowering their class grade.

LISTENING

CD2 TRACK 42

Now listen to a conversation on the same topic.

SPEAKING

Speak on the following topic.

The woman expresses her opinion of the administration's new policy. Explain what the university plans to do. Then explain why the woman agrees or disagrees with the policy.

INTEGRATED SPEAKING TASK 2

Listen to part of this lecture. You will then answer a question about it. You may take notes as you listen. After you hear the question, take 20 seconds to prepare your response, then speak for 60 seconds. (Check the Answer Key on page 229.)

LISTENING

Now listen to part of a lecture in an economics class.

SPEAKING

Speak on the following topic.

Explain what is meant by mass customization. Then explain how the examples presented in the lecture illustrate this concept.

Audioscript

LISTENING

PAGE 206, CONVERSATION 1

Student: Professor …

Professor: Yes, Mark.

S: About the assignment … can I ask a question?

P: Sure. I've got some time before my next class. What can I help you with?

S: Well, as I understand it, you want us to find examples of subjectivity, er … um … reporters putting their own opinions in news stories.

P: Yes, exactly.

S: Well, I was thinking about it, and it's just that the newspapers I read seem so straightforward, you know, just the facts, and I'm not sure how to find the reporters' opinions in there.

P: OK, well … I guess you read the local newspaper?

S: And sometimes national newspapers, but I don't read the, y'know, the tabloids. That's just gossip and sports.

P: The first thing I can tell you is to start to read more critically. Instead of reading the paper just to get the news, pay attention to the words reporters use. Ask yourself, "Why did the reporter use this specific word, this phrase?"

S: OK, I guess …

P: For example, you know every state has two senators, and when a politician is called a *junior* senator, that just means that the other senator from the same state has been in office longer. It's usually very neutral. But say you're reading a news story and you read the word *junior* again and again. What else does *junior* mean?

S: Well, it sounds like … y'know, junior, like a little kid—like, inexperienced and kind of naive.

P: A little kid! Exactly! Does the reporter want you to think *little kid* every time you read that politician's name? Now, for most stories, why is it at all important to know how long a senator has been serving? *Unless* you're trying to question that senator's experience and qualifications …

S: OK, I'm starting to see.…

P: That's what I mean by reading critically and paying close attention to the words. Not just the dictionary meaning, but the impression that you get—that the reporter wants you to get—from the words. And another thing is to read the same newspaper over a few days or weeks. Let me give you an example from the last election. There was a poll taken, and one candidate had a very slim lead, so the headline was "Election Race Too Close to Call." But a week later the situation had reversed, and the second candidate had a slim lead. But this time the headline said that the second candidate was "Surging into the Lead."

S: But it was the same slim lead?

P: Yes, exactly.

S: So the paper didn't … deal with them in the same way.

P: Not at all. But you really have to look at a newspaper over a period of time to notice.

S: OK, thanks. I think I get it now. This isn't going to be easy, but it should be pretty interesting.

Listen again to part of the conversation. Then answer question 5.

S: Well, it sounds like … y'know, junior, like a little kid—like, inexperienced and kind of naive.

P: A little kid! Exactly! Does the reporter want you to think *little kid* every time you read that politician's name?

5. Why does the professor ask this?

"Does the reporter want you to think *little kid* every time you read that politician's name?"?

PAGE 207, CONVERSATION 2

Student: I want to apologize for missing work on Friday. I hope you didn't have too much trouble finding a replacement.

Manager: I'm just glad you're back at work now. And there's no need to apologize. I understand emergencies happen. Is everything OK with your family?

S: Oh yeah, There wasn't any real emergency. It's not like they were in any danger or anything. It's just that, well, they live in Florida and I guess you know hurricane season is coming up.…

M: That usually starts in May, right?

S: Yeah. So at this time of year … I don't know if I told you … my father has a business renting out boats to fisherman, and he used to stay open year-round. But this year he decided to close for a few months. So there's a lot of work to do. He's got to get all the boats out of the water and into this indoor storage building. I thought I ought to go and help him.

M: But you never made it?

S: Well, I tried. I spent all day Friday and most of Saturday at the airport. My flight was canceled and then rescheduled, and that one was canceled and then rescheduled again. I wound up sleeping on the floor in the airport. I couldn't get a flight.

M: Well, we did have some terrible weather around here.…

S: I know, all the flights were canceled.

M: So, was he able to do all that work by himself?

S: Well, my mother was able to drive the car … er, the trailer to pull the boats. And one of the neighbors was able to help too.

M: That's good, I mean it's good that everything's OK. So, if you're ready to get back to work … I don't know if you heard, but we had quite an interesting weekend here.

S: What happened?

M: Well, as you know, we had quite a bit of rain and wind here too—not anything like a hurricane, but it certainly was wet.

S: I know. I couldn't even go outside the terminal at the airport.

M: So what happened was … we had a flood in the storage room.

S: Oh …

M: Now we've got to get an inventory of everything that's been damaged. I know that there were a lot of textbooks, notebooks, probably some copy paper … everything that was on the lower shelves in there … so a lot of stuff got wet.

S: OK …

M: So anything that got even a little wet, put it aside and make a list—book, title, author, and especially the price—that's important.

S: OK, I guess I'll get started. You said there's lots of stuff?

M: I'm sure it'll take at least a couple hours. And come back and see me when you're finished.

Listen again to part of the conversation. Then answer question 5.

M: That's good, I mean it's good that everything's OK. So, if you're ready to get back to work … I don't know if you heard, but we had quite an interesting weekend here.

5. Why does the manager of the bookstore say this?

"So, if you're ready to get back to work …"

PAGE 208, LECTURE 1

Professor: Over the course of this semester, I'm sure you've encountered a number of obstacles that you were certainly not used to dealing with before you entered college this school year. So, that's what I want us to talk about today—some of the challenges you've faced as first-year college students. Now, in case you're wondering, I want to talk about challenges because it's important to see that you're not alone in your first-year experiences. Every year, first-year students across the country go through some of the same things you do, and that's the point of this class, to help you deal with the college experience. And I think the best way to deal with it is to have a dialogue about your experiences as a first-year student—to talk about them so that you can help each other—you know, like, what's been challenging, and how have you dealt with it? OK, so, who wants to go first? Any volunteers?

Um … OK … no volunteers? How about this, why don't I start by telling you about one of the challenges I faced as a first-year college student? Let's see … well, I remember the first time I'd realized how unprepared I was for college. I showed up my first week of classes without books for any of the classes. …

Student 1: But how is that, Professor Hill? I mean, didn't they have a university bookstore at your school so that you could buy the books?

P: Well, yes, Chris, they did. But that wasn't the problem. You see, I was unaware of the fact that I needed to go to the bookstore to buy the books. I'd thought just by showing up to class with my backpack in hand and all of the school supplies I needed, I was ready. I didn't know I was required to use the names of the courses to help find the necessary books to purchase from the university bookstore. I didn't know anything about what to do, and my parents certainly didn't know because they had never been to college either.

Student 2: Oh wait, you mean you were an F-gen too? A, um, first-generation college student?

P: Why, yes. Are you saying that you are as well, Nora?

S2: Um well, yes, I am. My parents and their parents have never gone to college, and none of my brothers or sisters have either. So, I'm kind of in the same situation you were in—basically unprepared to succeed in college. I had my books for my classes, but I had other problems. Like, right now, I live at home, and this year has been really hard for me because I have no choice but to live there. My family couldn't afford the cost of me living in the university dorms, here on campus, so I've had to stay at home. I work part-time to help pay for school, but I'm also working to save up enough money to get an apartment near campus for next year.

I really don't want to have to live at home during my next year of school.

S1: Hey, well, it couldn't be that bad. Seems like you're doing really well in all your classes. Why would you want to leave home? I mean, if my parents lived closer, I would definitely commute from home. I'd be saving a lot of money that way.

S2: You're right. I am saving a ton of money, but you try studying in a place where your family keeps interrupting you because they don't understand how hard it is to do college work. The interruptions by my younger brother … who can study like that? Having a part-time job off campus doesn't help either. My boss keeps asking me to work late hours when I have class the next morning.

P: You know, Nora, everything you've just talked about—difficulties with balancing school, home, and work—are all common challenges that first-generation college students often face. Your family may support you, but because they have never gone through the college experience, they can only understand so much. Oftentimes, they haven't ever seen a family member so focused on life at college, a life separate from their own. It happens to many first-generation college students. So, believe me, I'm sure I'm not the only one who can relate to what you're going through. So now the question is … how can one effectively deal with the challenges of being a first-generation college student? Any thoughts?

S1: Well, I think talking about our experiences in class, like this, is really helpful.

S2: I agree. And what's great is that last month I found talking to one of the advisors at the university academic support office to be really helpful as well.

P: Right. Talking with fellow students and getting support from the university is definitely a start.

Listen again to part of the discussion. Then answer question 6.

P: OK, so, who wants to go first? Any volunteers?
Um … okay … no volunteers? How about this, why don't I start by telling you about one of the challenges I faced as a first-year college student?

6. Why does the professor ask this?

"Why don't I start by telling you about one of the challenges I faced as a first-year college student?"

PAGE 209, LECTURE 2

P: We've discussed some dolphin behaviors that are very well understood, like feeding and reproducing, and we talked a bit about dolphin communication, which isn't as well understood, but there's a lot of research going on in that area. So before we end for the day, let's look at one more behavior that I find really interesting, and that's how dolphins sleep.

Now let me first say that there are a lot of things we don't know about human sleep, and dolphin sleep is, I think, even more complicated and certainly harder to study, so you can imagine that the research is far from complete. But let's first look at sleep in general and then dolphin sleep.

OK, there are two ways we distinguish sleep from wakefulness—either by looking at behavior or by looking at physiology. And by physiology, I mean we usually look at electrical changes in the brain wave pattern and that's, well, for humans at least, it's easy to measure those changes. Umm … and looking at behavior, we say that an animal has reduced responsiveness to external stimulation. So, think of your own sleep—you're probably not responsive to things like voices unless they're very loud. And except for a few really uncommon conditions like sleepwalking, a sleeping person is inactive. OK, so if you want to know if a person or an animal is asleep, look at those two things: physiology and behavior.

But if you look at only those two things in a dolphin ... well, you're not going to get very far.

Let's start with brain wave patterns. As you know, human brains—and dolphin brains too, they're actually very similar—have two hemispheres ... two sides. We often talk about the right brain and the left brain. So when humans sleep, well, looking at the brain waves, you can tell that both halves of the brain are sleeping. There are distinctive sleep brain wave patterns. But with dolphins, what actually happens is one half of the brain stays awake and the other sleeps. And again you can measure this—measure the electrical activity in each half of the dolphin's brain. And throughout the night, or the time the dolphin's asleep, about every hour or so, the sides switch. The left side is awake and the right side sleeps, and then vice versa.

And the dolphins' behavior while half of its brain is asleep? Well, dolphins in a group will swim in a small circle. They won't vocalize, er ... communicate ... no clicks and whistles. They'll have one eye open and one closed. That's right, they'll sleep with one eye open. And periodically they'll rise to the surface to breathe.

So what's the advantage of having half a brain awake and half asleep? Well for starters, dolphins have to maintain some motor activity—they've got to get to the surface to breathe, and they need brain activity to tell them to do it. The other thing is with one eye open and half their brain awake, dolphins can continue to monitor their environment. Now, it's unclear whether they mainly want to watch for predators or keep in contact with the other members of their group, but again, they need part of their brain awake to do it.

And I should mention it's not just dolphins. There are a few other, uhh, aquatic mammals. Umm ... seals and sea lions. Some species of seals and sea lions have this same ability to have half their brain awake and half asleep. So they'll sleep just like dolphins. But just *some* species. Other species of seals sleep much as humans do. The entire brain sleeps. For these seals, well, what happens is they'll hold their breath for a few minutes, sleep, wake up, rise to the surface, breathe, hold their breath, fall asleep, wake up, rise to the surface, breathe, and continue that pattern throughout the night.

We're almost out of time for the day, but let me mention one more thing. We may be able to learn something about human sleep by looking at dolphin sleep. And let me say I'm not going to suggest that humans train themselves to sleep like dolphins. That's not where this is going. But what we are learning from experiments with dolphins shows that it's the brain, not the body, that needs sleep. So sleep serves a primary function for the brain, and it may be that the need for sleep is regulated locally within small portions of each side of the brain.

That's going to be it for today. Make sure to read the next chapter before Monday's class. See you then.

Listen again to part of the lecture. Then answer question 5.

OK, so if you want to know if a person or an animal is asleep, look at those two things: physiology and behavior.

But if you look at only those two things in a dolphin ... well, you're not going to get very far.

5. What does the professor imply when she says this?

"But if you look at only those two things in a dolphin ... well, you're not going to get very far"

Listen again to part of the lecture. Then answer question 6.

We may be able to learn something about human sleep by looking at dolphin sleep. And let me say I'm not going to suggest that humans train themselves to sleep like dolphins. That's not where this is going.

6. What does the professor imply when she says this?

"And let me say I'm not going to suggest that humans train themselves to sleep like dolphins. That's not where this is going."

WRITING

INTEGRATED WRITING TASK 1

PAGE 220, LISTENING

Professor: There's no doubt that giving to charities has declined in recent years, but there are good reasons to think it'll soon begin to go up.

Consider, for example, the fact that the number of elderly and retired people in our society keeps growing. Right now, elderly citizens who can't afford health care often rely on government programs to pay for it. But as the elderly population grows, government programs probably won't be able to cover the health care of those who need help. When there's a need for charitable assistance, Americans respond to that need. And since the need will be increasing, we should expect to see charitable giving rise accordingly.

There's another reason to be optimistic about the future of charitable giving. The disclosures of waste and bad management at major charities, and people's anger at this waste, are producing significant reforms. Overpaid managers have been forced to resign by the bad publicity. Charities are reducing their expenses and are now subject to closer public scrutiny. As a result, people are regaining confidence that the money they donate will support the causes they care about.

People's reaction to charity fraud is also evolving. In the short run, people don't want to donate because they're concerned with whether charities are honest. But in the long run, such skepticism makes people careful, not stingy. For example, many people now refuse to give money when they're asked to do so over the telephone. They insist on receiving proof and documentation before they donate. Just as people learn how to be careful consumers, most people are acquiring the skills needed to guard against charity fraud without stopping their support for worthwhile causes.

INTEGRATED WRITING TASK 2

PAGE 221, LISTENING

Professor: Now, let's consider how taking children on vacation when school is in session impacts their education. I believe the impact on children and their teachers can be quite negative.

While students have been traveling, their fellow students have been working. What do you think happens when they return to school? Well, they have to spend a lot of time "playing catch-up," you know, doing work that fellow students have already done. It's one thing to miss a day or two of school, but many parents take their children on vacation for weeks on end, and it's very difficult for any child to make up that much missed time. So, the missed learning has to be weighed against the benefits of traveling and learning about other cultures. On balance, what is lost is greater than what is gained.

When children come back to class after a long trip, they're excited about their recent adventures. Sounds good, but this enthusiasm can have a downside. Their excitement can make it difficult for them to fit back into the routine of the school day. School seems a little boring to them, so they're not attentive to their studies, and their restlessness can distract other students.

When a student is distracted or has to catch up on missed work, there's a negative effect on the teacher too. Teachers have lesson plans that detail, day by day, what they are going to teach. When a student is absent from the classroom, this interferes with a teacher's plan for that student. And if teachers spend time helping a few students catch up, they have less time for other students … so they suffer too.

SPEAKING

INTEGRATED SPEAKING TASK 1

PAGE 222, LISTENING

Student 1: I'm so glad the administration's finally doing something about this.

Student 2: Really? I mean, I didn't think it was a big enough problem to warrant an official policy.

S1: Are you kidding? At least once a week, I hear some kind of electronic symphony or some other ringing melody in the middle of a lecture. And, it's not just that. Some people even answer their phones and have conversations … in class … unbelievable! Who can concentrate with all that noise?! It gets worse every semester.

S2: The punishment seems pretty harsh though.

S1: Oh, that's what I like about it the most. If that part weren't in there, people wouldn't take it seriously. The problem's serious … and the punishment should be too. If they don't take a firm stand now, it's just going to keep getting worse.

S2: Yeah, I guess you're right. Maybe this policy is for the best.

INTEGRATED SPEAKING TASK 2

PAGE 223, LISTENING

Professor: Mass customization means using the techniques of assembly-line production to manufacture customized products—products that are personalized to meet the specific needs and desires of individual buyers. Mass customization is advantageous for both manufacturers and consumers. Because these products are made on assembly lines, which are quite efficient, manufacturers can keep production costs low. And because customers who buy these products pay only for the features they want and need, they can control the price too.

Here's an example. Suppose you want to buy a car. Well, you can go to the manufacturer's Internet Web site and select the model of car you want, and then choose the options you want. Do you want two doors or four doors? You choose. Do you want cloth seats or leather seats? Well, leather seats are pretty expensive, and maybe you don't want to spend the money. So you choose cloth seats. You specify your color, the size of engine—you can make dozens of choices. You get exactly the car you want, and you're not paying for options you don't want. And…because your car is being made on the assembly line, the production costs are reasonable. That's good both for the manufacturer and for you.

Mass customization also happens today in the shoe industry. Mostly for athletic shoes. Some manufacturers have Web sites where customers can order not just their size and the style they want but they can also select the fabric, and the color and…. They can make the top of the shoe red and the bottom yellow—or purple or green if that's what they want. The customers control the options, so they get just what they want at the price they can afford. And it's still relatively cheap for the manufacturer, because the shoes are being made on an assembly line.

Answer Key

LISTENING

Conversation 1

1. A	**3.** A	**5.** D
2. C	**4.** B	

Conversation 2

1. A, C	**3.** B	**5.** A
2. C	**4.** B	

Lecture 1

1. C
2. D
3. C
4. A
5. B, C
6. A

Lecture 2

1. C	**3.** A	**5.** B
2. A, B	**4.** C	**6.** C

READING

Reading 1

1. C	**5.** C	**9.** B	**13.** C
2. B	**6.** D	**10.** A	**14.** A, C, F
3. D	**7.** B	**11.** D	
4. A	**8.** A	**12.** B	

Reading 2

1. D
2. A
3. C
4. B
5. D
6. D
7. A
8. C
9. B
10. C
11. A
12. B
13. D
14. B, E, and F

WRITING

Integrated Writing Task 1

<u>Key points</u>

Points made in the lecture counter claims made by points of the reading passage.

LECTURE POINT	READING PASSAGE POINT
Charitable giving will probably rise in the future as the growing costs of public services create the need for private funding.	Charitable giving will not rise because the government has replaced charities.
Anger at the disclosures of mismanagement at charities has led to reforms that are giving donors more confidence their money will be properly used.	Disclosures of mismanagement at charities will lead to a permanent decline in charitable giving.
People are learning how to avoid giving to fraudulent charities.	People will react to charity fraud by not giving to any charity, honest or not.

Integrated Writing Task 2

<u>Key points</u>

Points made in the lecture counter claims made by points of the reading passage.

LECTURE POINT	READING PASSAGE POINT
The disadvantages of needing to catch up on schoolwork outweigh the benefits of learning about other cultures firsthand.	Learning from visiting other places and cultures cannot be duplicated in a classroom.
The excitement that returning students bring to the classroom can distract them and other students from classroom studies.	Students who have not been away become bored, so the enthusiasm of students returning from travels is an educational benefit for the whole class.
Returning students disrupt a teacher's teaching plan for the class because a teacher needs to spend time with students who have missed work.	It is easy and useful for teachers to incorporate the vacation experiences of returning students into their classroom teaching.

SPEAKING

Integrated Speaking Task 1

Key points

1. The university plans to penalize students who do not turn off their cell phones before entering classrooms (or whose cells phones ring during class time).

2. The woman agrees with the plan because:
   - She cannot concentrate on the lecture when cell phones ring and people hold conversations in class.
   - She thinks strict punishment (such as asking people to leave class or lowering their grades) is the only way students will take the policy seriously.

Integrated Speaking Task 2

Key points

1. Mass customization uses assembly-line production techniques to make personalized products.

2. Mass customization benefits both manufacturers and consumers:
   - Production costs are low because making products on assembly lines is efficient. Both cars and shoes are manufactured on efficient assembly lines.
   - Customers can select the options they want or need. In car manufacturing, the options might include the number of doors, cloth or leather seats, and color. In shoe manufacturing, the options might include fabric, color, style, and size.
   - Customers control costs because they pay only for the options they choose.

Use the TOEFL iBT Scoring Rubrics on the following pages to assess responses to Integrated and Independent Tasks. For more detailed information and explanation of these rubrics, see the *NorthStar: Building Skills for the TOEFL iBT Teacher's Manual.*

TOEFL® iBT Test—Integrated Writing Rubrics

Score	Task Description
5	A response at this level successfully selects the important information from the lecture and coherently and accurately presents this information in relation to the relevant information presented in the reading. The response is well organized, and occasional language errors that are present do not result in inaccurate or imprecise presentation of content or connections.
4	A response at this level is generally good in selecting the important information from the lecture and in coherently and accurately presenting this information in relation to the relevant information in the reading, but it may have minor omission, inaccuracy, vagueness, or imprecision of some content from the lecture or in connection to points made in the reading. A response is also scored at this level if it has more frequent or noticeable minor language errors, as long as such usage and grammatical structures do not result in anything more than an occasional lapse of clarity or in the connection of ideas.
3	A response at this level contains some important information from the lecture and conveys some relevant connection to the reading, but it is marked by one or more of the following: • Although the overall response is definitely oriented to the task, it conveys only vague, global, unclear, or somewhat imprecise connection of the points made in the lecture to points made in the reading. • The response may omit one major key point made in the lecture. • Some key points made in the lecture or the reading, or connections between the two, may be incomplete, inaccurate, or imprecise. • Errors of usage and/or grammar may be more frequent or may result in noticeably vague expressions or obscured meanings in conveying ideas and connections.
2	A response at this level contains some relevant information from the lecture, but is marked by significant language difficulties or by significant omission or inaccuracy of important ideas from the lecture or in the connections between the lecture and the reading; a response at this level is marked by one or more of the following: • The response significantly misrepresents or completely omits the overall connection between the lecture and the reading. • The response significantly omits or significantly misrepresents important points made in the lecture. • The response contains language errors or expressions that largely obscure connections or meaning at key junctures, or that would likely obscure understanding of key ideas for a reader not already familiar with the reading and the lecture.
1	A response at this level is marked by one or more of the following: • The response provides little or no meaningful or relevant coherent content from the lecture. • The language level of the response is so low that it is difficult to derive meaning.
0	A response at this level merely copies sentences from the reading, rejects the topic or is otherwise not connected to the topic, is written in a foreign language, consists of keystroke characters, or is blank.

TOEFL® iBT Test—Independent Writing Rubrics

Score	Task Description
5	**An essay at this level largely accomplishes all of the following:** • effectively addresses the topic and task • is well organized and well developed, using clearly appropriate explanations, exemplifications, and/or details • displays unity, progression, and coherence • displays consistent facility in the use of language, demonstrating syntactic variety, appropriate word choice, and idiomaticity, though it may have minor lexical or grammatical errors
4	**An essay at this level largely accomplishes all of the following:** • addresses the topic and task well, though some points may not be fully elaborated • is generally well organized and well developed, using appropriate and sufficient explanations, exemplifications, and/or details • displays unity, progression, and coherence, though it may contain occasional redundancy, digression, or unclear connections • displays facility in the use of language, demonstrating syntactic variety and range of vocabulary, though it will probably have occasional noticeable minor errors in structure, word form, or use of idiomatic language that do not interfere with meaning
3	**An essay at this level is marked by one or more of the following:** • addresses the topic and task using somewhat developed explanations, exemplifications, and/or details • displays unity, progression, and coherence, though connection of ideas may be occasionally obscured • may demonstrate inconsistent facility in sentence formation and word choice that may result in lack of clarity and occasionally obscure meaning • may display accurate but limited range of syntactic structures and vocabulary
2	**An essay at this level may reveal one or more of the following weaknesses:** • limited development in response to the topic and task • inadequate organization or connection of ideas • inappropriate or insufficient exemplifications, explanations, or details to support or illustrate generalizations in response to the task • a noticeably inappropriate choice of words or word forms • an accumulation of errors in sentence structure and/or usage
1	**An essay at this level is seriously flawed by one or more of the following weaknesses:** • serious disorganization or underdevelopment • little or no detail, or irrelevant specifics, or questionable responsiveness to the task • serious and frequent errors in sentence structure or usage
0	**An essay at this level** merely copies words from the topic, rejects the topic, or is otherwise not connected to the topic, is written in a foreign language, consists of keystroke characters, or is blank.

TOEFL® iBT Test—Integrated Speaking Rubrics

Score	General Description	Delivery	Language Use	Topic Development
4	The response fulfills the demands of the task, with at most minor lapses in completeness. It is highly intelligible and exhibits sustained, coherent discourse. A response at this level is characterized by all of the following:	Generally well-paced flow (fluid expression). Speech is clear. It may include minor lapses, or minor difficulties with pronunciation or intonation patterns, which do not affect overall intelligibility.	The response demonstrates effective use of grammar and vocabulary. It exhibits a fairly high degree of automaticity with good control of basic and complex structures (as appropriate). Some minor (or systematic) errors are noticeable but do not obscure meaning.	Response is sustained and sufficient to the task. It is generally well developed and coherent; relationships between ideas are clear (or clear progression of ideas).
3	The response addresses the task appropriately, but may fall short of being fully developed. It is generally intelligible and coherent, with some fluidity of expression though it exhibits some noticeable lapses in the expression of ideas. A response at this level is characterized by at least two of the following:	Speech is generally clear, with some fluidity of expression, though minor difficulties with pronunciation, intonation, or pacing are noticeable and may require listener effort at times (though overall intelligibility is not significantly affected).	The response demonstrates fairly automatic and effective use of grammar and vocabulary, and fairly coherent expression of relevant ideas. Response may exhibit some imprecise or inaccurate use of vocabulary or grammatical structures or be somewhat limited in the range of structures used. This may affect overall fluency, but it does not seriously interfere with the communication of the message.	Response is mostly coherent and sustained and conveys relevant ideas/information. Overall development is somewhat limited, usually lacks elaboration or specificity. Relationships between ideas may at times not be immediately clear.
2	The response addresses the task, but development of the topic is limited. It contains intelligible speech, although problems with delivery and/or overall coherence occur; meaning may be obscured in places. A response at this level is characterized by at least two of the following:	Speech is basically intelligible, though listener effort is needed because of unclear articulation, awkward intonation, or choppy rhythm/pace; meaning may be obscured in places.	The response demonstrates limited range and control of grammar and vocabulary. These limitations often prevent full expression of ideas. For the most part, only basic sentence structures are used successfully and spoken with fluidity. Structures and vocabulary may express mainly simple (short) and/or general propositions, with simple or unclear connections made among them (serial listing, conjunction, juxtaposition).	The response is connected to the task, though the number of ideas presented or the development of ideas is limited. Mostly basic ideas are expressed with limited elaboration (details and support). At times relevant substance may be vaguely expressed or repetitious. Connections of ideas may be unclear.
1	The response is very limited in content and/or coherence or is only minimally connected to the task, or speech is largely unintelligible. A response at this level is characterized by at least two of the following:	Consistent pronunciation, stress, and intonation difficulties cause considerable listener effort; delivery is choppy, fragmented, or telegraphic; frequent pauses and hesitations.	Range and control of grammar and vocabulary severely limits (or prevents) expression of ideas and connections among ideas. Some low level responses may rely heavily on practiced or formulaic expressions.	Limited relevant content is expressed. The response generally lacks substance beyond expression of very basic ideas. Speaker may be unable to sustain speech to complete task and may rely heavily on repetition of the prompt.
0	Speaker makes no attempt to respond OR response is unrelated to the topic.			

TOEFL® iBT Test—Independent Speaking Rubrics

Score	General Description	Delivery	Language Use	Topic Development
4	The response fulfills the demands of the task, with at most minor lapses in completeness. It is highly intelligible and exhibits sustained, coherent discourse. A response at this level is characterized by all of the following:	Speech is generally clear, fluid and sustained. It may include minor lapses or minor difficulties with pronunciation or intonation. Pace may vary at times as speaker attempts to recall information. Overall intelligibility remains high.	The response demonstrates good control of basic and complex grammatical structures that allow for coherent, efficient (automatic) expression of relevant ideas. Contains generally effective word choice. Though some minor (or systematic) errors or imprecise use may be noticeable, they do not require listener effort (or obscure meaning).	The response presents a clear progression of ideas and conveys the relevant information required by the task. It includes appropriate detail, though it may have minor errors or minor omissions.
3	The response addresses the task appropriately, but may fall short of being fully developed. It is generally intelligible and coherent, with some fluidity of expression, though it exhibits some noticeable lapses in the expression of ideas. A response at this level is characterized by at least two of the following:	Speech is generally clear, with some fluidity of expression, but it exhibits minor difficulties with pronunciation, intonation or pacing and may require some listener effort at times. Overall intelligibility remains good, however.	The response demonstrates fairly automatic and effective use of grammar and vocabulary, and fairly coherent expression of relevant ideas. Response may exhibit some imprecise or inaccurate use of vocabulary or grammatical structures or be somewhat limited in the range of structures used. Such limitations do not seriously interfere with the communication of the message.	The response is sustained and conveys relevant information required by the task. However, it exhibits some incompleteness, inaccuracy, lack of specificity with respect to content, or choppiness in the progression of ideas.
2	The response is connected to the task, though it may be missing some relevant information or contain inaccuracies. It contains some intelligible speech, but at times problems with intelligibility and/or overall coherence may obscure meaning. A response at this level is characterized by at least two of the following:	Speech is clear at times, though it exhibits problems with pronunciation, intonation or pacing and so may require significant listener effort. Speech may not be sustained at a consistent level throughout. Problems with intelligibility may obscure meaning in places (but not throughout).	The response is limited in the range and control of vocabulary and grammar demonstrated (some complex structures may be used, but typically contain errors). This results in limited or vague expression of relevant ideas and imprecise or inaccurate connections. Automaticity of expression may only be evident at the phrasal level.	The response conveys some relevant information but is clearly incomplete or inaccurate. It is incomplete if it omits key ideas, makes vague reference to key ideas, or demonstrates limited development of important information. An inaccurate response demonstrates misunderstanding of key ideas from the stimulus. Typically, ideas expressed may not be well connected or cohesive so that familiarity with the stimulus is necessary in order to follow what is being discussed.
1	The response is very limited in content or coherence or is only minimally connected to the task. Speech may be largely unintelligible. A response at this level is characterized by at least two of the following:	Consistent pronunciation and intonation problems cause considerable listener effort and frequently obscure meaning. Delivery is choppy, fragmented, or telegraphic. Speech contains frequent pauses and hesitations.	Range and control of grammar and vocabulary severely limits (or prevents) expression of ideas and connections among ideas. Some very low-level responses may rely on isolated words or short utterances to communicate ideas.	The response fails to provide much relevant content. Ideas that are expressed are often inaccurate, limited to vague utterances, or repetitions (including repetition of prompt).
0	Speaker makes no attempt to respond OR response is unrelated to the topic.			

CD 1 TRACKING LIST

CD 2 TRACKING LIST